SCHOENBERG'S
MODELS FOR BEGINNERS
IN COMPOSITION

Schoenberg in Words

General Editors
Sabine Feisst and Severine Neff

Volume 1: *Schoenberg on Form,*
  including Fundamentals of Musical Composition,
  edited by Áine Heneghan

Volume 2: *Schoenberg's* Models for Beginners in Composition,
  edited by Gordon Root

Volume 3: *Schoenberg on Counterpoint,*
  including Preliminary Exercises in Counterpoint,
  edited by Severine Neff

Volume 4: *Schoenberg on Performance,*
  edited by Avior Byron

Volume 5: *Schoenberg's Program Notes and Musical Analyses,*
  edited by J. Daniel Jenkins

Volume 6: *Schoenberg's Correspondence with Anton Webern,*
  edited and translated by Benjamin Levy

Volume 7: *Schoenberg's Correspondence with Alma Mahler,*
  edited and translated by Elizabeth L. Keathley
  and Marilyn McCoy

Volume 8: *Schoenberg's Early Correspondence,*
  edited and translated by Ethan Haimo and Sabine Feisst

Volume 9: *Schoenberg's Correspondence with American Composers,*
  edited and translated by Sabine Feisst

SCHOENBERG'S
MODELS FOR BEGINNERS IN COMPOSITION

EDITED BY GORDON ROOT

OXFORD
UNIVERSITY PRESS

OXFORD
UNIVERSITY PRESS

Oxford University Press is a department of the University of Oxford. It furthers
the University's objective of excellence in research, scholarship, and education
by publishing worldwide. Oxford is a registered trade mark of Oxford University
Press in the UK and certain other countries.

Published in the United States of America by Oxford University Press
198 Madison Avenue, New York, NY 10016, United States of America.

© Oxford University Press 2016

First issued as an Oxford University Press paperback, 2017

Library of Congress Cataloging-in-Publication Data
Schoenberg, Arnold, 1874–1951.
[Models for beginners in composition]
Schoenberg's Models for beginners in composition / edited by Gordon Root.
pages cm.—(Schoenberg in words; Vol. 2)
Includes bibliographical references and index.
ISBN 978-0-19-538221-1 (hardcover : alk. paper)—ISBN 978-0-19-970031-8 (ebook)
ISBN 978-0-19-086565-8 (paperback : alk. paper)
1. Composition (Music) I. Root, Gordon, editor. II. Title. III.
Title: Models for beginners in composition.
MT40.S33M6 2016
781.3—dc23
2015030567

To the imagination and inspiration
of a creative mind

In the memory of Bonnie Root

Contents

Preface

On the History of
Models for Beginners in Composition

On February 9, 1943, Carl Engel, Arnold Schoenberg's editor at the American classical music publishing company Schirmer, congratulated Schoenberg on the completion of his new textbook, *Models for Beginners in Composition*:[1]

> On my return to the office today I find at last the printed copy of your "Models." It was a difficult birth, I admit, but now that the child is with us, I hope that it will meet the father's satisfaction and that it will enjoy a long and happy life.

Some seventy years after the initial printing of *MBC*, most of Engel's wishes for the longevity of Schoenberg's diminutive syllabus have come true. Since its publication in February 1943, this outline for the study of tonal form and school composition has appeared in three English editions (the present one excluded) and in Chinese, French, German, Spanish, and Russian translations. Its "difficult birth" took place over the short span of seven months, from August 1942 to February 1943—for Schoenberg, a time filled with numerous problems related to its publication.

Schoenberg was motivated to create *MBC* by the need for a syllabus designed to cover precisely a semester's worth of material in a single six-week summer course, Beginning Composition 105a at UCLA. In the summer of 1942 Schoenberg and his assistant at the time, the pianist and musicologist Leonard Stein (1916–2004), finished a first version of the syllabus consisting only of musical examples.[2] Schoenberg then paid Golden West Music Press of Los Angeles to make photostat copies of these handwritten examples, which he offered to the students enrolled in his course for $1.25.

Encouraged by its success as a syllabus for Composition 105a, Schoenberg sought to make it available to a broader audience. On August 8, 1942, he wrote to Engel:

> Today I mailed to you a syllabus: "Models for Beginners in Composition."
> I made this syllabus, because I was at first desperate to teach students, who
> have no special talent for composition, in *six* weeks matters which only the
> best could master in a regular semester of 16 weeks.[3]

After receiving a letter of acceptance from Engel, Schoenberg secured a contract on September 10, 1942, along with the first $100 installment of his $500 advance. However, Engel also stipulated that the final acceptance of *MBC* would be contingent on several conditions. He required the inclusion of a preface that would "enable the teacher or pupil to understand the 'Models' more intelligently." Secondly, he specified that Schoenberg write it in German rather than English and that Schirmer be responsible for a translation ultimately to be approved by the composer.[4]

Schoenberg wrote a preface and explanatory text to accompany the syllabus, and as Facsimile 1.1 demonstrates, its earliest drafts are in German, as Engel requested (see also the transcription in Example 1.1). In this draft, Schoenberg's language drifted increasingly in and out of German and English as he struggled to express himself in his native language. He found that the ideas necessary for explaining the nuances of composition and form no longer came naturally to him in German. Finally, with only a few pages written, he

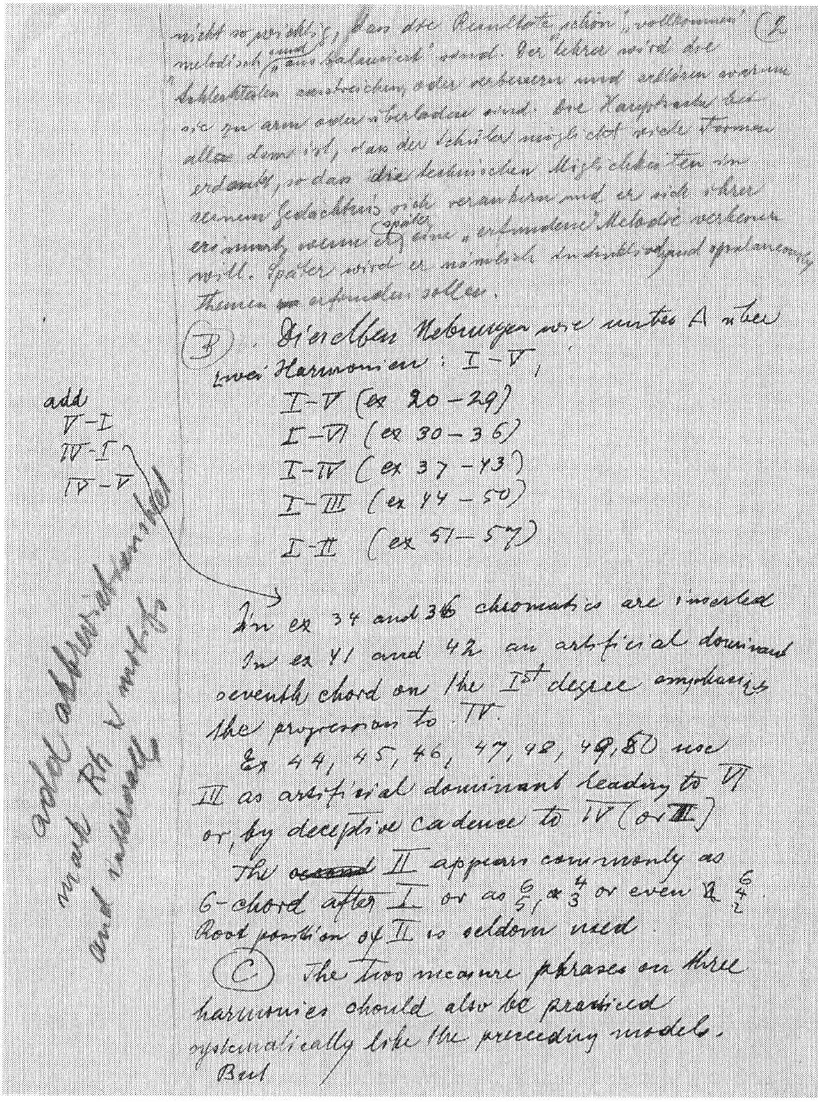

nicht so wichtig, dass die Resultate schön "vollkommen"
melodisch und "ausbalanciert" sind. Der "Lehrer" wird die
Schlechtalen ausstreichen, oder verbessern und erklären warum
sie zu arm oder überladen sind. Die Hauptsache bei
allem dem ist, dass der Schüler möglichst viele Formen
erdenkt, so dass die technischen Möglichkeiten in
seinem Gedächtnis sich verankern und er sich ihrer
erinnern, wenn er eine "erfundene" Melodie verkürzen
will. Später wird er nämlich in sinnvollgeordnet
themen erfinden sollen.

(B). Dieselben Uebungen wie unter A über
zwei Harmonien : I–V,

    I–V (ex 20 – 29)
    I–VI (ex 30 – 36)
    I–IV (ex 37 – 43)
    I–III (ex 44 – 50)
    I–II (ex 51 – 57)

In ex 34 and 36 chromatics are inserted
In ex 41 and 42 an artificial dominant
seventh chord on the I^{st} degree emphasizing
the progression to IV.
Ex 44, 45, 46, 47, 48, 49, 50 use
III as artificial dominant leading to VI
or, by deceptive cadence to IV (or II)
The II appears commonly as
6-chord after I or as $\frac{6}{5}$ & $\frac{4}{3}$ or even a $\frac{6}{2}$.
Root position of II is seldom used.
(C) The two measure phrases on three
harmonies should also be practiced
systematically like the preceding models.
But

add
V–I
IV–I
IV–V

add abbreviations!
mark Rh & motifs
and intervals

	nicht so wichtig, dass die Resultate „schön" „vollkommen" „melodisch und „ausbalanciert" sind. Der Lehrer wird die Schlechtesten ausstreichen, oder verbessern und erklären warum sie zu arm oder überladen sind. Die Hauptsache bei alle dem ist, dass der Schüler möglichst viele Formen erdenkt, so dass die technischen Möglichkeiten in seinem Gedächtnis sich verankern und er sich ihrer erinnert, wenn er später eine „erfundene" Melodie verbessern will. Später wird er nämlich instinctively and spontaneously Themen erfinden sollen.

add
V-I
IV-I
IV-V
	B. Dieselben Uebungen wie unter A über zwei Harmonien: I-V,
	        I-V (ex 20-29)
	        I-VI (ex 30-36)
	        I-IV (ex 37-43)
	        I-III (ex 44-50)
	        I-II (ex 51-57)

Add abbreviation sheet
mark **Rh v** motifs and intervals
	In ex 34 and 36 chromatics are inserted
	        In ex 41 and 42 an artificial dominant seventh chord on the Ist degree emphasizes the progression to IV.
	        Ex 44, 45, 46, 47, 48, 49, 50 use III as artificial dominant leading to VI or, by deceptive cadence to IV (or II)
	        The ~~second~~ II appears commonly as 6-chord after or I as $^6_5$, ~~or~~$^4_3$ or even $^{6}_{2}\text{4}$.
	        Root position of II is seldom used.
	C. The two measure phrases on three harmonies should also be practiced systematically like the preceding models. But

EXAMPLE 1.1

Transcription of Facsimile 1.1. Courtesy Arnold Schönberg Center.

Note: Schoenberg's German text in Example 1.1, a draft of page 5 from *MBC*, is translated as follows: not so important that the results are "beautiful," "perfect," "melodic," and "balanced." The teacher will either strike out the worst of them or improve them and explain why they are too poor or overloaded. The main thing about all of it is that pupils devise as many forms as possible, so that the technical possibilities become embedded in their memories and that they can recall them when they want to improve an "invented" melody. Later on they should be able to invent themes instinctively and spontaneously. B. The same exercises as in A on two harmonies:

abandoned this text for one exclusively in English. On September 12, 1942, he contacted Engel regarding this decision:

I started to write in German, but suddenly I wrote English. I felt the whole time that I was translating from bad English into worse German. So I started all over again in English. Now I am conscious of the shortcomings of my English, and I hope you will help me to correct it. I have a copy of the entire manuscript. Therefore it will not be necessary to return the manuscript with your corrections. The best is to send a questionary [*sic*] (two copies, so that I can keep the one and send you the other with my answers (agreements—I suppose). I would like to know how you find it now.[5]

Engel granted Schoenberg's request. He empathized with Schoenberg's humorous description of having to "translate" his thoughts from "bad English into worse German," and he described his own similar vacillation between the two languages:

> As concerns your English text: I can well understand that you are beginning to live in that unhappy state in which I have passed the last thirty-five years of my life—of losing control over German and not acquiring full command of English. It is a devil of a state to be in. You need not apologize for your English. It is probably good enough for oral delivery in a classroom where any questionable point can be easily clarified by added explanations. For a printed record, as you have sensed yourself, it is not good enough. Therefore Mr. Reese and I shall be glad to "correct it," *liebevollst*. But it cannot be done with a questionnaire, as you suggest. We shall have to go over the whole text and send you a completed revision, which you can then criticize if you think that in any place your meaning has been obscured instead of having been made more intelligible.[6]

Schoenberg was indeed aware of "the shortcomings" of his English and of the imperfection of language in his American texts. However, as he made clear in a letter to his editors at Schirmer, Willis Wager and Gustave Reese, he felt that certain kinds of excessive editing could be detrimental to the individuality of his thought:

> Dear Mr. Wager:
>
> I want to thank you and Mr. Reese most cordially for the excellent way in which you made my English as perfect as possible. I think it can stand now as it is. I realize that there are some differences in the way of thinking which are distinctly mirrored in the organization of my style. But I also think that it

would rather destroy the individuality of my writing if one would correct also these differences. Probably a mere translation would have produced a more perfect result as regards to the English language, but it seems to me that, being now nine years in this country, I have to write English, even if it is less perfect, than formerly my German writing. I am afraid you will have to correct also much of the glossary, though I think I have learned to avoid some of my errors.

Many thanks again.

Most cordially, yours[7]

Occasionally problems during the editorial process stemmed from Schirmer's desire to replace Schoenberg's literally translated German terms with conventional American ones. For example, Schoenberg translated the German terms *Vordersatz* and *Nachsatz*, or "fore-" and "after-sentence" to describe the parts of a period—terms which the editors at Schirmer replaced with the English "antecedent" and "consequent."[8] Regarding this point, Schoenberg expressed disbelief that his literal translations of the German terms might cause confusion, but in the end he acquiesced.[9] And it is in part due to this concession that we owe the clear distinction between terminology related to sentence and period forms in Schoenberg's written works.

Not all the correspondence regarding text editing was amicable. One particularly heated and mildly entertaining exchange occurred between Schoenberg and Felix Greissle, his son-in-law and a music editor at Schirmer. In a letter dated October 6, 1942, Greissle wrote to Schoenberg regarding a few problematic wordings in the syllabus. Regarding one of these passages, Greissle took a conciliatory tone, explaining how he had attempted faithfully to follow his father-in-law's wishes by making only slight grammatical changes to the text, but that in doing so he distorted the meaning. In such cases, he explained, it was sometimes necessary to "use slight circumscriptions." Consequently, he suggested that Schoenberg write a glossary to explain his terminology. Schoenberg's response three days later was both swift and sharp. "I am very frightened," he wrote, "about the 'corrections' in my text,"—"especially," he emphasized, "about the circumscriptions."[10] In a second response several days later, Schoenberg addressed the problem once again, specifically in relation to what he regarded as specious allegations of parallel octaves in Example 227:

The idea that I might have misunderstood your question comes to me suddenly. Did you want to say that perhaps students or teachers might think that these are wrong parallels? I admit that this can happen. If this was your idea, why did you not formulate it? I suggest adding a footnote to this example: something like this is not unusual in piano style—these are not wrong parallel octaves.[11]

After such correspondence on the text and one day before his sixty-eighth birthday (September 12, 1942), Schoenberg ultimately mailed his completed draft of *MBC* to Carl Engel:

Dear Friend: Usually 2 or three days before my birthday I finish a work. Yesterday, 2 days before my 68th, I finished the "Models for Beginners in Musical Composition." Today I airmailed it and had just received the contract. I hope you do not mind that it became so much larger. Will it not be almost double of what it was? Frankly I hope you will be glad, that it is now so much richer. The preface alone comprises 16 typewritten pages, and there are 113 new examples. I am very enthusiastic about it. It must be a success.[12]

Once they received Schoenberg's text, Schirmer immediately purchased all the available copies of Schoenberg's 1942 self-published version (through Golden West) from the UCLA bookstore. While their action eliminated the problem of unauthorized copies, it created a new one for Schoenberg: he had counted on the book's being ready in time for classes, which began on October 12.[13] Schoenberg's immediate solution was to have Schirmer return twenty copies of the Golden West syllabus to be sold to his class. However, in an effort to protect their financial interests, Schirmer had destroyed all copies of it. Editor Gustave Reese's immediate countersolution was to quickly prepare copies of pages 3–21 of the new edition and arrange for students to pay the full $2.00 price for this excerpt—with the understanding that they would receive the complete version by December 1, 1942. This date, however, was entirely unsatisfactory to Schoenberg, although it was one he would no doubt have accepted had he known that the first printing would be delayed until February 1, 1943.

When December passed and the syllabi did not appear, Schoenberg first grew impatient with Schirmer and then ultimately despondent with the result. Had he known that it would take so long, he would have either suggested a "good copyist" or spent the time improving the unnecessarily rushed examples:[14]

> I am desperate. Tomorrow are examinations, and I am afraid the result will be terrible, though I did perhaps three times as much for my classes than in the summer session. Please, *bitte tausendmal,* can you do something that I get it now? The student's cooperative store has ordered 100 copies. The second semester starts a few days after examinations. I have based my teaching this time entirely upon the assumption that the students will study the syllabus. It is very difficult now to change. I am sorry to have to bother you, but I am really in trouble now.[15]

The new book ultimately arrived for the 1943 composition class at the beginning of the spring semester.[16] The rush to complete the text caused countless errors to appear in its initial printing.[17] Moreover, the executives at Schirmer were reluctant to jeopardize their potential profit by correcting the imperfect manuscript in an immediate reprinting. They opted for a temporary solution instead—an errata sheet, which Schirmer pasted to the inside front cover of the first printing (Example 1.2).[18]

In February 1943 *MBC* began to fill the shelves of music stores across the United States, selling for the substantial sum of $2.00 a copy. In their advertisements, the executives at Schirmer wholeheartedly supported their product and its author, describing Schoenberg as a composer known for "advanced tendencies" and at the same time "profoundly imbued with the spirit of the masters" (see Example 1.3, 18). This "new book of first importance" would "lead the student directly into the process of composition," laying out "the whole process, from the invention of a melodic phrase through larger entities to complete small forms." And if this promise failed to attract the aspiring composer, the convenient layout in two separate volumes (a design Schoenberg had proposed in correspondence with Engel "for ease in use in connection with the examples") would dispel any hesitations.

ERRATA

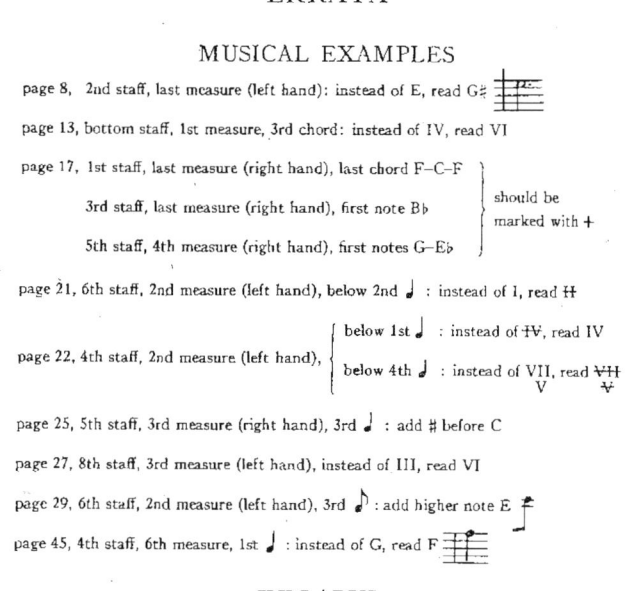

MUSICAL EXAMPLES

page 8, 2nd staff, last measure (left hand): instead of E, read G♯

page 13, bottom staff, 1st measure, 3rd chord: instead of IV, read VI

page 17, 1st staff, last measure (right hand), last chord F–C–F

    3rd staff, last measure (right hand), first note B♭   } should be marked with +

    5th staff, 4th measure (right hand), first notes G–E♭

page 21, 6th staff, 2nd measure (left hand), below 2nd ♩ : instead of I, read II

page 22, 4th staff, 2nd measure (left hand), { below 1st ♩ : instead of IV, read IV
V

    { below 4th ♩ : instead of VII, read VII
V

page 25, 5th staff, 3rd measure (right hand), 3rd ♩ : add ♯ before C

page 27, 8th staff, 3rd measure (left hand), instead of III, read VI

page 29, 6th staff, 2nd measure (left hand), 3rd ♪ : add higher note E

page 45, 4th staff, 6th measure, 1st ♩ : instead of G, read F

SYLLABUS

page 6, line 31: instead of 91, read 92

page 8, lines 25 and 26: instead of 217, read 220

page 9, last sentence on page should be transferred to end of preceding section

page 10, 6th line from bottom: instead of 13, read 18

EXAMPLE 1.2
Errata sheet in Models, first printing. Courtesy G. Schirmer.

Later that year Schoenberg again contacted his editors, this time to discuss the creation of a new edition of the syllabus. Ultimately, his plan was to add a number of new harmonic patterns for thematic structures, models for varied recapitulations, alternate harmonic frameworks for contrasting middle sections, and several new minuets and scherzos—but the project never came to fruition.[19] The executives at Schirmer had been receptive to the idea, but as Schoenberg explained in a letter to Engel (April 10, 1944), several factors, including illness, had forced him to reprioritize his activities. As a result, the completion of his new counterpoint text would take precedence over the syllabus. Engel's sudden death less than a month later, on May 15, 1944, ended any further possibilities of revision. After that, Schoenberg's relations with Schirmer rapidly deteriorated.

EXAMPLE 1.3

Advertisement for MBC, from "Bulletin of New Music Published and Imported by G. Schirmer, New York," Bulletin No. 8, 1943. Courtesy G. Schirmer. Appears as a loose-leaf paper in Schoenberg's annotated copy of MBC, S142.C3. Courtesy Arnold Schönberg Center.

One of several contributing factors to these soured relations appears to have been Schirmer's refusal to grant Universal or Dyname Editions the rights for *MBC*'s German or French translation, respectively. Eventually, the long-term unavailability of *MBC*, combined with Schirmer's alleged failure to account for proceeds from performances, rentals, and sales of his Theme and Variations for Band, Op. 43b (1943), Suite in G Major ("in Ancient Style") for String Orchestra (1934), and the Concerto for Cello and Orchestra after Keyboard Concerto by Georg Matthias Monn (1933) led Schoenberg to seek the advice of the Los Angeles–based lawyer Milton S. Koblitz.

Schoenberg maintained correspondence with Koblitz over several years. However, his clearest account of the case against Schirmer appears in a letter from June 9, 1947 (Facsimile 1.2).

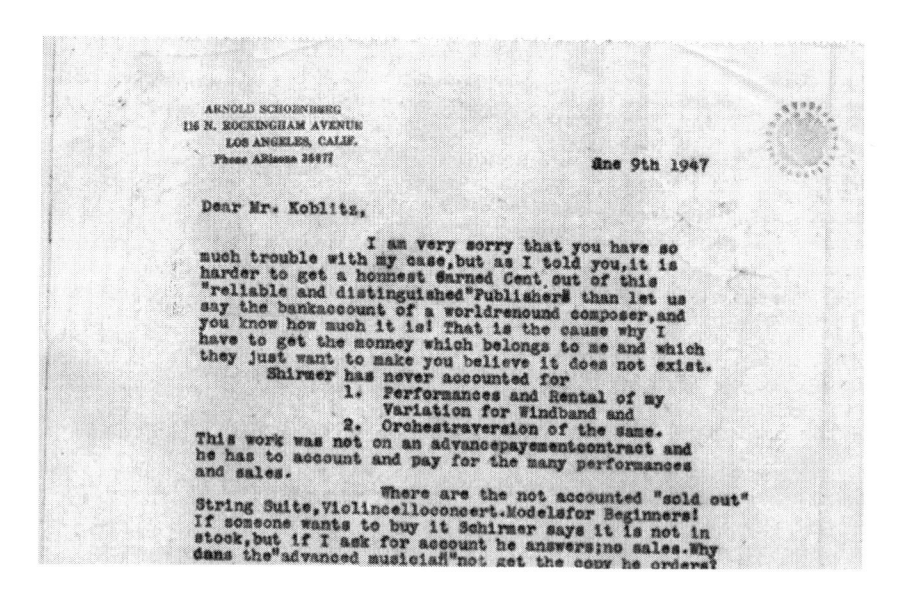

FACSIMILE 1.2

Schoenberg's letter to Milton S. Koblitz, June 9, 1947, excerpt. Courtesy Arnold Schönberg Center

Ultimately, Koblitz was unable to recover Schoenberg's royalties. As Schirmer explained it, they had already "over-paid" Schoenberg through advances, a claim that Schoenberg was unable to disprove but felt was false. Furthermore, the replacement of Engel by both William Schuman and Hans Heinsheimer signaled an unfavorable shift in attitude toward Schoenberg's music. Schuman, chief advisor of publications, was at best indifferent to Schoenberg's music. Ultimately he championed a more conservative brand of tonal composition for Schirmer's catalog—one that included many of his own works.[20]

If poor health, changing priorities, and problematic relations with Schirmer had made any subsequent editions of *MBC* unlikely, the posthumous publication of *SFH* in 1954 and *FMC* in 1967 relegated *MBC* to a footnote in the discussion of Schoenberg's ideas on music—and it remained a work that was somehow associated with, but ultimately deemed unessential to, an understanding of his theoretical output as a whole. This lack of attention is perhaps best typified by Alexander Goehr's otherwise insightful and pioneering 1974 article on Schoenberg's theoretical works, in which he condenses all discussion of *MBC* into a single terse and exceedingly nondescript statement: "In addition, there is a short work, *Models for Beginners in Composition*."[21] Goehr's focus on *TH, FMC*, and *SFH*, is understandable. His tacit value judgment is predicated on the belief that the content of *MBC* is included in these other texts—even though, very simply, it is not. *MBC* reveals the complex array of different issues confronting Schoenberg in his attempt to fashion a practical manual for the understanding of formal functions and composition of school forms in the American classroom. In this sense, *MBC* stands alone.

Acknowledgments

I am grateful to all those who have helped bring this new edition of *Schoenberg's Models for Beginners in Composition* (*MBC*) to fruition. Special thanks to Nuria Schoenberg Nono and to Ronald and Lawrence Schoenberg, who have generously allowed me to publish their father's manuscripts. Their devotion to the dissemination of his work and thought is truly a model for anyone interested in Schoenberg's music.

I wish also to thank the Arnold Schönberg Center for awarding me an Avenir Grant to travel to Vienna in order to study the classroom notes of Leonard Stein and Gerald Strang, as well as Schoenberg's manuscripts and corrections for *MBC*. During my stay, the archivists Therese Muxeneder and Eike Fess generously shared their knowledge at every step. The assistant director, Karin Nemec, was always helpful during my stays in Mödling.

I am indebted to my friend Adam Shanley for copying the majority of the musical examples, to my colleague Matthew Wilson for his final formatting of these examples and sound engineering for the companion website, and to my colleague Dmitri Novgorodsky for performing the musical examples in *MBC*. My appreciation is extended to several readers, including John Jansen, Jim Davis, Sean Doyle, Michael Markham, and Paul Murphy, and to

Pieter van den Toorn, who made many useful comments and suggestions for early versions of the commentary. In addition, I acknowledge Julia Bungardt, whose expertise with Schoenberg's handwriting proved vital for preparing the transcription of Facsimile 1.1; Grant Chorley for his editing and German translations; and my friends and colleagues Joel Hunt and Paul Coleman for the valuable criticism they contributed to the manuscript at its final stage. My thanks as well to Severine Neff, who edited several drafts of my work with great care; to Sabine Feisst, who provided indispensable comments on the final version; and to Áine Heneghan for her help with several important manuscripts. I also extend a note of thanks to the staff at the UCLA Library, Special Collections, for providing the 1930s and '40s course catalogues. I am grateful to Suzanne Ryan for making this edition possible, and to her assistants Adam Cohen and Andrew Maillet for their help at several points. Finally, I thank my wife Wenzhuo and our son Weilin, for their love and support.

Permissions

I thank the following publishers and individuals for permission to reproduce excerpts from the works cited below.

The Arnold Schönberg Center

Manuscripts from the Leonard Stein and Gerald Strang Satellite Collections. All manuscript and book sources related to *MBC* (see Appendix 1).

Austrian Public Library

Special thanks to Peter Prokop for his help in securing permission for excerpts from Fonds 21 Berg 55.

Belmont Music Publishers

For permission to publish *Models for Beginners in Composition* and to reproduce excerpts from Op. 43a. Specific thanks to Lawrence Schoenberg, Nuria Schoenberg Nono, and Ronald Schoenberg for these permissions.

Faber and Faber

International permissions for:
  Chart of the Regions, SFH, 20.
  Chart of the Regions in Minor, *SFH*, 30.
  Example 19, Derivation of the substitute tones, *SFH*, 9.
  Example 55, Chart of Transformations, *SFH*, 38.
  Example 59, *SFH*, 40.
  Scale degrees as inclusive classes from *TH*, 387.
  Example 183, *TH*, 246.

The Kirchner Heirs, Lisa and Paul Kirchner

Kirchner's Minuet for Composition 105, 1941, Appendix 3, Facsimile 6.5.
Special thanks to the Kirchner heirs, Lisa and Paul Kirchner, for allowing
  me to reproduce their father's minuet (Facsimile 6.5), a student work
  composed in 1941 for Schoenberg's Beginning Composition course,
  Music 105, at UCLA.

The Arnold Schönberg Center and Belmont Music Publishers

Schoenberg's correspondence.

Schirmer

Errata Sheet in *Models*, first printing.
Advertisement for *MBC*, from "Bulletin of New Music Published and
Imported by G. Schirmer, New York," Bulletin No. 8, 1943.

UCLA

1930s and 40s Course Catalogues.

University of California Press, Berkeley

Scale-degree chart, *TH*, 246.
Example 183, *TH*, 246.

W. W. Norton

U.S. permissions for:
  Chart of the Regions, *SFH*, 20.
  Chart of the Regions in Minor, *SFH*, 30.
  Example 19, Derivation of the substitute tones, *SFH*, 9.
  Example 55, Chart of Transformations, *SFH*, 38.
  Example 59, *SFH*, 40.
  Scale-degree chart, *TH*, 387.
  Example 183, *TH*, 246.

Editorial Notes

This edition of *MBC*, with critical commentary, supplemental materials, and newly transcribed musical examples, incorporates the author's 1944 corrections. Owing to the book's original function as a course syllabus, many of Schoenberg's theoretical concepts such as transformation, regions, and the relationship between harmony, form, and motivic development, remain only briefly outlined in Schoenberg's original text—at UCLA, students would have had a background in these topics from taking other required music theory courses (e.g., Structural Functions of Harmony, Music 106A and B; Form and Analysis, Music 104A and B). The extensive analytical commentary and appendices in this new edition explore relevant theoretical topics not covered in detail in *MBC* and situate them within Schoenberg's collected music-theoretical output.[22] Further appendices including Schoenberg's teaching schedule at UCLA and related pedagogically oriented manuscripts complete this most recent edition.

Schoenberg's handwritten 1944 corrections, incorporated into this text, are found in three separate copies of the book housed at the Arnold Schönberg Center in Vienna (ASC), call numbers S142.c1, S143.

c3, and S143.c4 (see their description in Appendix 1). Most, but not all, of these corrections made their way into the 1972 edition of *MBC* published by Belmont Music Publishers and edited by Schoenberg's former teaching assistant Leonard Stein. Example 2.1 shows the corrections new to this edition of *MBC*.[23]

Location	1972 Edition	Present Edition	Source of Correction
Ex 85, m. 2	 *[music notation, m. 85]*	 *[music notation, m. 85]*	S143.C3
Ex. 193, m. 1	 *[music notation, m. 193]*	 *[music notation, m. 193]*	S143.C3
Ex. 198, m. 4	 *[music notation, m. 198]*	 *[music notation, m. 198]*	S143.C3
Ex. 220, 2nd ending	 *[music notation]*	 *[music notation]*	S143.C3
Ex. 220	VI	~~VI~~	S143.C3
Ex. 225, m. 2	 *[music notation]*	 *[music notation]*	S143.C3
Ex. 225, m. 4	 *[music notation]*	 *[music notation]*	S143.C3
Ex. 231a Alternative 1	 *[music notation]*	 *[music notation]*	S143.C3
IX. Phrases, Half Sentences, etc., Ex. 12, m. 1	 *[music notation, m. 12]*	 *[music notation, m. 12]*	S143.C2

Additional corrections of errors in harmonic analysis, page references, and courtesy accidentals are shown below.

EXAMPLE 2.1

Editorial changes to the current edition of MBC *based on Schoenberg's corrections*

ii

Location	1972 Edition	Present Edition	Rationale
Text, p. 7. "The examples are based…"	V-IV	IV-V	Accurately reflects the content of Example 167b
Exx. 44-48	III	~~III~~	Strikethrough reflects chromatic alteration of chord.
Ex. 91	II and IV	~~II~~ and ~~IV~~	Chromatic alterations
Ex.109	cautionary treble clef	deleted	unnecessary
Ex.149	VI and II	~~VI~~ and ~~II~~	Chromatic alterations
Text, Page 9. "For this purpose…"	pp. 30-33	pp. 38-41	Mistake in 1942 and 1972 edition
Ex.152	*[musical example]*	*[musical example]*	Beaming in motive *a* made identical to that of *a*1
Ex.167	a) VI - II b) IV - II c) VI - IV d) III - VI	a) VI - II (~~V~~ - ~~II~~) b) IV - II (~~IV~~ - ~~II~~) c) VI - IV (VI - ~~IV~~) d) III - VI (~~III~~ - VI)	Chromatic alterations
Ex. 210	*[musical example]*	*[musical example]*	Beaming of b1 in current edition of *MBC* now matches beaming of b.
Example 220	VI, II, and III	~~VI~~, ~~II~~, and ~~III~~	Chromatic alterations
Example 225			
Example 228 mm. 1-2.	*[musical example]* 228 Period No. 1 (*on same Model as Ex. 227*)	*[musical example]* 228 Period No. 1 (*on same Model as Ex. 227*)	Added motivic labels in m. 1 reflect motivic relationships.
Ex. 21, p. 39	II	~~II~~	Chromatic alterations
Ex.245, Alt.	*[musical example]* Alternatives	*[musical example]* Alternatives	Clarification (courtesy accidental)

EXAMPLE 2.1

(Continued)

Column 1 presents each pertinent passage in the 1972 Belmont edition, column 2 the correction in the present edition. Column 3 shows the ASC call number of the source manuscript for the corrections. All corrections are derived from one of three hand-annotated copies of *MBC* housed in the Leonard Stein Satellite Collection. By far the most frequent source of these corrections is the copy catalogued as S143.C3, the cover of which features the handwritten description "with corrections and remarks for a new edition." The text of the syllabus here includes Schoenberg's own corrections, written in red pen. Although Schoenberg had intended for this "new edition" to appear shortly after the original publication date, it was published only posthumously in 1972, and even then not all of the corrections were incorporated. Additional corrections in harmonic analysis, page references, and courtesy accidentals are shown below.

Beyond the correction of misspelled words and necessary missing punctuation, this edition contains no emendations of Schoenberg's manuscripts. Original versions of the correspondences may be accessed at the Arnold Schönberg Center website: http://www.schoenberg.at/. Critical notes are offered whenever Schoenberg's other writings can enrich the meanings of prose passages or music examples.

Abbreviations

ASC	Arnold Schönberg Center, Vienna
ASS	*Arnold Schönberg in seinen Schriften: Verzeichnis, Fragen, Editorisches.* Edited by Hartmut Krones. Vienna: Böhlau, 2011.
FMC	Schoenberg, Arnold. *Fundamentals of Musical Composition.* Edited by Gerald Strang and Leonard Stein. London: Faber and Faber, 1967. Reprint 1980.
HHS	Stuckenschmidt, H. H. *Schoenberg: His Life, World and Work.* Translated by Humphrey Searle. New York: Schirmer Books, 1978.
HL 1911	Schoenberg, Arnold. *Harmonielehre.* Vienna: Universal Edition, 1911.
HL 1922	Schoenberg, Arnold. *Harmonielehre*, 3rd edition. Vienna: Universal Edition, 1922.
JASC	*Journal of the Arnold Schönberg Center*
JASI	*Journal of the Arnold Schoenberg Institute*
MBC 1942	Schoenberg, Arnold. *Models for Beginners in Composition.* Los Angeles: Self-published, 1942.
MBC 1943	Schoenberg, Arnold. *Models for Beginners in Composition.* New York: G. Schirmer, 1943.

MBC 1947   Schoenberg, Arnold. *Models for Beginners in Composition.*
              New York: G. Schirmer, 1947.

MBC 1972   Schoenberg, Arnold. *Models for Beginners in Composition.* Edited by
              Leonard Stein. Los Angeles: Belmont Music Publishers, 1972.

MBC (Ger.)   *Modelle für Anfänger im Kompositionsunterricht.* Edited and
              translated by Rudolf Stephan. Vienna: Universal, 1972.

MI   Schoenberg, Arnold. *The Musical Idea and the Logic, Technique, and
              Art of Its Presentation.* Edited and translated by Patricia Carpenter
              and Severine Neff. Bloomington: University of Indiana Press, 2006.

MFK   Krehl, Stephan. *Musikalische Formenlehre (Kompositionslehre).*
              Berlin: G. J. Göschen, 1914.

MTS   *Music Theory Spectrum*

MTWS   Dudeque, Norton. *Music Theory and Analysis in the Writing of
              Arnold Schoenberg (1874–1951).* Burlington, VT: Ashgate, 2005.

PEC   Schoenberg, Arnold. *Preliminary Exercises in Counterpoint.* Edited
              by Leonard Stein. London: Faber and Faber, 1963.

PNM   *Perspectives of New Music*

Rufer   Rufer, Josef. *The Works of Arnold Schoenberg: A Catalogue of His
              Compositions, Writings and Paintings.* Translated by Dika Newlin.
              London: Faber and Faber, 1962.

SFH   Schoenberg, Arnold. *Structural Functions of Harmony.* Revised
              edition. Edited by Leonard Stein. New York: W. W. Norton. 1969.

SI 1950   Schoenberg, Arnold. *Style and Idea.* Edited and translated by Dika
              Newlin. New York: Philosophical Library, 1950; Reprint 2010.

SI 1975   Schoenberg, Arnold. *Style and Idea: The Selected Writings of Arnold
              Schoenberg.* Edited by Leonard Stein. Translated by Leo Black.
              Berkeley and Los Angeles: University of California Press, 1975;
              Reprint, 1984; 60th anniversary edition with a foreword by Joseph
              Auner, 2010.

SMN   Dineen, Murray. "Gerald Strang's Manuscript Notes to Arnold
              Schönberg's Classes (1935–1937)." *JASI* 4 (2002): 104–18.

SNW   Feisst, Sabine. *Schoenberg's New World: The American Years.*
              New York: Oxford University Press, 2011.

SW   *Schoenberg and His World.* Edited by Walter Frisch. Princeton: Princeton University Press, 1999.

TH   Schoenberg, Arnold. *Theory of Harmony.* Translated by Roy E. Carter. Berkeley and Los Angeles: University of California Press, 1978; 100th anniversary edition with a foreword by Walter Frisch, 2010.

UCLA University of California at Los Angeles

USC   University of Southern California

ZKIF   Schoenberg, Arnold. *Coherence, Counterpoint, Instrumentation, Instruction in Form.* Edited by Severine Neff. Translated by Charlotte M. Cross and Severine Neff. Lincoln: University of Nebraska Press, 1994.

About the Companion Website

Models for Beginners in Composition features a password-protected companion website with recorded performances of all the musical examples in *MBC*. Additionally, the website offers complete performances and transcriptions of Schoenberg's numerous alternative solutions for the many school compositions in his syllabus. Hearing Schoenberg's examples not only enlivens the exercises of *MBC*, but it also facilitates Schoenberg's original objectives for students of the syllabus. Schoenberg believed that studying *MBC* would improve ear training and formal comprehension, and that a firm grasp of its principles would enhance the "understanding of the technique and logic of musical construction." Readers are encouraged to take advantage of these additional web-based resources while exploring Schoenberg's 1942 pedagogical exercises and school compositions.

SCHOENBERG'S
*MODELS FOR BEGINNERS
IN COMPOSITION*

Commentary

What experiences in California motivated Schoenberg to begin writing his American theory texts? In the preface to the 1972 edition of *MBC*, Leonard Stein claimed it was pedagogical necessity—a sort of "teacher's emergency." Schoenberg, the newly arrived émigré, "felt the necessity of providing his ill-prepared students" with basic training in theory and composition. Certainly not all of Schoenberg's American students could have been "ill-prepared," as Stein claims. However, if the majority had been less knowledgeable about classical music than their European counterparts, it would not be surprising. Schoenberg's European students (including Alban Berg and Anton Webern) had been fortunate enough to experience the concert music of the late Romantic era as a living art. The southern California teenagers in Schoenberg's 1930s and '40s classes at USC and UCLA did not have these advantages.

Logically, Schoenberg should have modified or even changed his approach after his emigration to the United States in 1933—but as we shall see, a comparison of his European and American teaching materials indicates that he did not necessarily follow this path. Instead of the pedagogical about-face that we might infer from Stein's description, he both preserved and reinterpreted his European pedagogy.[24] Indeed, in California, Schoenberg's European ideas about tonal theory and its pedagogy grew in originality and scope.

Whether in Europe or the United States, Schoenberg valued students' interpretation of musical materials—their compositional possibilities and the logic of their presentation. As a result, the content of *MBC* is meant to awaken the student composer's musical intuitions, rather than to increase knowledge of any particular style. Specifically, *MBC* presents a step-by-step consideration of various structures called "models," constituting the basics of European compositional presentation.[25] First, students learn to compose two-measure melodic or thematic units modeled after particular motives; second, they add invented accompaniment to them. These two-measure units ultimately expand into thematic structures called the sentence and the period. These in turn generate sections of pieces—school forms such as the minuet or scherzo. The ensuing remarks will explore this compositional-pedagogical path, its history, and the structural models associated with it.

Berg's Models

From 1907 to 1911 Schoenberg taught Alban Berg free composition rather than harmony and counterpoint—and fortunately, his workbooks for this study are extant. Schoenberg's method focused on Berg's grasp of compositional possibilities and their presentational logic. His initial student notes entitled "Anfang des Menuetts ["Beginning of the Minuet"] commence with an exploration of motives for an opening theme and continue with the various methods of combining and harmonizing them; in essence, Berg learned motivic, melodic, and harmonic models for composition.

Schoenberg used precise methods to teach Berg the compositional implications of such motivic and harmonic structures. Typically he would illustrate these technical procedures in diagrams revealing compositional possibilities in concrete terms—that is, as models. As a case study, consider the materials in Berg's notes from his first lesson in free composition. Schoenberg gave Berg the matrix of motivic successions in Facsimile 3.1 (transcribed in Example 3.1) presenting a systematic way to consider the order and relation of motivic

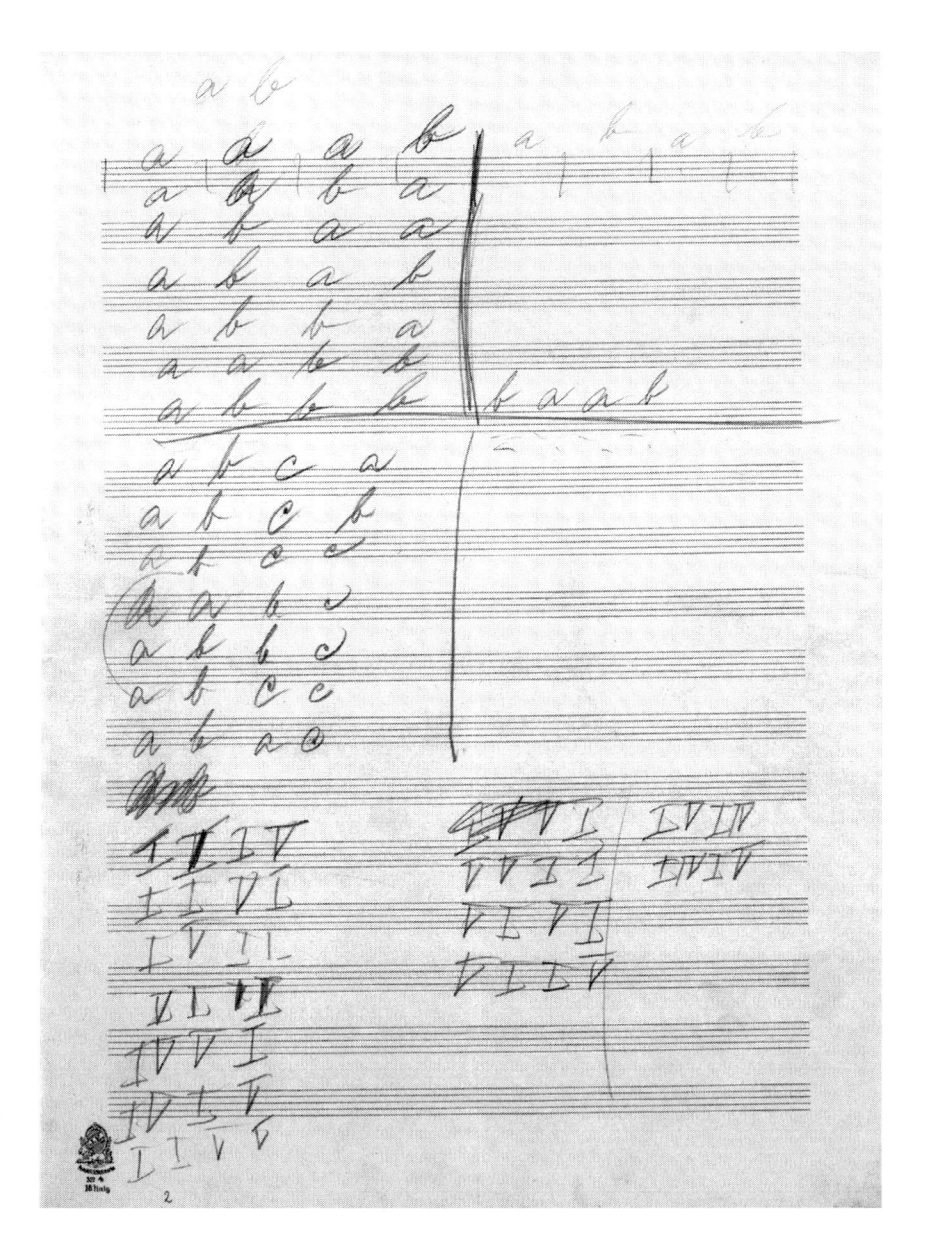

Facsimile 3.1. Schoenberg's motivic matrix from Berg's first composition lesson with Schoenberg, 1907 (Fonds 21 Berg 55/I, f. 2, Österreichische Nationalbibliothek, Vienna). Courtesy Austrian National Library.

1)	a	a	a	b
2)	a	a	b	a
3)	a	b	a	a
4)	a	b	a	b
5)	a	b	b	a
6)	a	a	b	b
7)	a	b	b	b
8)	a	b	c	a
9)	a	b	c	b
10)	a	b	c	c
11)	a	a	b	c
12)	a	b	b	c
13)	a	b	c	c
14)	a	b	a	c

EXAMPLE 3.1
Transcription of Schoenberg's motivic matrix.

materials.[26] It specifically tallies all possible orderings of a four-motive succession via a set of implicit rules.[27] The chart presents successions (nos. 1–3)
in which three *a* motives contrast with one *b* motive; thus, these successions begin with minimal diversity. By contrast, successions 4–6 contain an
equal representation of *a* and *b*, each stated twice. Succession 7 is the mirror
image of succession 1 and features maximal diversity within this arrangement: one familiar motive and three contrasting ones.[28] Finally, in the maxi-
mally diverse successions 8–14, *a* is combined with two distinctly contrasting
elements, *b* and *c*. In its development from minimal to maximal diversity,
Schoenberg's matrix progresses naturally from the most basic mode of musical presentation, repetition, to a more complex one emphasizing contrast,
thus systematically offering a student the broadest spectrum of compositional
choice.

The order and presentation of motives in the matrix is governed by an
implicit set of rules:

Rule 1. Each succession must begin with *a*
Rule 2. Each succession must contain no more than three *distinct* components (a, b, c) and no fewer than two (a, b)

Rule 3. Each succession must introduce its components incrementally, in alphabetical order:

Repeat	Return	Not allowed!
abbc	abca	acba

RULE 3

Illustration of Rule 3. Two resultant patterns: return and repeat.

Principle A: Once introduced, components may return in any order, as long as they follow Rules 1–3.

Within this set of rules, the orders of motivic successions in Schoenberg's matrix are exhaustive.[29]

Schoenberg's matrix also naturally defines the relation of a motive to its positions within a succession. On the one hand, position 1 must present *a* and is thus always expository. Analogously, position 4 is always cadential. On the other hand, position 2 may be contrasting (if it presents *b*) or developmental (if it varies *a*). The function of position 3 is variable in that it depends upon the number of motives in the unit (two or three). In a two-motive design, as in successions 1–7, position 3 is always developmental—a varied repetition of either *a* or *b*. In a three-motive design, position 3 may either be developmental, if it presents *a* or *b* (as in *abbc*, i.e., succession 12) or contrasting, if it introduces *c* (as in *abcc*, i.e., succession 10).

The basic layout of Schoenberg's motivic matrix ensures a certain degree of both coherence and development. Since each line begins with the same motive (*a*), each presents a variation both on the original combination of motives *a* + *b*, or *a*, *b* + *c*. Any four-motive succession with fewer than four distinct units involves at least one instance of motivic repetition, ensuring a sense of internal cohesion. For example, the succession *abbc* in line 12 includes all three motivic units *a*, *b*, and *c*, yet it is internally coherent in its repetition of motive *b*. Through this repetition, the resultant phrase develops a characteristic sound, defined by its "abundance" of *b* material. This abstract motivic succession comes to life in the periodic phrase structure of Example 3.3a, discussed below.

After constructing his motivic matrix, Schoenberg designs a harmonic matrix analogous to Example 3.1, using only tonic and dominant chords (see the harmonic matrix, Example 3.2).[30] Its structural materials progress from near-maximal similarity to maximal diversity; however, since the matrix uses only two distinct harmonies, diversity is limited. Schoenberg begins his matrix with a framework of three tonic chords and one dominant, with successions 1–3 exhausting the combinations of this arrangement. Successions 5–10 exhaust all combinations with two dominants and two tonics.[31] The contrasting element, V, can now begin the succession (see successions 4, 8, 9, and 10). This allowance accounts for the greater number of equally balanced two-plus-two combinations in the harmonic matrix than in the motivic one. To the right of the tonic and dominant section of the matrix, Schoenberg begins a new section including three chords (I, IV, and V) (i.e., a tonic with two contrasting components), which he quickly discontinues. It is tempting to attribute this abrupt termination of the matrix to the awkward syntax resulting from successions such as V–IV–I–I and I–I–V–IV (if all permutations are exhausted). However, in *TH,* Schoenberg includes this very root motion (V–IV) as a perfectly viable "superstrong" (*überstark*) progression—although he urges the student to use it sparingly.[32]

a. I and V

1)	I	I	I	V
2)	I	I	V	I
3)	I	V	I	I
4)	V	I	I	V
5)	I	V	V	I
6)	I	V	I	V
7)	I	I	V	V
8)	V	V	I	I
9)	V	I	V	I
10)	V	I	I	V

b. I–IV– V

1)	I	V	I	IV
2)	I	IV	I	V

EXAMPLE 3.2
Transcription of Schoenberg's harmonic matrix.

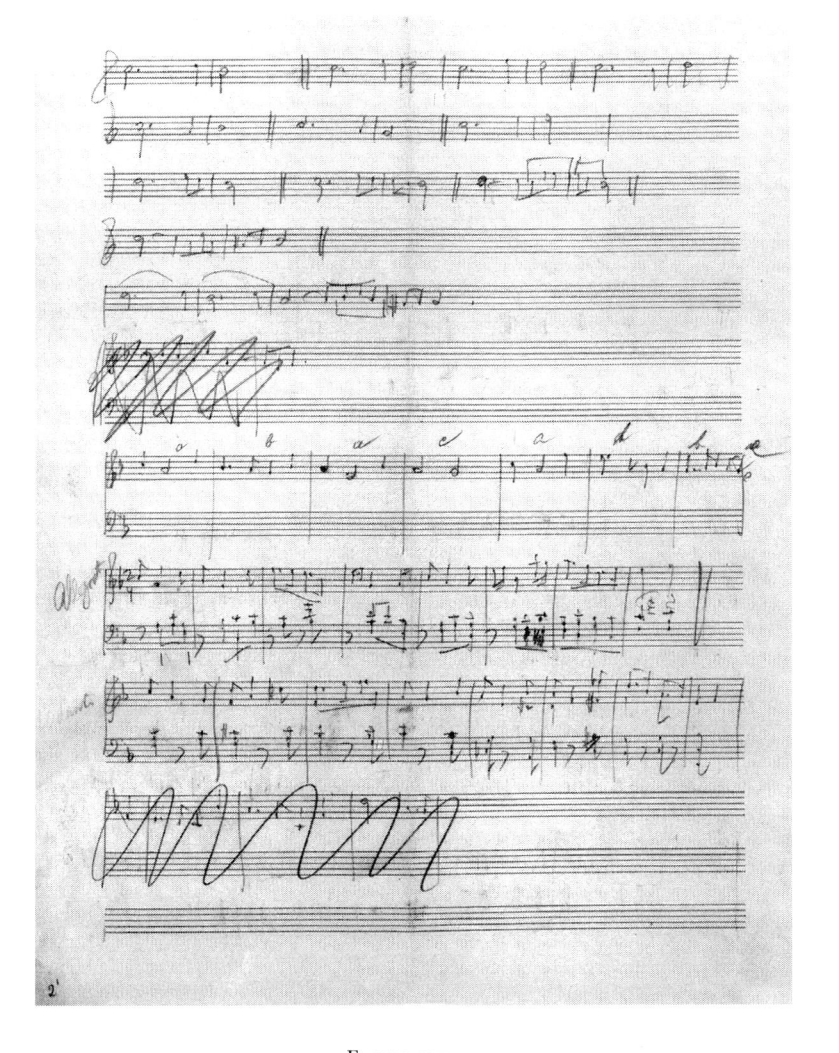

FACSIMILE 3.2
*Schoenberg's musical contextualization of the motivic procedures from Facsimile 3.1
(Fonds 21 Berg 55/I, f. 2', Österreichische Nationalbibliothek, Vienna) (middle of page).
Courtesy Austrian National Library.*

Schoenberg uses his presentation of matrices to compose an eight-bar period (though he does not label it explicitly as such).[33] The theme features an antecedent phrase based on motivic succession 14 (*abac*) (Example 1) and a consequent on motivic succession 12 (*abbc*) (center of Facsimile 3.2, transcribed as Example 3.3).[34]

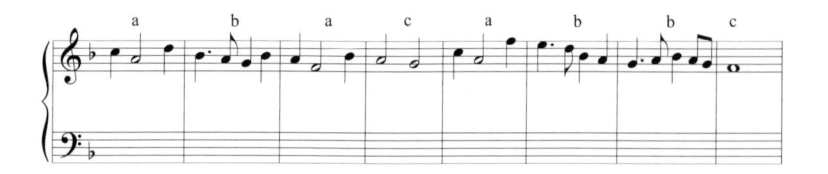

EXAMPLE 3.3

Transcription of Schoenberg's musical contextualization of the motivic procedures from Facsimile 3.1.

The first two *a* motives (mm. 1–3) are exact transpositions of each other; the third (m. 5) expands the final interval from a fourth to a sixth.[35] The two *c* motives in mm. 4 and 8 are assigned to cadential figures, the first with an embellishing suspension.[36] In contrast to motives *a* and *c*, motive *b* and its variations derive their similarity through rhythmic relatedness rather than intervallic variation.

Furthermore, Example 3.4 illustrates the hypothetical process by which the *b* motive in m. 7 can be understood as an inversion of the initial *b* (m. 2).[37] Stage 1 shows the tonal inversion of this motive; stage 2, its tonal transposition a third lower; and stage 3, the addition of the embellishing tone A to generate motive *b* (m. 7). System 2 shows the hypothetical evolution of motive *b* from m. 2 as it morphs into motive *b* from m. 6. In stage 1 this motive is transposed tonally by a fourth; in stage 2 the second interval of the motive is expanded from a second to a third; in stage 3 the direction of the final interval of the motive is reversed; and in stage 4 it is contracted from a third to a second.[38]

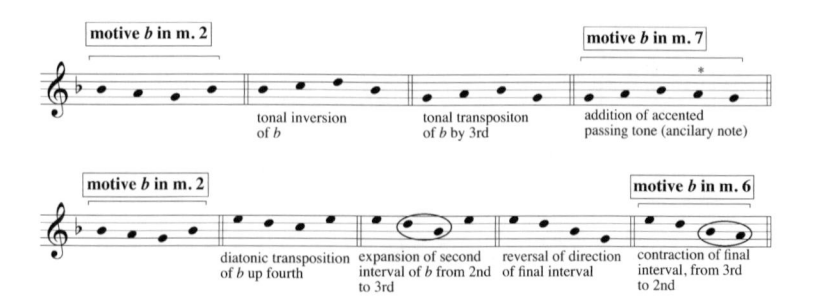

EXAMPLE 3.4

Relationship between b motives in Schoenberg's F major period.

EXAMPLE 3.5
Schoenberg's F major period varying the motives from Example 3.3.

Example 3.5 shows Schoenberg's ultimate use of motive *a* to generate a new period composed of motivic successions 2 and 11, which are accompanied by a bass in a "complementary rhythm"; the bass fills "the gaps in the movement" of the upper voices in order to achieve a sense of rhythmic independence between the accompaniment and melody (see also Facsimile 3.2, penultimate phrase).[39]

The goals of this exercise are twofold. On the one hand, Schoenberg's example illustrates how a student might vary an existing theme with an appropriate balance between the rhythm of the melody and its accompaniment.[40] On the other, a student learns to handle the interaction of motivic work in all voices—a skill required for the technique of *developing variation*, which Schoenberg favored throughout his career.[41] Never at a loss for variation, Schoenberg follows this period with yet another (see Example 3.6 and Facsimile 3.2, bottom), before the student is allowed to invent a similar theme.

EXAMPLE 3.6
Schoenberg's period in F, using variations on motives in Examples 3.3 and 3.5

Examples 3.7 and 3.8 show Berg's initial efforts to compose his own period (see also Facsimile 3.3, "Allegro").[42] The *aabc* motivic structure (with one motive per measure), the antecedent of Berg's first four-bar period (Example 3.8), features succession 11 from the motivic matrix, while the consequent (*abac*) uses succession 14.[43] Berg's four-plus-four-bar phrase structure is conventional in its harmonic structure, with a half-cadence in m. 4 answered by an authentic cadence in m. 8. His subsequent attempt at an eight-bar period, reproduced in Example 3.8, reveals his skill in motivic variation, the Schoenbergian hallmark of technical competence. Its arch-shaped contour ascends purposefully to a climatic F5 (m. 2) and then descends to G4 (m. 4; see Example 3.7). The corresponding phrase (Example 3.8) manages to replicate and expand upon the arching shape of the original. What was previously a G4 in the second measure of the original consequent is now transferred by an octave to G5. This shift leads to the sudden emergence from the inner voices of a climactic A5 before it descends via an octave transfer to usher in the cadence (m. 8).

In their overview, the topics in Berg's lessons incorporate Schoenberg's models and their compositional processes: the composition and harmonization of motives and possible permutations of their content, the joining of motives to create phrases and of phrases to create thematic groups, and finally the composition of school forms. Example 3.9 compares these general topics to those of *MBC*'s opening sections; the first column shows

FACSIMILE 3.3
Berg's periods in C major (Fonds 21 Berg 55/I, f. 3, Österreichische Nationalbibliothek, Vienna). Courtesy Austrian National Library.

EXAMPLE 3.7
Transcription of Berg's period in C major.

the headings in *MBC*, the second summarizes their content, and the third, the content of Berg's lessons. In the most general sense, the subject matter in *MBC*'s sections I, II, and IV is analogous to that of Berg's lesson. Clearly, Schoenberg preserved aspects of his European pedagogy in California. However, as we shall see, he also reinvented and expanded some of it.

New Models

The California composer Gerald Strang was one of Schoenberg's earliest students at USC and was also his teaching assistant at UCLA. Strang's class

EXAMPLE 3.8
Transcription of Berg's variation on the C major period.

MBC	Description of Content in *MBC*	Berg's Lessons
I. Coordination of Melody and Harmony	Begins with harmonization of the motive. First, simple "broken chord forms" on one, then two, and finally three harmonies.	I. Study of motives and their harmonization
II. Motive and Motival Features in Two-Measure Phrases	Adds rhythmic features, and eventually, accompaniment, and "enriched" harmony to the motives from I.	
III. Sentences	Composition of themes based on the motives from II (with new motives added).	II. Thematic composition based on the motives from I, and based on a four plus four period.
IV. Periods		

EXAMPLE 3.9
Outline of topical framework common to Berg's lessons and MBC.

notes for Schoenberg's summer composition course (Composition 108a) at USC, dated June 24, 1936, were written twenty-nine years after Berg's 1907 lessons and six years before the earliest edition of *MBC*.[44] They include a lesson on motives analogous to Berg's in topic, method, and design. Specifically, Strang copied out a chart presenting possibilities for the permutation and harmonization of motives and a subsequent theme based on these models (see Facsimile 3.4 (recto) and Example 3.10, a transcription of Facsimile 3.4, verso).[45]

Example 3.10 contains two groupings each including four distinct motives with a possible repetition or variation of one of these. Although this results in motive successions of five components, AABCD and ABBCD, rather than the four-element successions of Berg's lesson, the pedagogical aim of Strang's exercise—composing a four-bar phrase while working with a limited number of motives—is identical to that of Berg's lesson. Interestingly, whereas Berg's notes are consistent and continuous in topics, Strang's notes related to a motivic matrix cease abruptly. Perhaps this model was too rigid to accommodate Schoenberg's increasingly nuanced teaching of motivic succession during the mid-1930s and early '40s.

No longer was the motive confined to the single-measure configuration seen in Berg's notes. Rather, it was now a flexible structure capable of straddling the boundary between two measures, or even saturating the measures through multiple, varied statements of itself. In this process, the motive acquired the sort of pliability it had always exhibited in Schoenberg's nonpedagogical compositions. Moreover, Schoenberg's motives in pedagogical works now overlapped with or nested within each other; they could be primarily rhythmic or intervallic—or neither, or both. As a result, more than four motives could appear in a four-bar phrase, a development rendering the 1907 motive matrix obsolete—even in modified form.[46]

MBC's Example 3.11 illustrates this flexibility of motives. In the opening two-measure phrase, four motives (*abcd*) nest and overlap with each other. Moreover, Schoenberg's analytic notation separates two different *kinds* of motives; the angled brackets in *a* and *c* highlight rhythmic motives, while the horizontal brackets in *b* and *d* refer to intervallic ones.[47] Such overlapping and nesting of motives in Example 3.11 were crucial for the developmental procedures of the "sentence"—a configuration beginning with a two-measure unit immediately repeated in variation and carried further through a continuation, liquidation and cadence. *MBC* contains the first discussion of the sentence structure in Schoenberg's published writings, and the first one with the pedagogical aim of teaching a student how to compose this thematic structure.[48] Thus, the mid-1930s and early '40s marked a change in Schoenberg's pedagogy—one particularly geared toward an emphasis on the sentence and its characteristic grouping: the two-measure phrase.

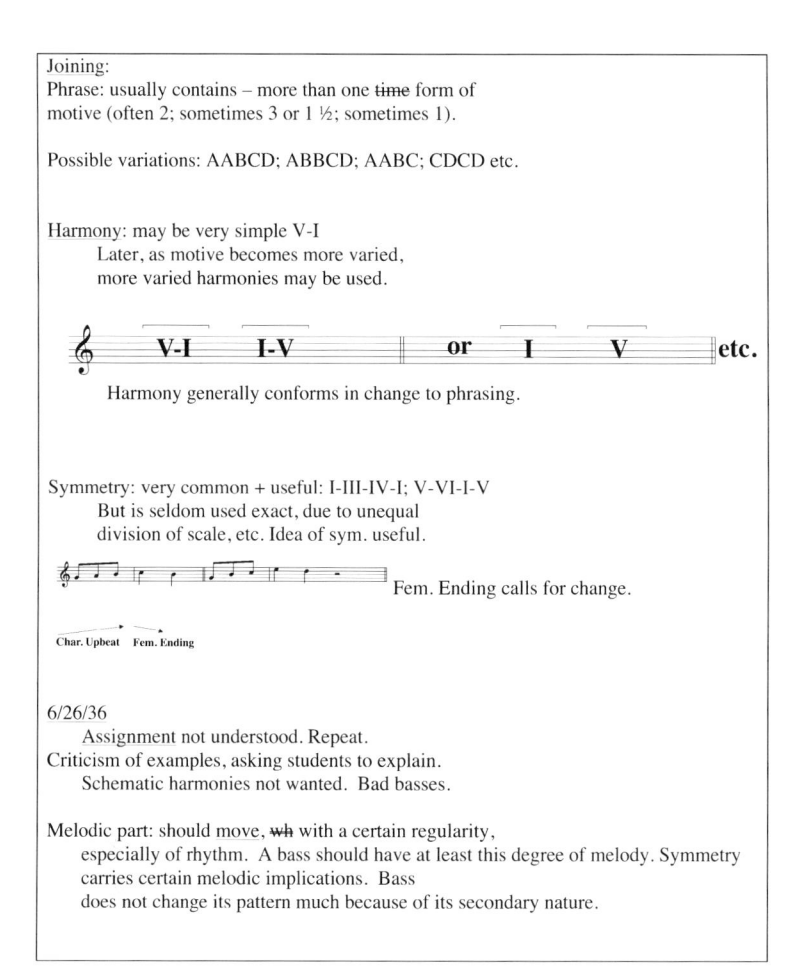

Joining:
Phrase: usually contains – more than one ~~time~~ form of
motive (often 2; sometimes 3 or 1 ½; sometimes 1).

Possible variations: AABCD; ABBCD; AABC; CDCD etc.

Harmony: may be very simple V-I
  Later, as motive becomes more varied,
  more varied harmonies may be used.

V-I I-V   or   I   V   etc.

  Harmony generally conforms in change to phrasing.

Symmetry: very common + useful: I-III-IV-I; V-VI-I-V
  But is seldom used exact, due to unequal
  division of scale, etc. Idea of sym. useful.

              Fem. Ending calls for change.

Char. Upbeat   Fem. Ending

6/26/36
  Assignment not understood. Repeat.
Criticism of examples, asking students to explain.
  Schematic harmonies not wanted. Bad basses.

Melodic part: should move, ~~wh~~ with a certain regularity,
  especially of rhythm. A bass should have at least this degree of melody. Symmetry
  carries certain melodic implications. Bass
  does not change its pattern much because of its secondary nature.

EXAMPLE 3.10

*Transcription of Facsimile 3.4 (Strang's notes for Beginning Composition 108a,
June 24, 1936), verso.*

The Two-Measure Phrase as a New Model

Strang's notes, which feature an assignment focusing on the two-measure phrase, clearly demonstrate Schoenberg's new pedagogical emphasis. The assignment requires students to join two forms of a one-bar motive together to create a phrase, and to "build a second [two-bar] phrase" to complete a

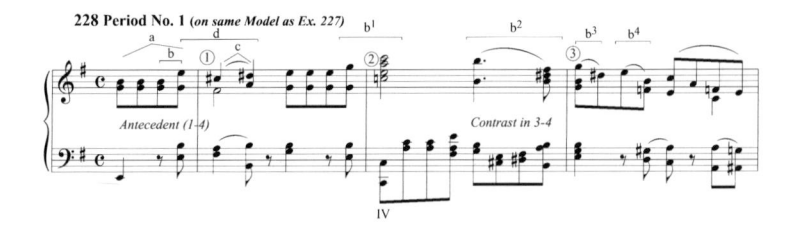

EXAMPLE 3.11
Schoenberg's analysis of motives in Example 228 from MBC.

four-bar thematic statement (Facsimile 3.4 verso, transcribed in Example 3.12).[49] The verso of this page (transcribed above in Example 3.10) features harmonic models for these two-measure phrases (the palindromic V–I | I–V and the simplified I–V successions).[50] Below this, Strang's notes show the opening two-measure phrase of a theme, above which is written "Symmetry: very common + useful."[51]

Unfortunately, the class failed to grasp the significance of two-plus-two-bar symmetry in the example, and Schoenberg asked them to repeat the assignment.[52] At the beginning of the next class meeting (June 26, 1936), Strang's notes explain that the "melodic part should move with a certain regularity, and that "symmetry carries certain melodic implications" (Example 3.10). Strang then transcribes Schoenberg's example, correctly illustrating these concepts (Facsimile 3.5, transcribed in Example 3.13).

Example 3.13 illustrates the antecedent phrase of a period encompassing a pair of clear two-measure phrases (mm. 1–2 and 3–4). The first two-measure phrase states two motives *a* and *b*, followed in the second phrase by their variations. Motive *a*[1] varies *a* by retaining its contour transposed up a third, and expanding the interval spanned by pitches three to five in *a* (from a third to a fourth). Motive *b*[1] retains the initial contour of the dotted-eighth figure, transposed up a fourth, retaining the same basic rhythm of *b* while inverting and expanding the minor second B–C to a descending fifth; D–G (in the accompaniment, the dotted-quarter rhythm from the tenor of *b* is heard in the bass of *b*[1]).

FACSIMILE 3.4
Gerald Strang's notes for Beginning Composition 108a, USC (June 24, 1936) (Gerald Strang Collection, Folder 51, Arnold Schönberg Center), verso. Transcribed as Example 3.10. Courtesy Arnold Schönberg Center.

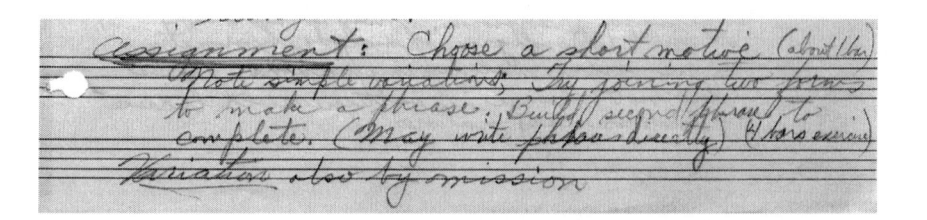

FACSIMILE 3.4
Gerald Strang's notes for Beginning Composition 108a, USC (June 24, 1936)
(Gerald Strang Collection, Folder 51, Arnold Schönberg Center), recto. Courtesy
Arnold Schönberg Center.

Assignment: Choose a short motive (about 1 bar)
        Note simple variations; Try joining two forms
        To make a phrase: Build second phrase to
        Complete. (May write phrases directly) (4 bars exercise)
        Variation also by omission

EXAMPLE 3.12
Transcription of Facsimile 3.4 (Strang's notes for Beginning
Composition 108a, June 24, 1936), recto.

Schoenberg's focus on the two-measure phrase in these examples typifies his emphasis on the sentence during the mid 1930s and '40s.[53] As mentioned above, he had briefly touched on this thematic type in *ZKIF* (1917) and in more detail in *MI* (1934–36)—even as early as the *TH* of 1911, he refers to "liquidation," a concept later associated with the continuation of a sentence.[54] He had composed sentences as early as 1897 in the Waltzes for String Orchestra and subsequently in the opening of his song, "Erwartung," *Vier Lieder*, Op. 2 No. 1 (1899).[55] However, it is only with the publication of *MBC* in 1943 that Schoenberg initially explained in published form the nuances of this iconic thematic design.[56] Whatever the origin of the concept in Schoenberg's pedagogical thinking, it played no explicit role in Berg's 1907 lesson, nor in the others that survive.[57] Even the two-measure phrase, so crucial for the sentence form, remains only a latent possibility.

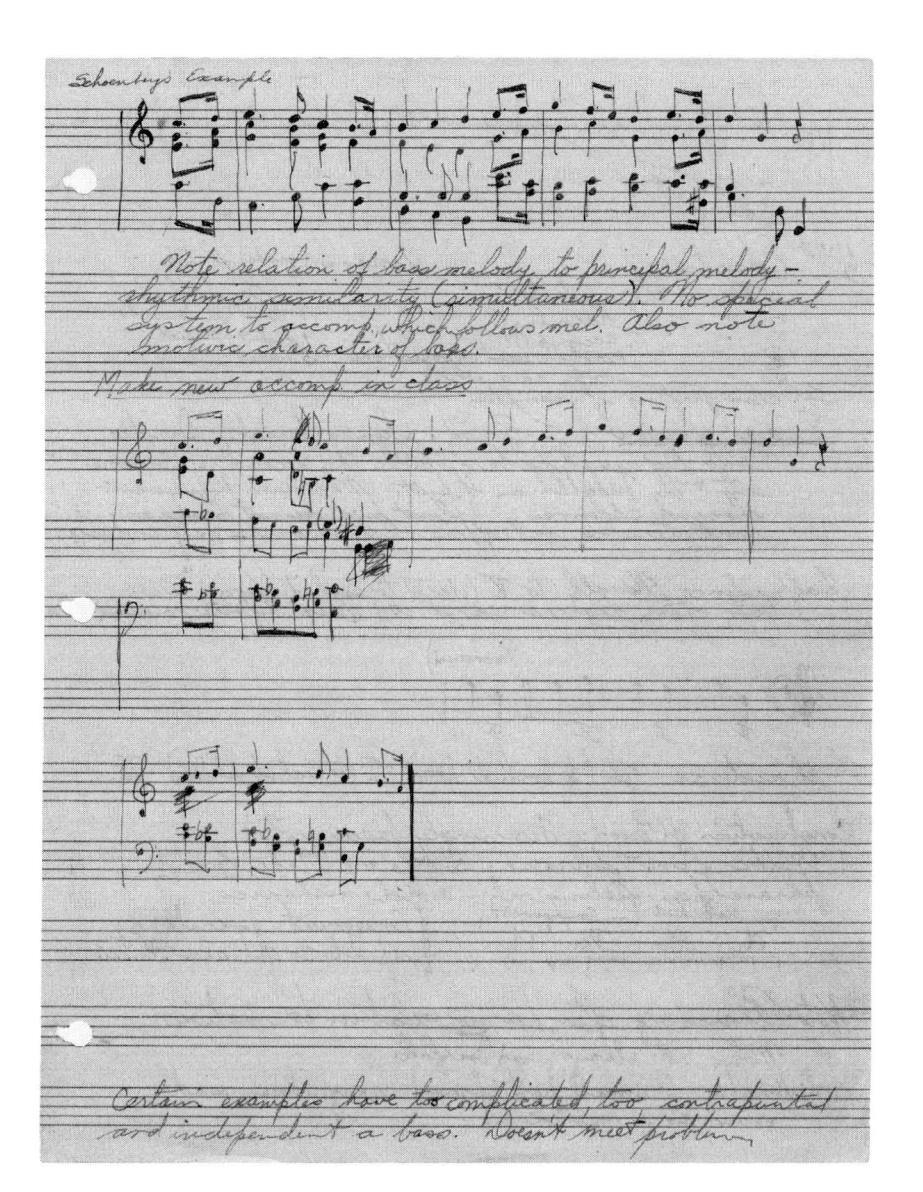

FACSIMILE 3.5
Continuation of Strang's notes for Beginning Composition 108a (June 26, 1936)
(Gerald Strang Collection, Folder 51, Arnold Schönberg Center), recto.
Courtesy Arnold Schönberg Center.

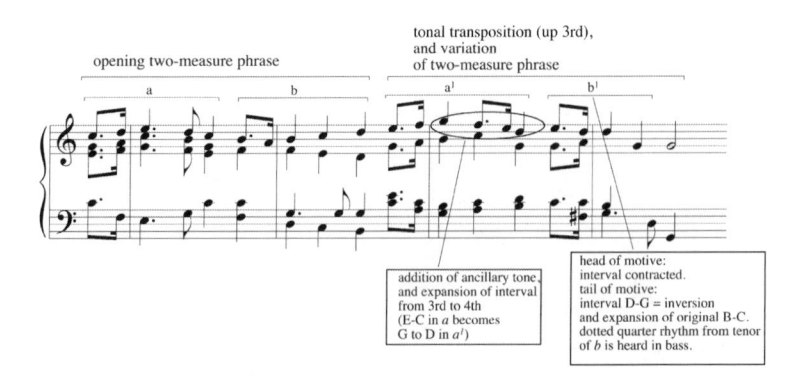

EXAMPLE 3.13
Transcription of Schoenberg's antecedent phrase at the top
of Facsimile 3.5 (brackets and analytical notation are added to emphasize
the two-measure phrase).

In *MBC*, Schoenberg introduces the two-bar grouping in conjunction with motives on broken chord forms (Ch. I. A), models for their harmonization (Ch. I. B–D) and the addition of their rhythmic features (Ch. II. A–C). Example 3.14 provides excerpts of the main sections in Ch. I–II of *MBC*. In stark contrast to Berg's lessons focused on the four-bar grouping, their content shows that all topics in *MBC*—harmony, motives, and even variation— relate to the composition of two-measure phrases.[58]

Schoenberg's two-measure phrases can be traced to the work of earlier theorists such as Koch, Lobe and Adolf Bernhard Marx, the latter whom Schoenberg particularly admired.[59] A simple example of the two-measure phrase in Marx's treatise is found in his Example 27, which presents a four-bar *Satz* divided into "zwei deutlich unterscheidbare Hälften," or two clearly distinguishable halves (Example 3.15).[60] Although he offers no specific terminology for these "halves," they are clearly analogous to Schoenberg's two-measure phrases in *MBC*, which are divisible precisely in this way. As in Schoenberg's pedagogy, the two-bar unit is implicit as the basic building block for Marx's well-known *Satz*.[61]

A lesser-known writer, composer and theory pedagogue at the Leipzig Conservatory during the early twentieth century, Stephan Krehl (1864–1924) similarly focused his introduction of harmony and form on the two-measure

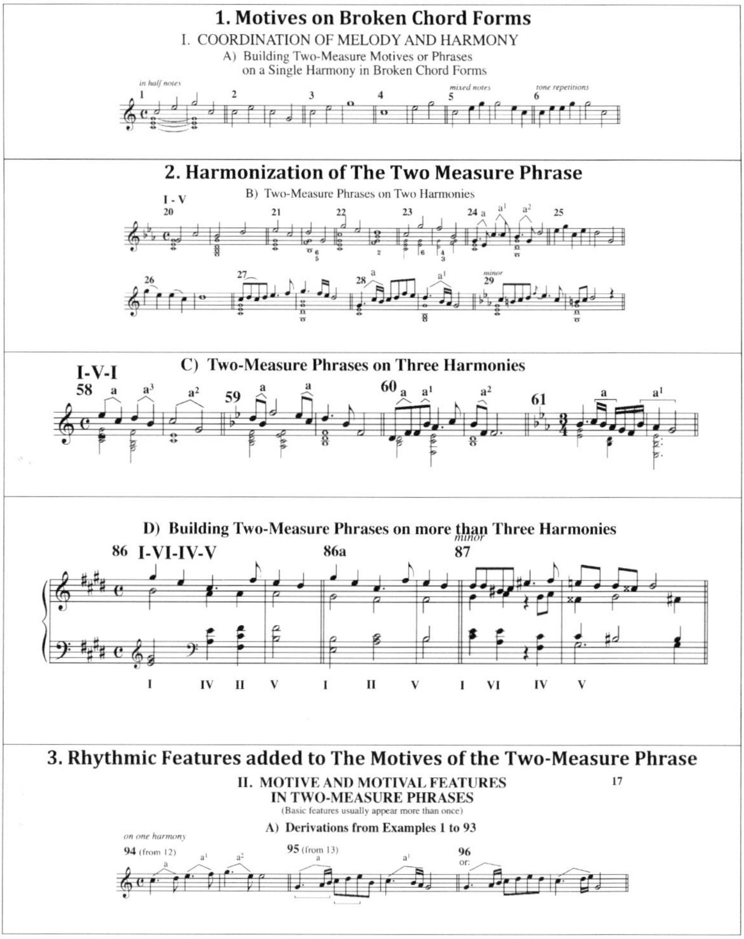

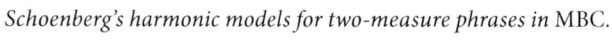

EXAMPLE 3.14
Schoenberg's harmonic models for two-measure phrases in MBC.

EXAMPLE 3.15
Two-measure grouping, early precursor to Schoenberg's two-measure phrases in MBC.
A. B. Marx, Musikalische Kompositionslehre, vol. 1 (1843), Example 27, p. 43.

phrase.[62] Schoenberg owned two of Krehl's books, including *Fuge, Erläuterung und Anleitung für Kompositionslehre* (1908) and *Musikalische Formenlehre (Kompositionslehre)*. Since the two men shared a student, Alexander Jemnitz (1890–1963), Schoenberg may have heard an account of Krehl's approaches to harmony and form. Jemnitz had studied with Krehl just before beginning his Berlin instruction with Schoenberg in 1913.[63] However, judging from the inscription on the title page of Schoenberg's copy of Krehl's *MFK*, the book was likely given to him not by Jemnitz, but by Josef Zmigrod (1902–1973), who studied with Schoenberg at the Prussian Academy of the Arts in Berlin from 1926–28 (and again in Paris, 1933), and eventually went on to become a success-ful international film composer.[64]

There are numerous annotations in this little book, now housed at the ASC, many belonging to Zmigrod rather than Schoenberg. However, several underlined passages and at least two annotations are Schoenberg's (on pages 110 and 137—the former in the characteristic red pencil he used for so many of his corrections and comments in other texts). Musicologists Julia Bungardt and Eike Fess at the Schönberg Center have dated the handwriting in the annotation on page 137 to Schoenberg's European period, and the one on page 110 to his time in the United States.[65] The decades separating the an-notations indicate that Krehl's book is one to which Schoenberg returned at various periods in his life. However, even if these annotations had not existed, the similarities between several of the ideas in Krehl's *MFK* and those in *MBC* are striking.

Both *MBC* and *MFK* introduce harmony in conjunction with the struc-ture of the "two-measure phrase," and in these discussions, harmonic ac-companiment is pointed toward specific compositional tasks. Example 3.16 shows Krehl's harmonic models for the *kleine Satz*, a structure identical to Schoenberg's two-measure phrase.[66] Like Example 3.16 in Schoenberg's Chapter I.B in *MBC*, Krehl's Example 25 begins with a setting in diatonic harmony, followed by increasingly chromatic realizations. All of his examples are based on four harmonies, i.e. a harmonic rhythm of one harmony per measure. By contrast, Schoenberg's presentation of harmony in Example 3.14 is graded, con-taining two-measure phrases first accompanied by only a single harmony (Ch. IA), then with two harmonies (IB), followed by three (IC), and so on.

25.

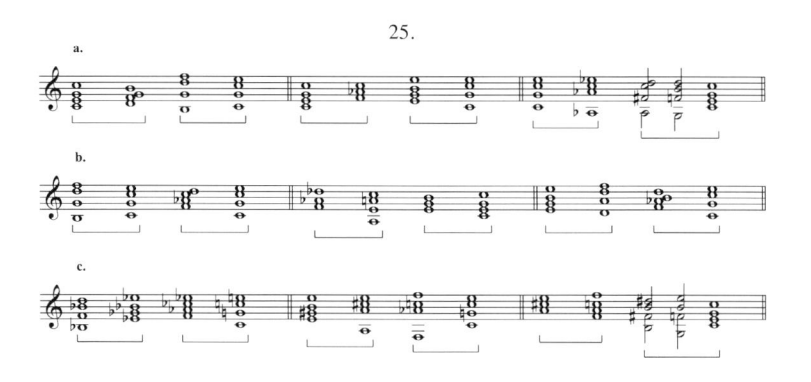

EXAMPLE 3.16

Krehl's harmonic models for the kleine Satz (MFK [1914], Example 25, p. 28). Compare
with Schoenberg's harmonic models for the two-measure phrase in Example 3.14.

Krehl also offers two possible motivic models for the *kleine Satz* distinguished by whether or not the initial motive is repeated (transposed or untransposed) or followed by a contrasting motive. In the first case, he describes the motivic structure as *Motiv* 1-1, in the second, *Motiv* 1-2. Example 3.17 shows Krehl's
bracketed grouping of the *kleine Satz* in Examples 16 and 19 from *MFK*.[67]

Example 3.18 illustrates the similarity between Krehl's analysis of
the opening of Beethoven's Op. 2, No. 3, and Schoenberg's analysis of
this same passage in *MBC*—both emphasize the two-measure phrase.
As Example 3.18 shows, Schoenberg and Krehl bracket the two-measure
groupings identically.

Krehl describes the opening of Beethoven's Op. 2, No. 3, as a simple
harmonization of one chord per motive, the abstract model of which could
consist of tonic or dominant for either motive—a description that points
toward Schoenberg's dominant- and tonic-form in the sentence. Krehl fur-
ther singles out Beethoven's I–V | V–I progression as the primary harmoni-
zation of the *kleine Satz* (See the opening progression in Example 3.16) and
as a palindrome.[68] He describes the I–V succession as a variation of V–I in
the simple two-chord model. Krehl writes:[69]

The first succession to examine here is, as in the very beginning of the forma-
tion of motives, the one from dominant and tonic. The succession of dominant

EXAMPLE 3.17

*Krehl's bracketed analysis of the kleine Satz from MFK, Examples 16 and 19,
pp. 22 and 24.*

a. Schoenberg's analysis of Beethoven's Op. 2 No. 3 in MBC.
Courtesy Belmont Music Publishers.

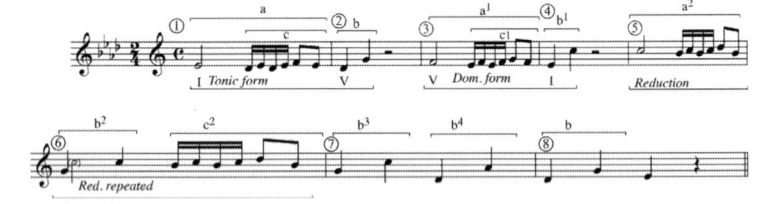

b. Krehl's analysis of Beethoven's Op. No. 3 in MFK.

EXAMPLE 3.18

*Comparison of Beethoven's Op. 2 No. 3, analyzed as the opening of a sentence in
Schoenberg's MBC, with Krehl's analysis in MFK.*

and tonic is conceivable for both motives. But for a well-rounded phrase, then, it is just as favorable if it goes in the first half from the tonic to the dominant and in the second half, the return follows from there to the tonic.[70]

By contrast, in Example 3.19 (from *MBC*), Schoenberg integrates the two-measure phrase into the standard sentence form having a continuation, liquidation, and cadence. Moreover, he explains the opening of the sentence as a "repetition of measures 1–2 accommodated to a contrasting harmony"—typically V. Like Krehl, Schoenberg offers the palindromic design, "I–V contrasted with the reverse succession V–I," as a typical framework for this opening segment (see Examples 190–91 and the alternatives 192–97). Schoenberg emphasizes the I – V | V – I succession throughout *MBC* and employs it in many of his original sentences (see Examples 190–197, and 199 {Example 3.19}).

Models for Harmonizing the Two-Measure Phrase

Schoenberg strongly believed in an integrated study of the subdisciplines of music theory. Thus his California students simultaneously enrolled in composition, harmony, and form: Structural Functions of Harmony 106, Form and Analysis 104, and Composition 105. As mentioned above, since *MBC* was conceived for students taking this program of study, the text's consideration of harmony and form was merely perfunctory. Moreover, the book's tight publication schedule, the prioritization of his new counterpoint text, and poor health, prevented Schoenberg from incorporating further pertinent materials from these other subdisciplines into *MBC*.[71] Thus, my Appendices 5–6 fill in the theoretical notions necessary for understanding the treatment of harmony in *MBC*.

As explained in Appendix 5, Schoenberg's theory of harmony was dependent on his concept of monotonality, which he describes in *SFH*:[72]

Every digression from the tonic is considered to be still within the tonality, whether directly or indirectly, closely or remotely related. In other words, there is only *one tonality* in a piece, and every segment formerly considered as another tonality is only a region, a harmonic contrast within that tonality.[73]

EXAMPLE 3.19
Schoenberg's use of the palindromic I–V | V–I succession as
the opening of the sentence in Examples 190–197 and 199 in MBC.
Courtesy Belmont Music Publishers.

Schoenberg describes such "contrasts" created by the establishment of regions in one of five ways: "direct and close," "indirect but close," "indirect,"
"indirect and remote," or "distant."[74]

    Through this network of relationships, Schoenberg views the establish-
ment of even distant harmonic regions as mere deviations subordinate to
the centripetal force of a tonic. Thus he is able to interpret all events in a
piece—whether thematic, motivic, or harmonic—within the main tonality.[75]

Schoenberg's monotonal harmonies are grounded on the "chromatic scale," rather than the diatonic. He explains:

> Once the chromatic scale is established as the basis for harmonic thought, then we shall be able to interpret even such modulations as these as functions of the key, and to assume, here also, that we do not leave the key. This is similar to what we are doing, even now, in our cadences, which will soon contain everything formerly regarded as modulatory, now serving just to express the key.[76]

For Schoenberg, the idea is straightforward: if a monotonal key is fully chromatic, then chromatic chords must still belong to the key. As a result, they function in reference to a region within the main tonality rather than a modulation in the traditional sense. Schoenberg refers to such chromatic chords as transformations: altered chords incorporating chromatic pitches called "substitute" tones borrowed from foreign tonal regions.[77]

The inclusion of such chromatic alterations in transformations may temporarily challenge the tonal cohesion of phrase structures, and this challenge often serves a particular formal function. For example, in sentence–forms, the harmony in the first two measures is usually diatonic, whereas the harmony of the continuation and tends to be chromatic, dependent on transformation chords.[78] Similarly, the antecedent of the period is diatonic, and the consequent can be either diatonic or chromatic.[79] In its coverage of the two-measure phrase, the pedagogical plan of *MBC* reflects this gradated approach in terms of harmonic complexity— from single-chord progressions (Example 3.14, Section IA), to two-chord progressions (IB, shown in Example 3.20), or those based on "more than three harmonies" (ID). All begin on the tonic and progress systematically to triads on every diatonic degree except VII, which Schoenberg understood as a substitute function for V.[80] Thus he shows a systematic thoroughness in teaching harmonic progression and its relation to thematic design and formal function.

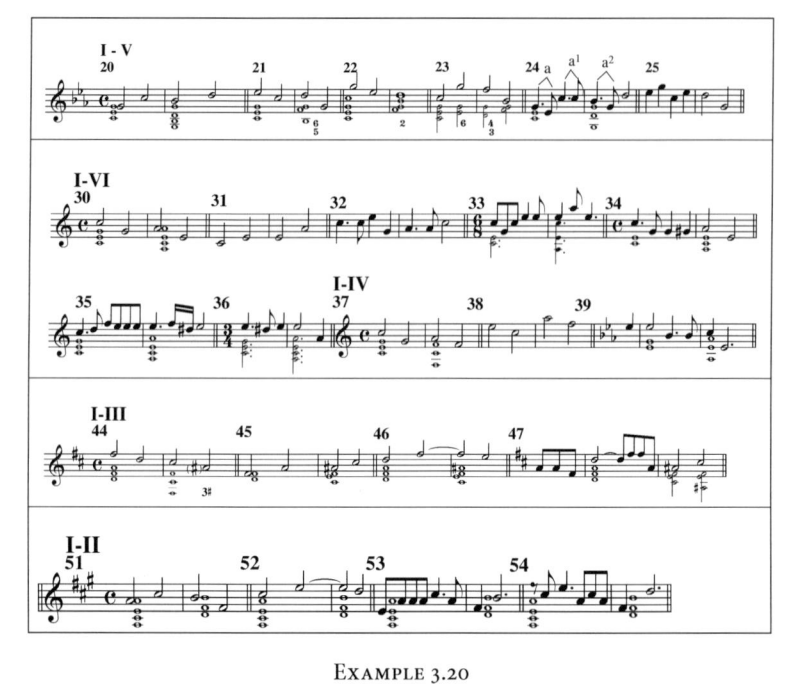

EXAMPLE 3.20
Schoenberg's diatonic harmonization of the two-measure phrase in IB from MBC.
Courtesy Belmont Music Publishers.

In *MBC*, the diatonic harmonization of the two-measure phrase serves an expository, or "establishing" function.[81] Harmonized in this way, the opening two-measure phrase can then be extended to form either a period or a sentence. In the sentence, a two-measure phrase is followed by its repeated variation extending into a continuation containing the identifying sentential characteristics: reductions of the principal motive, sequences, and a liquidation in which the characteristic features of the motive are gradually eliminated in preparation for the final cadence (see Example 3.21).[82] As in Example 3.21, the liquidation often makes specific use of reduced variants of *a*, labeled "halves of *a*" in Schoenberg's analysis.

Schoenberg's notion of harmony in the sentence also gives rise to the idea of *harmonic variation* first discussed in 1911 in *TH*.[83] As the examples throughout *MBC* demonstrate, harmonic variation may involve either elaborating a basic harmonic framework by "inserting" diatonic or chromatic

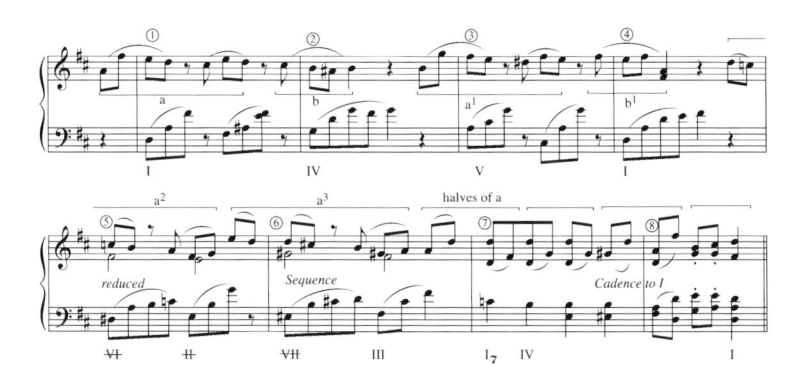

EXAMPLE 3.21
Sentence, Example 220 from MBC. *Courtesy Belmont Music Publishers.*

chords between principal harmonies, or by substituting transformed harmonies for diatonic ones.[84] The second of these techniques is illustrated
clearly in II.D from *MBC*, which features basic harmonic progressions such
as I–V for two-measure phrases, "enriched" through the insertion of one
or more harmonies, including II, IV, or VI.[85] In Example 3.21, *a3* is a harmonic variation in the latter sense—the transformed harmonies VI–II–VII
substitute for what would otherwise be a diatonic progression: VI–II–V–(I).
This variation is complementary to the simultaneous intervallic, motivic,
and rhythmic variants of motive *a*. For Schoenberg, harmonic variation
(*harmonische Variation*) was seldom a "fill-in-the blank" process. Rather,
he demanded that harmonic progressions must be "invented" (*erfunden*)
on the basis of their context. In order to "invent," the student must systematically learn to explore the possibilities at hand and to compose original accompaniments.[86] Crucially, Schoenberg taught his students that their
"invented" harmonies would coherently feed into the "constructive functions" of motivic and thematic structures—configurations used to generate
a work's form.[87]

Moreover, the constructive functions of harmony were predicated on the
notion that harmonic designs were crafted to fit the internal logic of a particular work.[88] Specifically, harmony had the inherent ability to "move" or
to "stand;" and such characters determined whether the phrase to which the

harmony belonged was "introductory, establishing, transitional, connecting, [or] closing."[89] For example, the constructive function of the opening phrase in Example 3.21 was one of "stability:" to establish the tonality in the opening two-measure phrase. Conversely, the constructive function of the chromatic harmony in the continuation of Example 3.21 (mm. 5–6) was meant to question the stability of a tonality. The concept of the constructive function of harmony is particularly relevant in relation to the sentence, a form often incorporating a balance of diatonic and chromatic harmony as a means of articulating its unique blend of establishing and developing functions.

In Example 3.22 (Schoenberg's chromatic recomposition of the sentence in Example 3.21), the opening is identical to the original theme, but with a more elaborate continuation involving a move to the dominant region and emphasis on its Neapolitan, through an artificial dominant (labeled as ♭VI) (mm. 5–8). The cadential formula of this passage features the common classical idiom ♭2–1–7, harmonized with Neap.6—Ħ—V (mm. 7–8, beginning beat 3) (in this pattern, as here, Ħ is typically a fully diminished seventh chord, applied to V as an artificial dominant). In terms of its motivic structure, Schoenberg's continuation has a "moving," or developmental function highlighted by an increase in harmonic rhythm and an emphasis on transformed harmonies.

Example 3.22 outlines the developmental character of this continuation through its systematic reduction and dense overlap of motivic variants. Example 3.22b shows the derivation of the initial motive of the continuation, which begins with a two-measure sequence based on a modified retrograde inversion of motive x. Example 3.22c illustrates the dense web of motivic development in this sequence, beginning with the retrograde inversion of x (m. 5) (#1, Example 3.22c) overlapping with a variation of itself (#2), its initial interval inverted to generate the motive A–G–B. This line is answered by a verbatim statement of the "tail" of motive b (#3), punctuated by a statement of the tail of x (the sixth-motive of the theme) (#4). The entire pattern, with the sixth-figure of motive x, now functioning as an anacrusis, is then sequenced in measure 6 (#6 and #7).

Measures 7–8 form a quintessential liquidation of the sentence, with the "characteristic features" of the original motive further fragmented and

a. Sentence, Example 221.

b. Derivation of RI(x) (mm. 4–5).

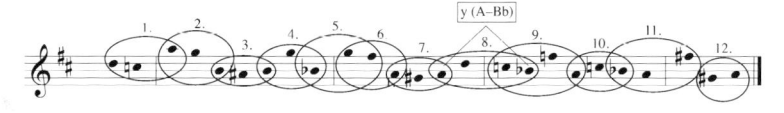

c. Motivic overlap and elision (mm. 5–8).

1.	RI(x)
2.	I(#1), first interval inverted
3.	y (tail of b)
4.	consecutive sixth motives (x)
5.	T1(original x)
6.	sequence of #2
7.	sequence of #3
8.	y, now encompassing a variation of x (contraction of initial motive)
9.	overlapping var. of x, contraction of initial motive
10.	var. of x, contraction of initial interval
11.	T−4(#1)
12.	fragment of y

EXAMPLE 3.22

Schoenberg's recomposition of the sentence in Example 2.22 with a chromatic continuation (appears as Example 221 in MBC). Courtesy Belmont Music Publishers.

abstracted as they loosen their previous obligations in preparation for the cadence.[90] This fragmentation, combined with a heightened tension between motive, harmony and meter, creates a momentum toward the conclusion of the theme in m. 8. First, motive *y*, functioning as a neighbor to B♭ (neap.), expands as A–D–C–B♭ (Example 3.22c, #8), so that it now cleverly embeds a contracted variation of *x* (A–C–B♭). This iteration of *y* then immediately overlaps with a statement of *x* cutting across tonal and metric boundaries (#9, C–B♭–F) (m. 7, beats 1 and 2), now beginning on a downbeat instead of an anacrusis and landing on an unstable artificial dominant (applied to the Neap.) (m. 7, beat 2) as opposed to a stable tonic harmony.

Due to the motivic saturation throughout the continuation, the associative power of motive *x* allows it to be heard despite the persistent pull of the artificial dominant resolving to the Neapolitan in A major (beats 1 and 3 of m. 7)—a pull that would normally prioritize B♭ (in conjunction with the conclusion of motive *y*). Melodically, the passage ends with a motivically nondescript stepwise figure (C–B♭–A) leading to the cadence through a resourceful overlapping statement of *x* (B♭–A–F♯) (#11), now employed as a cadential figure, followed by a final "residue" of *y* (G⊠–A) (#12).

The majority of the sentences in *MBC* (including Examples 222–24, 22) and the alternative endings in Example 220 feature continuations comparable in structure and character to those in Example 3.22.[91] The same constructive functions are featured later in the school compositions of *MBC*: the Minuet (Example 242), the Scherzo in G major (Example 245), and the untitled scherzo (Example 247).[92]

A Model School Composition: Schoenberg's Scherzo in D Major

Schoenberg's untitled scherzo (Example 3.23) opens with a hemiola-laden theme moving from the tonic to the dominant region (mm. 8–16).[93] Here, the modulatory portion of the theme (mm. 4–14) is larger and more tonally complex than analogous excerpts in *MBC's* other school compositions; it touches on the dorian (Em), submediant (Bm), and dorian of the

submediant (C♯m) regions before finally arriving at a half-cadence in the
tonic region in m. 16 (See Example 3.23).[94] In fact, the basic theme is followed by an "extension" (Schoenberg's label) which is itself a sentence
beginning with a two-measure phrase (mm. 9–10) sequenced upwards
stepwise (mm. 11–12), and answered by a continuation (mm. 12–16),
thus employing the same techniques of liquidation as the sentences in
Examples 3.21 and 3.22.

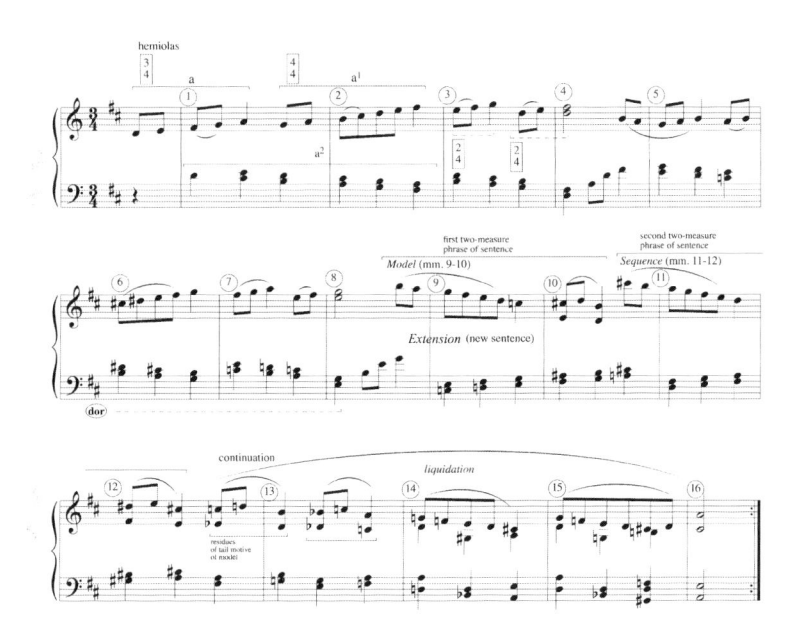

EXAMPLE 3.23
Untitled scherzo, A section (mm. 1–16), MBC. Courtesy Belmont Music Publishers.

However, in this case, the developmental function of the opening
theme (mm. 4–8) ultimately is extended through the modulatory character of the second sentence (9–16), so that mm. 4–16 encompass one large
developmental function. Motivically, the "extension" is a variant of the
initial theme—inverting not only the basic motive of the opening theme,
but also the accompanimental figure (mm. 9–10), the latter sequenced
stepwise upward to create tension and forward momentum (mm. 11–12),

which is symmetrically balanced by a release of tension through a *descending* stepwise sequence at the start of the continuation (mm. 13–14) (i.e. the pairs of harmonic centers in this sequence Bm—C♯m (mm. 10–12) and G—F (mm. 12–13), together balance symmetrically about A, the harmonic goal of this section.[95] In this way, the harmony in mm. 10–13 fulfills its constructive function of challenging the tonic while leading to momentary stability in the dominant region—first through symmetrical balancing, and then via a more traditional cadence. Moreover, the function of the liquidation—to release the tension of the previous developmental tendencies—is also clarified harmonically, through a repetition of the half-cadence (mm. 14 and 16).

The basic design for part of the continuation of Schoenberg's extension in the scherzo seems to have found its way into Schoenberg's Theme and Variations for Wind Band, Op. 43a, a work composed at the same time as he was preparing the text for *MBC*.[96] (Example 3.25 shows the opening sentence of the work with its characteristic two-measure phrases). Despite the harmonic complexity of these groupings, they remain recognizable as the same basic thematic unit. Example 3.24 shows how the continuation in Op. 43a overshoots its initial harmonic goal on the dominant in m. 6, traveling through the flat mediant of the mediant region en route to a half-cadence in the minor submediant (E♭ minor) (m. 9). Example 3.25 shows the similarity between the first four measures of this continuation (mm. 4–6), and the analogous passage in the scherzo.

Example 3.25 shows the similar function of each pattern as the opening of a continuation phrase; each features an identical internal intervallic pattern (+2, –3), which is then sequenced stepwise downwards; each employs the same d5-10 linear intervallic pattern. Finally, the two phrases of the continuation lead to similar half-cadences in their respective tonic regions. Considering that the continuation motive in Example 3.25 is itself a condensation of the opening motive in Op. 43, Schoenberg's untitled scherzo may have had some influence not only on the passage in mm. 4–6, but also on the theme itself.

The idea of writing a piece for amateur wind band certainly could have been on Schoenberg's mind when he began working on *MBC*. And in

EXAMPLE 3.24

Opening sentence of Op. 43a. Courtesy Belmont Music Publishers.

a. Op. 43a. Courtesy Belmont Music Publishers.

b. Untitled scherzo, *MBC*. Courtesy Belmont Music Publishers.

EXAMPLE 3.25

Comparison of continuations from untitled scherzo and Op. 43a.

hindsight, it is clear that the timing of Op. 43, its similar musical language, and its identically targeted performers—college-aged Americans—makes it a kindred work to *MBC*. In Op. 43 Schoenberg incorporates many of the methods of thematic design, motivic variation, and contrapuntal techniques that his California students had learned in their classes.

Modeling the Two-Measure Phrase as *Grundgestalt*: Schoenberg's Minuet in B♭

Each of the school compositions discussed above purposefully incorporates the pedagogical components outlined in *MBC*. Despite their clear didactic focus, these examples are often complex in character. Schoenberg's Minuet in B♭ is notable for its symmetrical harmonic design—one encapsulating in miniature the same principle of inversional balance that generates the Chart of Regions (*SFH*), and one that ultimately guides the tonal design of many of Schoenberg's early works, including *Verklärte Nacht* and the First String Quartet in D minor, Op. 7.[97] Example 3.26 shows the harmonic design of

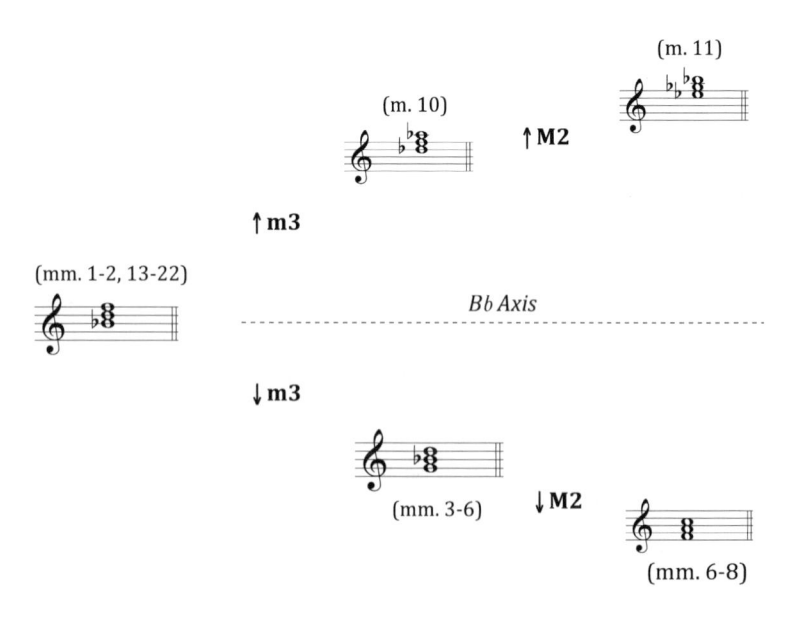

EXAMPLE 3.26
Inversional balance of harmonic regions in Schoenberg's Minuet, MBC.

Schoenberg's Minuet (A section), which moves from the tonic to the submediant (mm. 3–6), then to the dominant region (m. 8); the regions progress from B♭ to G minor to F (see lower half of Example 3.26). In the contrasting section, this pattern is inverted to (B♭)–D♭–E♭ minor (see upper half of Example 3.26). In this way, the initial move to G minor in the A section is answered by a tonicization of D♭ (the flat mediant) in the contrasting section, and the tonicization of F by a move to E♭ (the minor subdominant). Thus, B♭ in Example 3.26 is positioned as a central tonic axis, much like the tonic in the Chart of the Regions.

This symmetrical regional design is not only similar to the harmonic balance of the continuation in Schoenberg's untitled scherzo (Example 3.23), but is also analogous to the inversional mediant pattern in the Scherzo from Beethoven's Piano Sonata, Op. 31, No. 3 Indeed, Stein's notes demonstrate that Schoenberg had quoted the theme of this Scherzo (for its motivic, rather than harmonic, design) in Composition 105 (Facsimile 3.6 as transcribed in Example 3.27); moreover, he mentions this piece in connection with its truncated recapitulation in *MBC* (65).[98]

Although the inversional design in Beethoven's Scherzo is tonal rather than real, its basic structure is similar enough to warrant a comparison (see Example 3.28). Considering that both works immediately gravitate to a striking half-cadence in the submediant region near their openings, perhaps Schoenberg even had Op. 31 in mind as a model for his Minuet.

This symmetrical design recalls Schoenberg's lifelong preoccupation with inversional symmetry as means of achieving formal balance, whether through the pairing of inversionally combinatorial rows, the mirroring of motive forms, or inversional recapitulations (the most renowned being the Largo of the Fourth String Quartet, Op. 37).[99] Given the pedagogical context of this little minuet, the symmetry of this modulatory scheme also recalls Schoenberg's mention of inversional balance in *ZKIF* as a means of achieving coherence, and his discussion of symmetry as "one of the principles of form."[100] Although Schoenberg there failed to provide any significant elaboration of these points, the Minuet in *MBC* offers an effective demonstration of these principles.

FACSIMILE 3.6

Schoenberg's quotation of Beethoven's Scherzo Op. 31 No. 3 from his composition course at UCLA, undated, verso. (Leonard Stein Collection, Arnold Schönberg Center). Courtesy Arnold Schönberg Center.

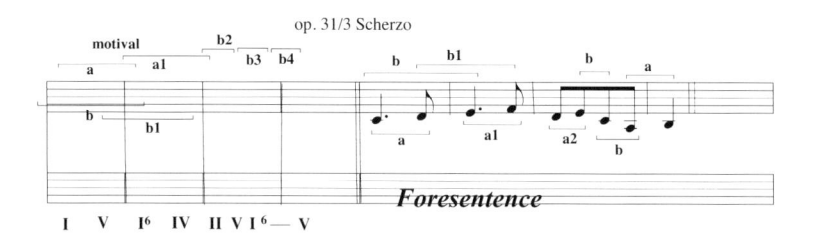

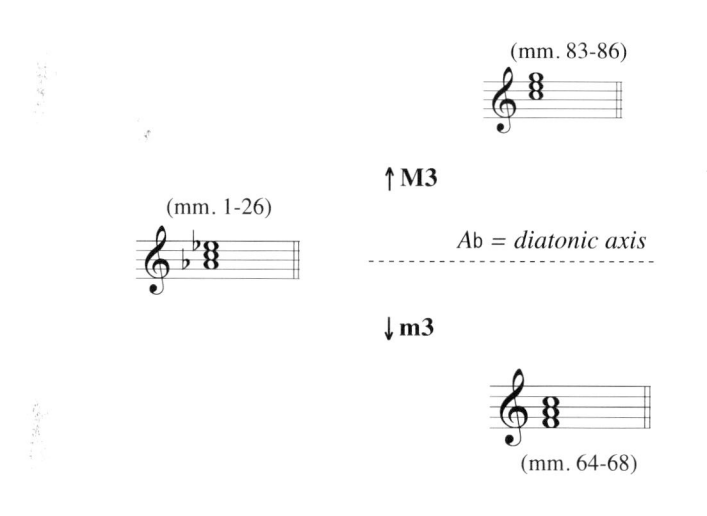

EXAMPLE 3.27

Transcription of Facsimile 3.6 (Schoenberg's analysis of the theme from Beethoven's Scherzo Op. 31 No. 3).

EXAMPLE 3.28

Inversional balance of harmonic regions in Beethoven's Scherzo Op. 31 No. 3.

Like most of the themes in *MBC*, the opening phrase of the Minuet may be grouped into a pair of two-measure phrases, which serve an expository function while unfolding the "tonal problem" of the work.[101] The first of these, the *Grundgestalt*, or basic shape, is composed of two motives (see Example 3.29). Motive *a* outlines the third D–B♭ through a stepwise descent followed by a brief nonharmonic neighbor figure, B♭–A–B♭. Owing to its potential for dual interpretation in either B♭ or G minor, this span of a third functions as the tonal problem of the Minuet—first confirming the tonic (m. 1) and then immediately spurring the work's earliest conflict by initiating a

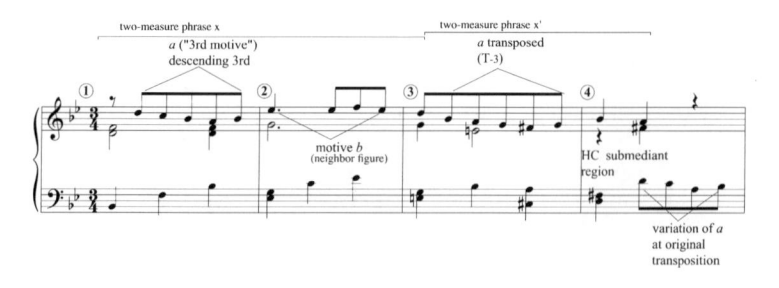

EXAMPLE 3.29

*Two-measure phrases and motivic structure in mm. 1–4 of Schoenberg's Minuet
from* MBC.

move to the submediant region, when it is heard in the upper voice (con-
densed) (m. 3, first beat) and again in the tenor (m. 4).

The second motive of the *Grundgestalt, b* (m. 2), elaborates the tail
neighbor figure of *a* (B♭–A–B♭), transposing, inverting, and expanding it diatonically from a semitone to a whole tone (E♭–F–E♭). This variation employs
what Schoenberg described as *Gliederung*, or the "division" of a work "into
functioning parts," in a lecture for his USC course Construction of Themes
(Facsimile 3.7).[102] Example 3.30 provides a transcription of Strang's notes for
this lecture.

Example 3.31 illustrates the way in which this second figure initiates
a larger, harmonically supported neighbor figure (mm. 2–3), completed
only when the decorated E♭ (m. 2) resolves to D5 (m. 3). Despite this
completion of the neighbor figure, a satisfactory resolution remains un-
supported as the harmony simultaneously shifts to a surprising artificial dominant chord (♯) to begin the second two-measure phrase (m. 3).
The goal of this second two-measure phrase, the dramatic half-cadence
in the submediant region (m. 4), only compounds the imbalance trig-
gered by the transformation in m. 3. This cadence and the subsequent
tonicization of G minor (mm. 4–6) realize the tonal problem implied by
the dual nature of motive *a*, and they eventually lead to the first attempt
at reconciliation: the symmetrical balancing of the submediant region
by the flat mediant in the opening of the B section (mm. 9–11) discussed
above (Example 3.30).

4.sc.0

Construction of Themes — Schönberg — Oct. 1935

Carry thru :— quotes Schopenhauer: "Every great idea can be expressed in 1 sentence", but to prove, establish such an idea requires carrying out its implication. Presentation from various sides.

Develope :— not an aim but means. Means growth. A method presenting in different lights.

Construction of themes : Themes _not_ confined to few types but of manifold character

Creation of parts — that fulfill demands of logic, clearness, transparency & sonority in their union

Manifold ways to   use, work out, use and develope musical ideas and build.

Homophonic-melodic method developes by variation. Joining of smaller parts to one another (simultaneous cadence dividing into parts).

Gliederung — ~~dividing~~ division into functioning parts. (glieder, gegleider)

Contrapuntal: materials not varied. Continuous flow (not broken by simultaneous cadences, except exceptional; parts not separated), secures succession of different forms of ideas thru varying contrp. combination.

Satz :— vertical joining of parts.   Satz-weise
part-combination   Setz-weise

10/15/35
Harmonize given theme; accompany; set for string orch; piano, violin, cello; flute, oboe, clarinet, bassoon, 1 horn, strings 5 solo strings.

FACSIMILE 3.7
Gerald Strang's notes for Schoenberg's Construction of Themes, USC, October 15, 1935 (Gerald Strang Collection, Folder 51, Arnold Schönberg Center), recto. Courtesy Arnold Schönberg Center.

Construction of Themes – Schönberg – Oct. 1935

Carry thru – quotes Schopenhauer: "Every great idea can be
    expressed in 1 sentence," but to prove, establish such
    an idea requires carrying out its implication. Presenta-
    tion from various sides.
Develop: — not an aim but means. Means growth. A method
    presenting in different lights.

Construction of themes: Themes not confined to few types but
    of manifold character

Creation of parts – that fulfill demands of logic, clearness,
    transparency & sonority in their union.

Manifold ways to   use, work out, use and develop
    Musical ideas and build.

Homophonic – melodic method develops by variation. Joining
    of smaller parts to one another (simultaneous cadence
    dividing into parts).
            division
Gliederung – ~~divided~~ into functioning parts. (glieder, gegliedert)

Contrapuntal: materials not varied. Continuous flow (not broken
    by simultaneous cadences, except exceptional; parts
    not separated). Secures succession of different
    forms of ideas thru varying contrap. combination.

Satz: – vertical joining of parts.   Satz-weise
        Part-combination   Setz-weise

10/15/35
        Harmonize given theme; accompany; set for string orch;
            piano violin, cello, flute, oboe, ~~cl~~ clarinet, bassoon, horn, trumpet
            5 solo strings.

EXAMPLE 3.30

*Transcription of Facsimile 3.7 (Strang's notes for Construction
of Themes, October 15, 1935, recto).*

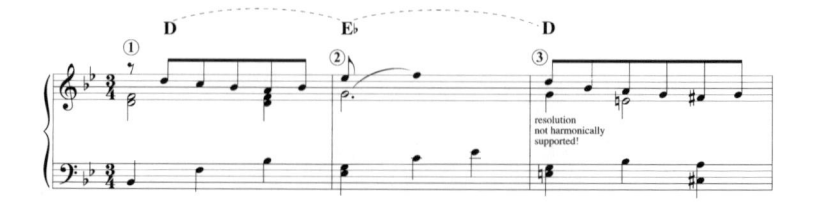

EXAMPLE 3.31

Schoenberg, Minuet, MBC: neighbor figure in mm. 2–3.

The first "implication" of the idea has thus been "carried out," as Schoenberg described it in his lecture (Example 3.30). But the idea has yet to be "proven," a bringing together that can be only completed with the return of the tonic key. Schoenberg's comment in this lecture regarding the "manifold ways to use, work out . . . and develop musical ideas" would seem to speak to the contextuality of the idea and the necessity of tailoring it to each work.

Schoenberg's symmetrical regional design in the Minuet may bear some similarity to earlier common-practice compositions, yet it arises naturally as a consequence of events within this work. In this way, harmony in the Minuet is both invented and constructed to create a tonal design fitting the work's specific motivic and formal needs. Schoenberg again touches on the contextual nature of composition in his 1935 lecture when he explains that "creation of parts" in any work must "fulfill [the] demands of logic, clearness, transparency, and sonority in their union." In the Minuet, this logic and "sonority [of] union" is heard in the way in which the harmonic third-relations (tonic/submediant and tonic/flat mediant) present themselves "from all sides" through motive *a* (e.g., D–B♭)—relations traced to the two-measure *Grundgestalt*.

The first stage of this presentation, summarized in Example 3.29, begins when motive *a* is transposed by descending third (m. 3) so that its progression mimics its own internal intervallic structure—an instance of Schoenberg's comment in Example 3.30 regarding the parts of a work fulfilling "the demands of logic, clearness, transparency, and sonority in their union." The transposition itself is real (see Example 3.29), so that the tail of *a* (B♭–A–B♭, m. 1) becomes G–F♯–G (m. 3). This figure is then analogously interpreted, with the F♯, like A (m. 2), functioning as a local leading tone. As a result, the passage proceeds with a sense of inevitability to the half-cadence in the submediant region mentioned above (m. 4).

This half-cadence and its inversional equivalent in the B section explore the implications of the descending third in motive *a* from the *Grundgestalt*. Taken as a whole, these passages constitute the first stage of the presentation of the musical idea; in Schoenberg's words, they "establish the idea." During this stage of presentation, the harmonic ambiguity of the *Grundgestalt* and its

its motives spawns several musical conflicts. The real transposition of motive *a* leads to the submediant, avoiding the consonant support of the neighbor figure (mm. 2–3) through harmonic transformation and through the thwarted passing motion from E♭ to E♮ (see the bass line in Examples 3.29 and 3.31), which in turn lead to subsequent attempts at balance in the contrasting section. This section quite literally strives for a sense of balance through inversional symmetry (see Example 3.26).

Example 3.32 demonstrates the degree to which the "demands of logic . . . through their union" inform the motivic development in the contrasting middle section of the Minuet (mm. 9–12). Example 3.32a shows the two-measure phrases constituting this contrasting middle section (mm. 9–10 and 11–12), the second of which is a variation of the first. The characteristic +3 and –1 intervallic succession, transferred to an inner voice (m. 11), exemplifies Schoenberg's notion of the "vertical joining of parts" or "part-combination" described in Example 3.30.

In Example 3.32b, the initial motive in the two-measure phrase (m. 9) is related to motive *a* at the opening of the piece. The relation constitutes a hypothetical three-stage process. In Stage 1 the original motive (m. 1) is shifted over to include E♭ from the downbeat of m. 2; in Stage 2 the succession of figures 1 and 2 constituting the motive are reversed (and figure 1 is transposed up a minor third and elided with figure 2); and finally, in Stage 3 the motive is adjusted to fit the harmonic region of the flat mediant (D♭) (see m. 11 of Example 3.32a), resulting in an expansion of motive *a*. Example 3.32c provides an alternative view of this process via transposition, inversion, and retrograde inversion.

Clearly, the inversional harmonic balance of Schoenberg's Minuet is closely wedded to the mirroring of the opening motive illustrated in Examples 3.32b and 3.32c—a pairing that provides a sense of balance between the opening and contrasting sections. However, the ultimate restoration of balance is achieved only when the opening theme is recapitulated in conjunction with the tonic return in mm. 13–22. As shown in Example 3.33, motive *a*, now in the bass, is harmonized with its characteristic interval of a third in counterpoint with the neighbor figure E♭–D from Example 3.33. This is where the idea is "proven," as Schoenberg explains it in his lecture.

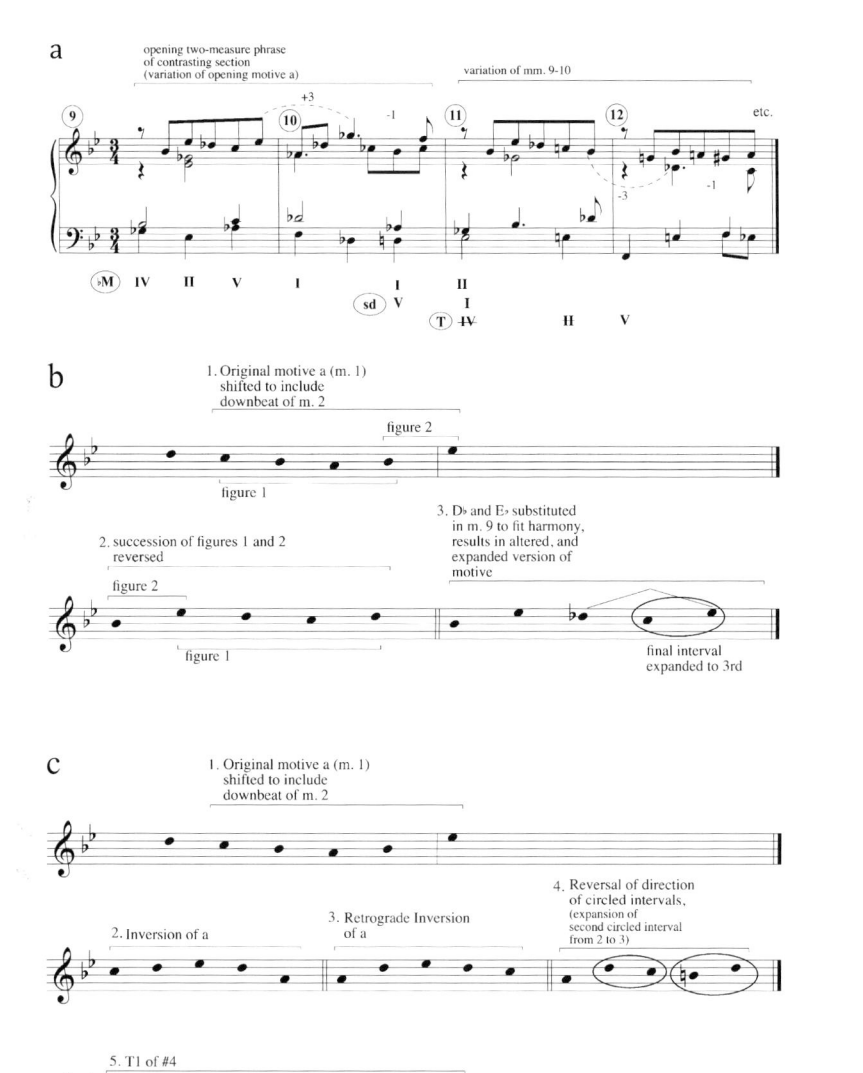

EXAMPLE 3.32

Schoenberg, Minuet, MBC: comparison of the contrasting middle sections with the second two-measure phrase of the theme.

Neighbor figure
E♭-D. Resolution
now provided with
consonant support

motive *a*

EXAMPLE 3.33
Schoenberg, Minuet, MBC: motive a and neighbor figure b combined at the start of the recapitulation.

In Example 3.34 motives *a* and *b* (the neighbor figure), once agents of tonal disruption, ultimately combine into a unified expression of reconciliation. In m. 15 (Example 3.34) motive *a* is transposed stepwise upward, where E♭ joins in a passing motion to F; this resolves the problem of the thwarted passing motion in the bass from mm. 2–4 (Example 3.29). Once this final stage of reconciliation is achieved, the closing dominant pedal begins (mm. 19–22).

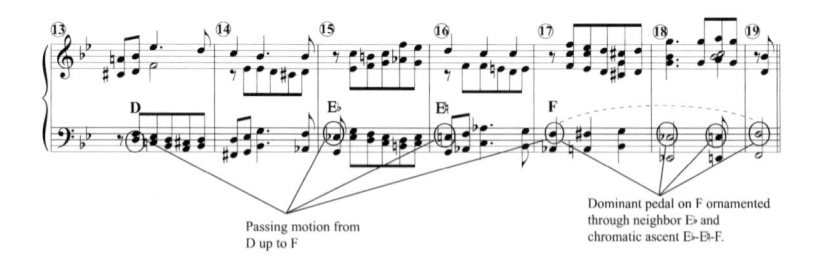

EXAMPLE 3.34
Schoenberg, Minuet, MBC: passing motion from D to F during the recapitulation (mm. 13–19).

As shown in Example 3.35, motive *a* and its characteristic third-span dominate the texture at both the surface and subsurface throughout the recapitulation. Whereas the transposition of motive *a* in the second two-measure phrase (m. 3) destabilizes the tonic, creating the imbalance necessary for a

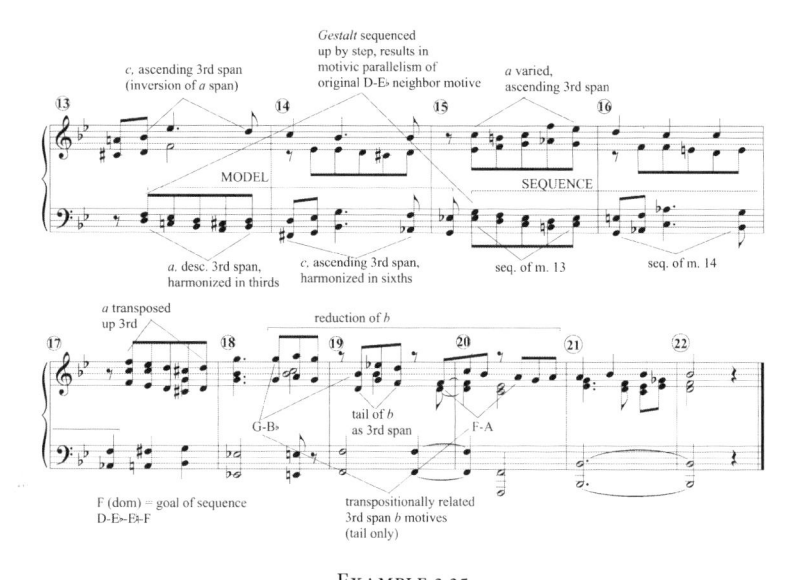

EXAMPLE 3.35

Schoenberg, Minuet, MBC: saturation of motive a and its characteristic third-span during recapitulation.

presentation of the musical idea, the omnipresent variations on this motive during the recapitulation (mm. 13–19) confirm the tonic region.

Conclusion

As Stein indicated in the preface to the 1972 edition of *MBC*, Schoenberg claimed to have written his American theoretical texts with the intention of supplying rudimentary knowledge for students lacking in it. Nevertheless, the Minuet and many of the other exercises in *MBC* reveal creative inspiration and compositional sophistication. Clearly Schoenberg refused to compromise the integrity of his ideas about music after immigrating to the United States. Rather, he continued not only to expand his pedagogical and theoretical concepts, but also to maintain a sense of consistency and conviction in his fundamental approach to teaching. This attitude is evident in the many individual concepts that he revised anew during the 1930s and '40s, concepts encompassing substitute tones and invented harmony, which were expanded into transformations and the constructive functions of harmony, respectively.

At the same time, Schoenberg's belief in the tenets of organicism and his faith in formal functions, musical logic, and the systematic exploration of compositional possibility continued to guide his pedagogical method.

One of the most important new aspects of Schoenberg's American teaching was his emphasis on the two-measure phrase, a model that *MBC* can truly claim as its legacy. This grouping became the vehicle not only for Schoenberg's presentation of thematic structures such as the sentence and period, but also for his introduction to harmony in Composition 105, a course that introduced the two-measure phrase as a foundation for motivic development. In Schoenberg's Minuet in B♭ and the untitled scherzo from *MBC*, the implicit power of this model was its ability to function as a vehicle for the presentation of a *Grundgestalt* and a musical idea. At this juncture *MBC*, the practical pedagogical manual begins to align with Schoenberg's theoretical and philosophical concepts. Here, *MBC* and the two-measure phrase confront the presentation of a musical idea; in this moment Schoenberg is both iconic composer and dedicated teacher, still composing with the same tenacity as in 1908, while at the same time imparting the basic principles of composition as he had always understood them.

Models for Beginners in Composition

Syllabus, Musical Examples, and Glossary
Arnold Schoenberg

Revised Edition with Corrections from *Schoenberg's Notes*
Original Revised Edition Edited by *Leonard Stein*
Newly Revised Edition Edited by *Gordon Root*

Editor's Preface to the 1972 Edition

From the beginning of his teaching career in American universities, Arnold Schoenberg felt the necessity of providing his ill-prepared students with basic texts in theory and composition. The many examples he prepared for them as "models" in harmony, counterpoint, and composition, were later collected and published, in enlarged form and with commentary. In the Summer of 1942, as Schoenberg's assistant, I gathered together, at his request, the accumulated examples of several years of class teaching in elementary composition at U.C.L.A. The original version of *Models for Beginners in Composition* consisted entirely of examples I copied by hand and was printed privately for use only by his classes. The following year, the second, revised and enlarged edition, with syllabus and glossary added, appeared under the imprint of G. Schirmer, Inc. Many of the concepts and procedures advanced here for the first time were subsequently developed at considerable length in *Structural Functions of Harmony* (completed in 1948; first published in 1954) and *Fundamentals of Musical Composition* (published posthumously, 1967). The present revised and corrected edition includes several handwritten additions to the text by Schoenberg, as well as corrections of the text and examples by the author and editor.[1]

LEONARD STEIN
Los Angeles, California 1972

Author's Preface
(Schoenberg's Preface to the 1943 Edition)

This is the second, revised and enlarged version of a syllabus which I prepared for beginners in composition in a summer session of six weeks at the University of California at Los Angeles. Though the first version was done in a great hurry and at a time when I was occupied with other affairs (composing, for instance, which is not a mere avocation of mine), and though I anticipated that I could perhaps teach some theoretical knowledge but not much technical skill, I was surprised by the success of this syllabus. It helped my students to such an extent that even those with little creative ability and musicianship could write a small minuet or even a scherzo that was not quite impossible.

This success induced me to interrupt my work, again to sacrifice composing to teaching, in order to produce this second version, hoping to make it more useful and effective.

The main objectives of this syllabus are: **ear-training,** development of a **sense of form,** and understanding of the **technique** and **logic** of musical construction.

Students who wish to become music teachers in colleges, high schools, or elementary schools are required to study composition. But, according to my experience, very few can write without the aid of the piano and even fewer possess a sense of the relation between melody and accompaniment. Besides, many of these students who might be good instrumentalists have no creative imagination, while often those who have talent think that today one may write everything: they have heard even in popular music unrelated dissonances and think they can apply them as well in their attempts at composing small but logically constructed forms.

Considering all these facts, I introduced several years ago a new method of achieving **coordination of melody and harmony,** which makes composing easier even to such students as have no desire or ability for musical creation, and which has also proved to contribute considerably to **ear-training.**

Great stress is laid in this syllabus upon the concept of variation, because this is the most important tool for producing logic in spite of variety. Even a beginner who has not a considerable creative talent will be able to write at least as well as is needed for a "passing grade" if he studies the manifold ways by which variation is applied to simple basic forms, and if he then tries to employ similar methods in his own attempts.

He will observe that even a change of the harmony-successions demands adaptation and thus produces new motif-forms. He should study very thoroughly the Models of Harmonies for Two-Measure Phrases. They reveal many ways of enriching the harmony; and if he understands the principles involved there, he will be able to apply these methods not only to phrases, but also to many other segments. This knowledge is very important in producing cadences to various degrees and, in the "elaboration"-section of the scherzo (see p. 66–67), in working out the "modulatory" harmony of the "models" and sequences. The student should become familiar with the "root progressions" which produce "roving" harmony.

Of course, not all those technical problems are within the reach of a beginner. But studying and analyzing the examples will make him acquainted with such procedures and might stimulate a future composer to write in a more dignified manner.

The student will also have to study the same forms in works of the classic masters. At first the study of Beethoven's piano sonatas is recommended, because his forms are generally simpler even than Mozart's or Haydn's. But the student must not be startled if he finds in the works of these masters features that are not discussed in this syllabus: in a brief course like this, it seems impossible to teach everything a master's imagination and fantasy might invent. There are "irregularities" which are only accessible to a really great talent, a higher technique, and—perhaps—only to genius. Besides, the student should realize that these models show merely **one way** of approach to the technique of composing. But he should not in any case think that a composer would work in such a mechanical manner. What produces real music is solely and exclusively the inventive capacity, imagination, and inspiration of a creative mind—if and when a creator "has something to express."

Nonetheless, a student should never write mere dry notes. At all times he should try to "express something." Marking tempo and character by such terms as *cantabile, agitato, con spirito, grazioso, playful, gay, vivace, grave,* etc., he may find that his imagination has been stimulated to make him produce pieces of a definite character such as a song, an agitated allegro, a witty scherzo, a graceful gavotte, or even a nocturne or rhapsody of vague, unidentifiable mood. Very early a student can thus write with more spontaneity, which need not exclude conscious application of his technical knowledge.

Los Angeles, California 1943

SYLLABUS

I

COORDINATION OF MELODY AND HARMONY

In order to obtain coordination of melody and harmony the student will in his first exercises use only the tones of the **underlying harmony.**

Tones foreign to the underlying harmony must be added to the tones of the broken-chord forms only as **passing notes, suspensions, grace notes,** and **other auxiliary notes,** according to the advice given under (c) and (d).

From the very beginning all exercises should be carried out in **several keys.** Thus the student will be at home in every key in a short time.

(A) Building Two-Measure Motives or Phrases on a Single Harmony[2]

   (a) In Exx. 1–4 only broken chord forms of the tonic are used in half- and quarter-notes. The student should try to find as many different ways of **breaking a chord** as he can.

   (b) In Exx. 5–11, the same and similar broken-chord forms are carried out in **different rhythms.** Tone repetitions contribute to **rhythmic variety** and often produce characteristic features.

   (c) **Addition of passing notes.** In the beginning they should preferably be used only on the weak beat (Exx. 12–15).

   (d) **Auxiliary notes** and other **embellishments** are added to basic forms (Exx. 16–19).

A student should always try for rhythmic variety. It may well be that not everything is "beautiful," or "melodious," or "perfectly balanced."* The

---

* The examples of this syllabus are also sometimes unbalanced, or even do not sound melodious. They are not made for beauty, but their purpose is exclusively to show the application of technical methods.[3]

teacher will correct or cross out the worst of his exercises and explain why they are too poor or overcrowded. At first the only important thing is to contrive as many different forms as possible. Incorporating thus the concept of variation and its technical possibilities in one's mind will be of great advantage when the student later tries to invent real melodies, instinctively and spontaneously.

Observe the **difference** between the **first** and the **second** measure of most of the phrases. Generally the second will contain fewer features and less movement than the first measure (Exx. 6, 8, 9, 10, 12, 13, 16, 18).

(B) Building Two-Measure Phrases on Two Harmonies

on I–V	(Exx. 20–29)
" I–VI	(" 30–36)
" I–IV	(" 37–43)
" I–III	(" 44–50)
" I–II	(" 51–57)

In Exx. 34 and 36, chromatics are inserted.

In Exx. 41 and 42, an **artificial dominant seventh** chord emphasizes the progression towards IV.

Exx. 44–50 use **III in the form of an artificial dominant (seventh) chord.**[4] This is especially advisable if the next measure should start on VI, or by a deceptive cadence on IV or II (Exx. 47a, 48a, 49a).

The **II** appears more frequently in its **first inversion** or as a $\frac{6}{5}$, $\frac{4}{3}$, or 2 chord. Beware of **parallel fifths** when using the root position.

(C) Two-Measure Phrases Based on Three Harmonies.
These should also be practiced as systematically as the preceding exercises. Sometimes, however, a student, even at this early stage, may have tried to "invent" such forms instinctively. In any case, the rhythmical and motival features and formations should stimulate him to produce material similar to that shown in the models.

Observe some of the rhythmic features, for instance the **syncopations** in Exx. 59, 64, 65, 79, and 83, and the augmentation of rhythmic features in Exx. 58, 61, 62, 67, 67a, 69, 75, and 76. Some of them are exact, some are free.

Again the **treatment of the second measure** should be studied. Its relation to the first measure might be compared to the relation of a strong to a weak beat. But just as a weak beat sometimes carries an accent, so a second measure of a phrase need not always represent a decline. Here one finds the augmentations mentioned above, and also reductions—that is, the omission of subordinate features (Exx. 60, 66, 78, 80, 81).

Watch further the multiple use of motival features, marked a, a¹, a², etc. Advice for this technique might be given as follows: **If the rhythm is exactly or approximately the same, the interval may be changed freely,** because rhythm is more noticeable than interval. Often a **rhythm is "shifted"** from a strong to a weak beat and vice versa (Exx. 59, 65, 76, and 79).

(D) Two-Measure Phrases on more than Three Harmonies

A few examples are given in Exx. 86–93. It would be too difficult for a beginner to write such exercises in the mechanical manner of the preceding assignments. It will be easier to do that when he has digested the ways of inserting "passing" harmonies shown in Exx. 167–188.[5] In studying all these models the student should realize that the basic assumption for richer harmony is a semi-contrapuntal movement of the bass, in which the other accompanying voices cannot fail to participate. It is the tendency of independent voices that produces a richer movement of the harmony. The alternatives 86a, 90a, 91a, and 93a show that even fewer harmonies would suffice.

Observe the (imitative) use of motival features in the accompaniment of Exx. 90 and 92.

II

Motive and Motival Features in Two-Measure Phrases[6]

In phrases, motival features usually appear more than once. Thus a motive might be established which in the continuation will appear in more and richer variations, developing more and other phrases and other segments of various size and function.

> (A) Most of these phrases are merely variations of the primitive examples of the beginning. Thus 94 is built from 12; 95, 96, and 97 are built from 13, etc.

(B) Various other Ways of Utilizing Motival Features

The student will observe that all these examples contain in one way or another the beginning three notes (or their rhythm) of Ex. 119. They appear in simple repetitions, in transpositions, in inversions, in augmentations, shifted to other beats, etc.

The student should apply all these treatments to his own exercises.

Many of these examples are unbalanced, at least without a proper accompaniment. But Ex. 132, a variation of Ex. 131, is used later (Exx. 226 and 231) to build a sentence and a period. It pays to try changes and variations of the kind indicated even if the result is very poor.

The examples 147 to 150 derive from the forms 140 and 141. There they are based on I–V. But Exx. 148–150 use a much richer harmony, though they also begin on I and end on V. But even examples like 130 and 144, distinctly overcrowded, can be of some usefulness if treated like 130a and 144a.[7]

(C) Some Models of Accompaniment

In **piano style** the harmony need not be present in full at every beat. On the contrary, if it is not for the expression of a certain character, the insertion of pauses in one or more voices will provide transparency and often produce a characteristic **"motive of the accompaniment,"** i.e., a rhythmic pattern that should be used, with slight accommodating alterations, in the continuation. Not only can such a model, even within one small phrase, consist of different elements, e.g. Exx. 152, 155, 156, 157, etc.; but also one element alone can be useful, e.g. the "march-like" forms of Exx. 158, 159, 161, and 163. **Independent movement** of one or more voices—if it does not interfere with the harmony and even obscure it—is always valuable, for instance in Exx. 159, 164 (of which later a sentence and a period are built, Exx. 224 and 230), 165, and 166. Mostly the independence of those voices is not considerable. They merely follow the movement of the melody. Ex. 162a shows that this model could also be accompanied without such movement, but Ex. 162b shows a freer treatment.

(D) Models of Harmonies for Two-Measure Phrases

Ex. 167 shows—in the beginning systematically—some of the most dependable harmony-successions. Attention is directed to the use of inversions of triads and seventh chords and to the use of "transformations" of the chords on some degrees: artificial dominants, diminished sevenths, etc. These transformations are produced by the use of "substitute tones" derived from "related regions" of the key.[8] The examples are based on "strong" or "ascending" and "super-strong" root-progressions according to the model V–I, V–III, V–VI, and IV–V, respectively.[9] Of course, not everything possible could be included, though weak progressions are avoided. In minor especially not every progression might be usable.

Exx. 172–188 show how much such harmonies could be used in phrases. Much of that will seem difficult to a beginner without a thorough knowledge of harmony. But to understand the principles of such treatment will widen the student's scope, even if only theoretically.

Attention should be directed again to the accompaniment, to the frequently independent movement of the voices, and to the fact that the rhythms of the harmonic pattern might be altered.

III

Sentences[10]

(A) First Four Measures only

What is here called the "dominant form" (measures 3 and 4) is in the most simple cases a repetition of meas. 1–2 accommodated to a contrasting harmony: Ex. 189, I contrasted with V; Exx. 190 and 191 (and the alternatives of 192–197), I–V contrasted with the reversed succession V–I. Even here the dominant form should not become merely transposed. This is primitive and monotonous. At least such alterations as have been marked by (+) are advisable. Of great interest are transformations like 193 to 197. Still more interesting are repetitions like Ex. 198, in which meas. 3–4 are based on (II)–V–I, a free repetition of the I–(IV)–V of meas. 1–2. Sequential repetitions are also sometimes useful, Exx. 200, 201, 205, 206. Of course, as there is here no I–V relation, the term dominant has to be understood in a metaphorical meaning.[11]

(B) Completion of the Sentence (meas. 5–8)

The sentence-form which is taught here does not pretend to be more than a "school form," a way of dealing with an elementary problem in a manner within reach of a beginner. Nevertheless, it should be mentioned that there are many similar examples in Beethoven. See, for instance, the Exx. 207–210, from his piano sonatas; even the first theme of his Fifth Symphony uses this form.

It will not be too difficult to construct this form according to the following suggestion: Measure 5 is usually a reduced form of the content of the first phrase. This reduction is achieved by omitting some features more or less subordinate (Ex. 212), or by connecting elements of the first phrase in a different manner (Ex. 213) or in a different order (Exx. 214, 215, 216). Measure 6 is generally a kind of repetition of meas. 5: a strict repetition (Exx. 210, 211), or an accommodation to another degree (Exx. 207, 212, 213, 214, 215), or a strict (Exx. 220, 221, 222, 225) or free sequential repetition. In contrast to that, in Ex. 223 only the motival "residues" of meas. 2 are repeated along a chromatic ascent in the melody: D–D♯–E–E♯–F♯; and Ex. 224 elaborates elements of the basic measures above a flowing succession of harmonies.

Measure 7 prepares for the cadence on I (Exx. 220, 223, 225, and 226), or V (Exx. 220, 2nd ending, 221, 224), or III (Exx. 220, 3rd ending, 222, 227).

Observe the **"condensation" of the harmony in the cadential segment.**[12] There are generally more harmonies used at this place than in the preceding measures.

Observe also the treatment of the main voice in this segment. In general, further reduced basic elements, above a moving harmony, pass into less obligatory forms.

It might help the student to approach a solution of these technical problems by writing at first a great number of sketches, even mechanically, and then selecting the best ones. While so doing, he should often return to the methods of developing new motif-forms by variation, as discussed in the beginning.

IV

Periods

The main difference and also, to a beginner, the main difficulty in writing periods lies in the necessity of using in meas. 3–4 "more remote" motif-forms. To all of the four periods in Exx. 228, 229, 230, and 231 are added two alternatives: all of these periods end on I, or on V, or on III or VI. The use of basic intervals, marked a a^1 a^2 etc., and of basic rhythms, marked a a^1 a^2 etc., illustrates the relation to the first phrase. The student should analyze in order to acknowledge the "destiny" of the motive, and try as many similar developments himself.

In Ex. 228 the interval of a fourth b is used in a "chain-like" construction in measures 2–3 of the antecedent; the consequent uses only the upbeat and the rhythm, but employs many changes of the interval. This period is built from the motif No. 8 on p. 42.

Inversion of a melodic part of the phrase (meas. 2–3 of Ex. 228b) can be recommended.

Observe in Exx. 230 and 230b, meas. 4, the shift of rhythm a to the first beat.

Similar shiftings of intervals and rhythms are used in Ex. 231.

The **caesura** (meas. 4) and the ending (meas. 8) are chiefly produced by the harmony. While the end (meas. 8) is always carried out by a full cadence (IV–V–I or II–V–I, transposed to the region in which one is at that moment), the caesura in meas. 4 can be approached by a half-cadence (IV–V or II–V, or also VI–V). Generally in the measure before the final degree, one will already observe an enrichment of the harmony: more harmonies are usually used there than in the beginning.

The melody in those cadential segments moves with more richness than in the preceding measures. The caesura, furthermore, is usually characterized by a rest, at least in the accompaniment, producing the effect that a comma or semicolon produces in punctuation.

The consequent is usually a free repetition of the antecedent. However, one, two, or even three measures could be exactly repeated. But in higher art mechanical repetition is not too dignified—variety should always be the aim of a good composer.

In Exx. 228, 228a, and 228b, only the up-beat is repeated exactly, while all the rest show a new use and a rearrangement.

In Ex. 229 one full measure is used, but the harmony is changed.

Two measures are repeated in the consequent of Ex. 230a. But Exx. 231 and 231a start at once with derivatives of the basic features.

In general, in cadential segments (e.g. Ex. 232, meas. 7–8) the strict use of motive forms is abandoned ("liquidated") and a freer melodic contour concludes this section, generally on V, sometimes on III.[13]

V

Contrasting Middle Section of the Ternary (a-b-a¹) Form[14]

The important problem in writing this section is to make it **contrasting and coherent.**

The decisive contribution to the contrast is made by the harmony.[15] For this purpose forty-eight schemes are to be found on pages 94–97.[16] Some of them are too complicated for the first attempts of a beginner, but might be tried by a student who possess considerable skill in harmony. Some of them, which have been starred (*), can be used not only in major, but also in minor. And some of the schemes given in minor (42–48) can perhaps even be of use also in major (in C major or transposed).

Structurally, the contrast will be achieved by using the motive forms or even new derivatives from them in a different order. Observe, for instance, in Ex. 236 the shifting of the features $\overset{a}{\wedge}$ and $\overset{b}{\wedge}$ of Ex. 229 to other beats, and the inversion of the interval $\overset{c}{\sqcap}$ in meas. 10.

Exx. 238, 239, and 240 show more complicated forms in the harmony and in the motival elaboration. They also use semi-contrapuntal imitations of a prominent rhythm in the accompanying voices.

VI

Recapitulation (a¹)

The **recapitulation (a¹) of the "a" section** after the contrasting middle section may in primitive cases consist of a mere repetition, on the condition that the first a-section end on I. Thus a full a–b–a¹ form could be composed by adding to Ex. 220 (no matter whether the first, second, or third ending was used) one of the two contrasting middle sections (Ex. 236 or 237) and thereafter simply repeating Ex. 220 with the first ending on I. The same would be right if Ex. 221 or 222 would be used as an a-section. It would perhaps be more interesting to use Ex. 223 as the a¹-section in all these cases, because a varied repetition is always more artistic than a literal one. Thus in masterpieces much variation is often found in structure, harmony, accompaniment, and even in size, the segment being sometimes reduced (to six, four, or an uneven number of measures, see Beethoven's piano sonatas Op. 2, No. 1, Adagio; Op. 2, No. 2, Rondo; Op. 7, Rondo; Op. 2, No. 2, Largo, seven measures), or being extended (to ten measures, Op. 7, Largo).

If the period Ex. 230 should be the a-section and Ex. 239 its contrasting middle section, the recapitulation has to be composed anew, in order to end on I. This is carried out in Ex. 241.

VII

Minuet

The form of the minuet is in most cases ternary. Sometimes one finds in classic examples the contrasting middle section longer (6, 8, or more measures) and more elaborate (Beethoven, Op. 2, No. 2; Op. 10, No. 3, Op. 22; etc.). Sometimes the recapitulation is shortened (Op. 31, No. 3). Sometimes one finds the addition of one or more codettas in the a-sections, or of an episode in the b-section. Irregular construction of phrases or segments will also be found. The accompaniment has often a "stylized" touch of dance accompaniment. But this might also occur in every other kind of ternary form.

The model given in Ex. 242 is complicated, harmonically and motivally. Especially the contrasting middle section, which turns in meas. 11 to the region of [the] subdominant minor, might be interesting. Observe, furthermore, that the recapitulation is extended to ten measures and begins with a remote variation of the first phrase in the left hand, to which the right hand adds a countermelody (compare meas. 10 to meas. 13), and that in measure 18 the feature d^1 is detached from b^2 and is used three times as material for the extension.

The alternatives (a), (b), and (c) show how the a-section could end on I or III, or (with a half-cadence) on V. The alternative (d) offers a different use of the material in the contrasting middle section. The way in which this section is extended to eight measures is interesting and emphasizes the "up-beat harmony" (V) in two measures (15–16). The following measures 13–20 bring a richly varied repetition of the a-section.

Ex. 243 shows that the antecedent, with slight harmonic changes, could end on V in instead of III, and that nevertheless meas. 5 could begin on VI.

Ex. 244 illustrates the use of a sequence (meas. 9–10 and 11–12) and, more interesting, a procedure which is excellent in its effect: in meas. 13 and 14 the melody remains unchanged while the harmony moves constantly.[17]

VIII

Scherzo[18]

The form of the scherzo is also ternary and differs from the preceding a–b–a[1] forms only in its middle section, which is a **modulatory** contrasting middle section and is called the **elaboration.** Its harmony, though roving (that is moving from region [generally miscalled "key"] to region), does not fail to establish at the beginning of each segment (called "model," "sequence," "reduction," etc.) at least temporarily the tonic of a region or key. Such points are marked by stars (*) in Ex. 245 at meas. 9, 14, 19; in Ex. 246 at meas. 9, 13, 17, 19, 21; in Ex. 248 at meas. 9 and 11; and in Ex. 249 at meas. 17, 21, 25, and 27.

A "school-form" of the **elaboration** of the scherzo can be constructed by building a model of two or more measures, using motif-forms or derivatives in a different order above a preconceived harmony-progression which leads to a region other than that of its beginning. Generally its ending harmony should be suitable for introducing the sequence which then follows (see Ex. 245, meas. 9–13; Ex. 246, meas. 9–12; Ex. 248, meas. 9–10; Ex. 249, meas. 17–20.

The **sequence,** if it deserves its name, must be a complete and exact transposition to another degree. But in selecting the transposition, the student should avoid deviating too far from the related regions. For instance, in C major one would scarcely go to F♯ major or to B♭ minor or B major. But Beethoven in the Scherzo of Op. 2, No. 2, arrives at G♯ in A major, which is quite far. A master may do this; a student would better avoid it. Generally the model now undergoes a process of **"liquidation,"** which is a method of getting rid of the obligations of the motif. Here it is done gradually, by at first omitting subordinate features and reducing the four measures to two (mostly followed here by a sequence). The liquidation thereafter reduces the model to one measure and even smaller units. In general, the place to approach the up-beat harmony (V) is at or after the two-measure model.

Often a little segment is added to mark the end of the roving section: a standstill on V, in many cases a pedal (Ex. 245, meas. 30 ff., Ex. 246, meas. 25–28).

The **recapitulation** often demands far-reaching new construction, especially if the ending of the a-section started early to move towards V or III (Ex. 246, meas. 5–8). Endings, on I, to the two alternatives, (a) and (b), are given at the end of Ex. 247.

It must be mentioned that many scherzos contain codettas in the a- and a¹-sections and episodes in the b-sections. **Codettas** are cadences primarily. If the end of any section should be short and not perfectly convincing, there would be reason to establish the fact of the ending more firmly. But such an addition is the result of the resourcefulness of an inspired composer rather than the problem of a beginner, struggling for form. Therefore, it seems superfluous to illustrate it here, and better to advise the student to study the examples of the masters.

IX

Phrases, Half-Sentences, Antecedents, and "a"-Sections of Ternary Forms

This material can be used by the student if at some time he might not be able to build a phrase or another segment himself. But they can also be profitably used for practice in dealing with various problems, such as producing several types of forms, building cadences to various degrees, working out harmonization and accompaniment, etc.

All this material has been used in classes and at examinations, and has proved to be not too difficult, and quite instructive.[19]

May they also be helpfull to the students of this syllabus!

Arnold Schoenberg
September 12, 1942

MUSIC EXAMPLES

MUSIC EXAMPLES

I. COORDINATION of MELODY and HARMONY

A) Building Two-Measure Motives or Phrases on a Single Harmony in Broken Chord Forms

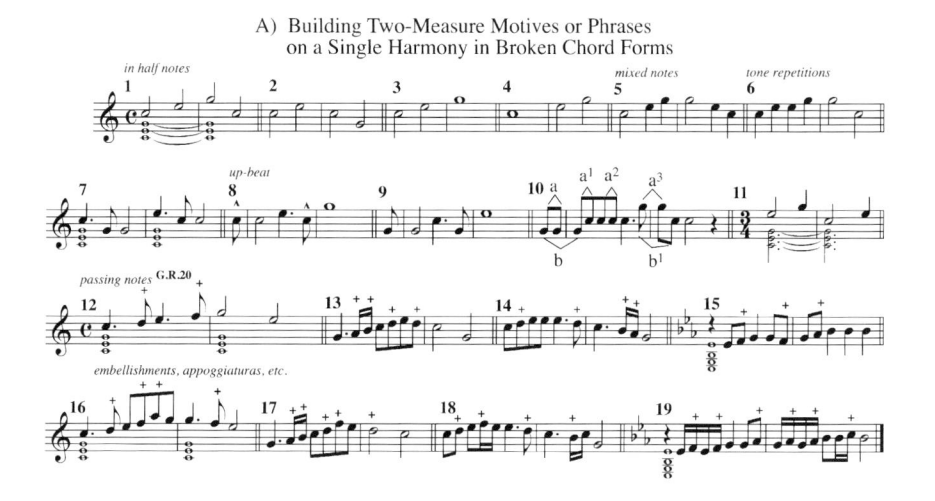

B) Two-Measure Phrases on Two Harmonies

C) Two-Measure Phrases on Three Harmonies

*Through passing-harmony melodious part-leading is achieved.

D) Building Two-Measure Phrases on more than Three Harmonies

I-VI-IV-V
86   86a   minor 87^G.R.24

I   IV II V   I II   V   I VI IV V

I-VI-II-V
88   Minuetto 89   Andante 90

I   IV II V

90a   Moderato 91^G.R.25   91a

I   IV   I VI IV II ——— V

Andante 92   93   93a

I   VI IV   II V   I III VI IV II   V

II. MOTIVE AND MOTIVAL FEATURES
IN TWO-MEASURE PHRASES
(Basic features usually appear more than once)

A) Derivations from Examples 1 to 93

B) Various other Ways of Utilizing Motival Features

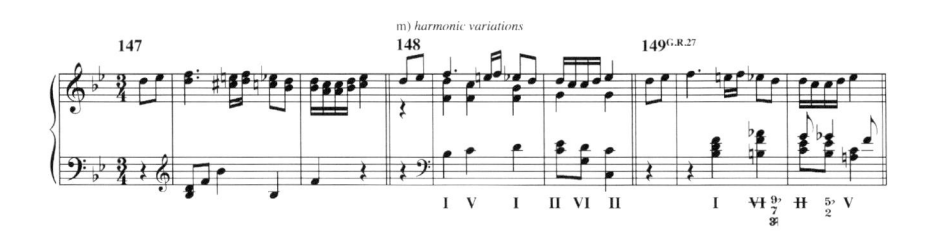

C) Some Models of Accompaniment

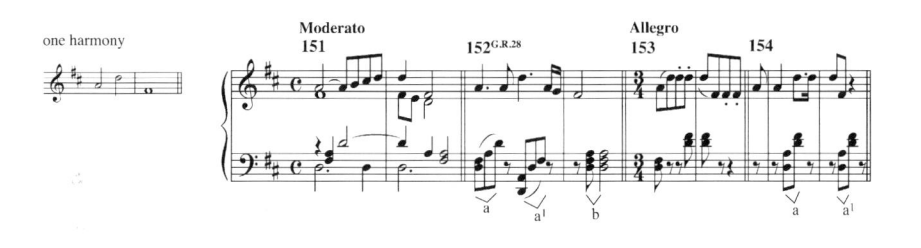

two harmonies

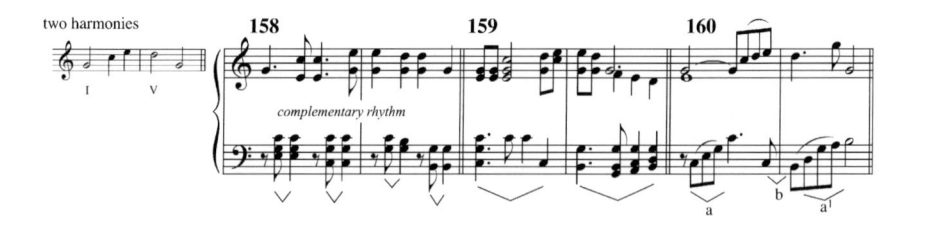

D) Models of Harmonies for Two-Measure Phrases enriched by insertion of one or more Harmonies[G.R.29]

167 Between I-V one may insert II, IV, or VI
ONE harmony inserted

a) II

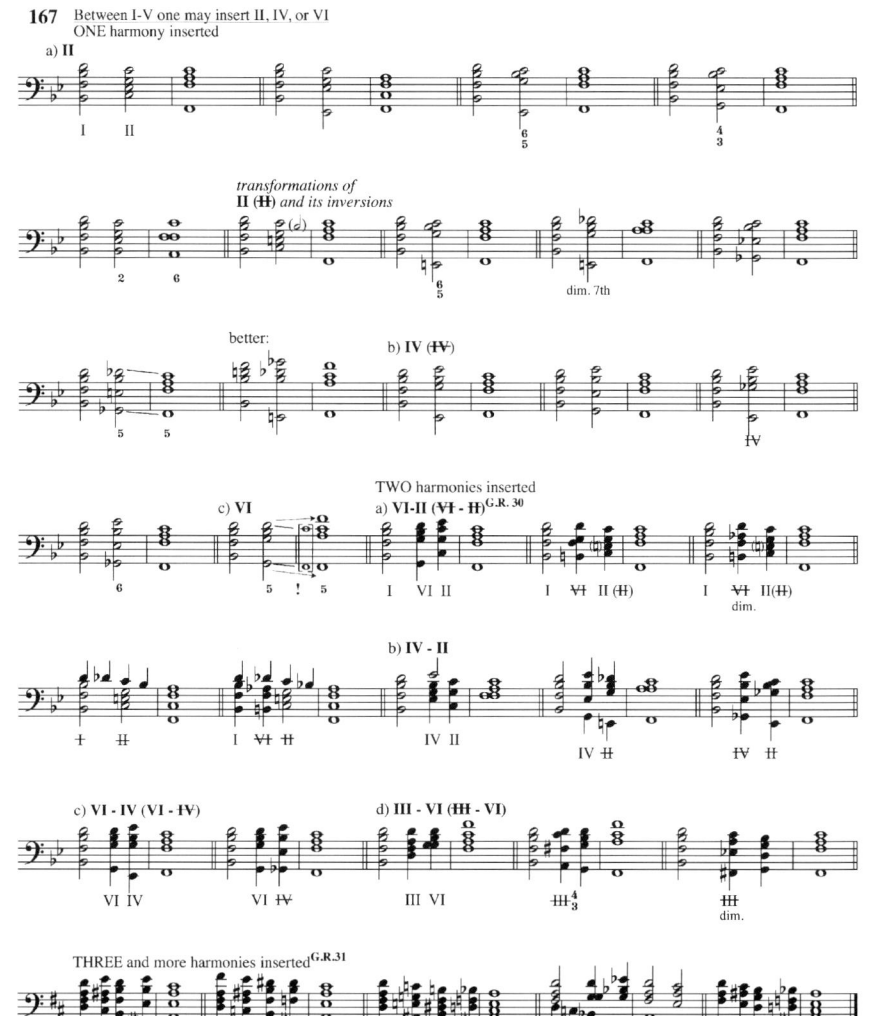

transformations of
II (H) *and its inversions*

better: b) IV (IV)

TWO harmonies inserted
c) VI   a) VI-II (VI - H)[G.R. 30]

b) IV - II

c) VI - IV (VI - IV)   d) III - VI (III - VI)

THREE and more harmonies inserted[G.R.31]

168 <u>Between I - VI one may insert III, V, or VII</u> (only a few examples; more may be
built according to a procedure similar to **I - V**)

a) **III** (*one or more*)

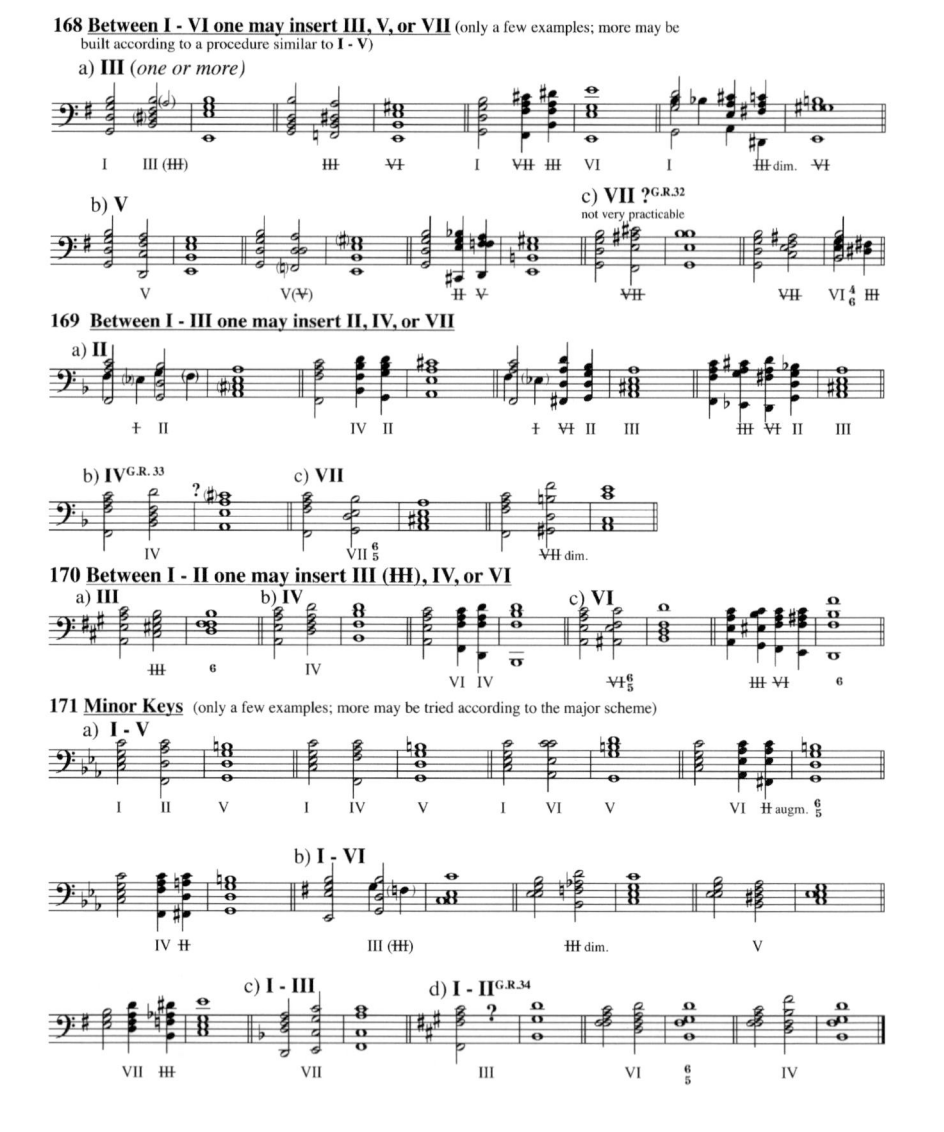

169 Between I - III one may insert II, IV, or VII

170 Between I - II one may insert III (III), IV, or VI

171 <u>Minor Keys</u> (only a few examples; more may be tried according to the major scheme)

III. SENTENCES[G.R.36]

A) First Four Measures only

B) Completion of the Sentence

Measures 5-8

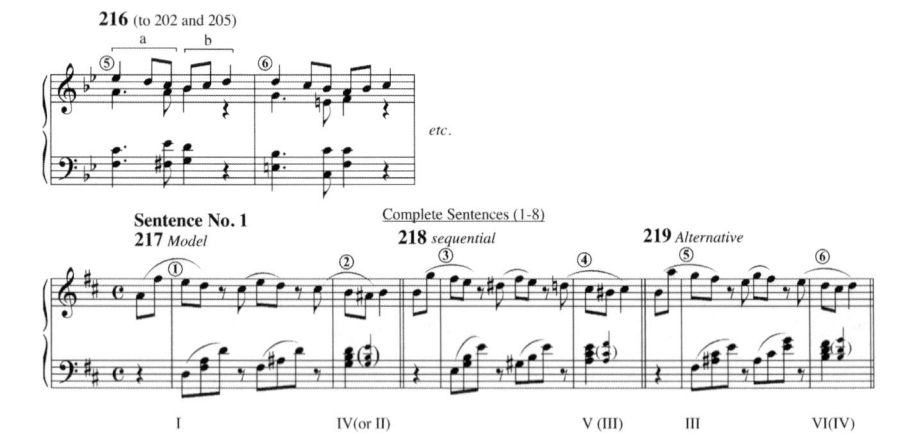

IV. PERIODS
based on Models of foregoing Sentences

The motive forms marked * are variants of the motive of meas. 1.

232 Period No. 5
(Sentence No. 3, 225)

V. CONTRASTING MIDDLE SECTIONS

"b"-section of the Ternary (a-b-a¹) Form
to preceding Sentences and Periods
on Harmonic Schemes, pages 30 - 33

233 No. 1 *(to sentences 190, 214)*

234 No. 2 *(same sentence)*

* *H S:* see pages 30 - 33, Harmonic Schemes (HS) for Contrasting Middle Sections.

235 No. 3 *(to Period No. 5, 232)*

D minor

III   I   VI   IV   VII   I   IV   V   I   II   V

etc.

236 No. 4 *(to Period No. 2, 229)*

H S 5

V   I   VI   II   II   V

etc. to
Repetition
of a

237[G.R.45] **No. 5** *(same period)*

H S 12

V   III   VI   II   V   I (plagal)   V

etc. to
Repetition
of a

238 No. 6 *(to Sentence No. 4, 226)*

H S 18

V   ♭III   ♭II neap. 6   V   I   II   V

239 No. 7 *(to Period No. 3, 230, second ending)*

240 No. 8 *(to Sentence No. 5, 227, second ending)*

* passing harmony

Harmonic Schemes
for Contrasting Middle Section[G.R.46]

C major

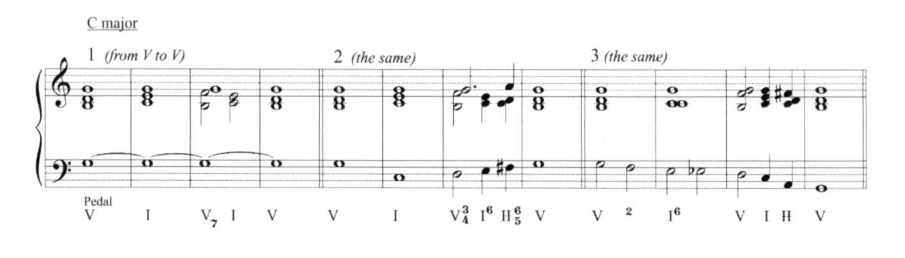

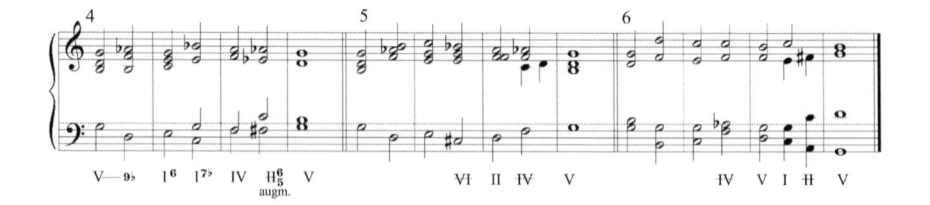

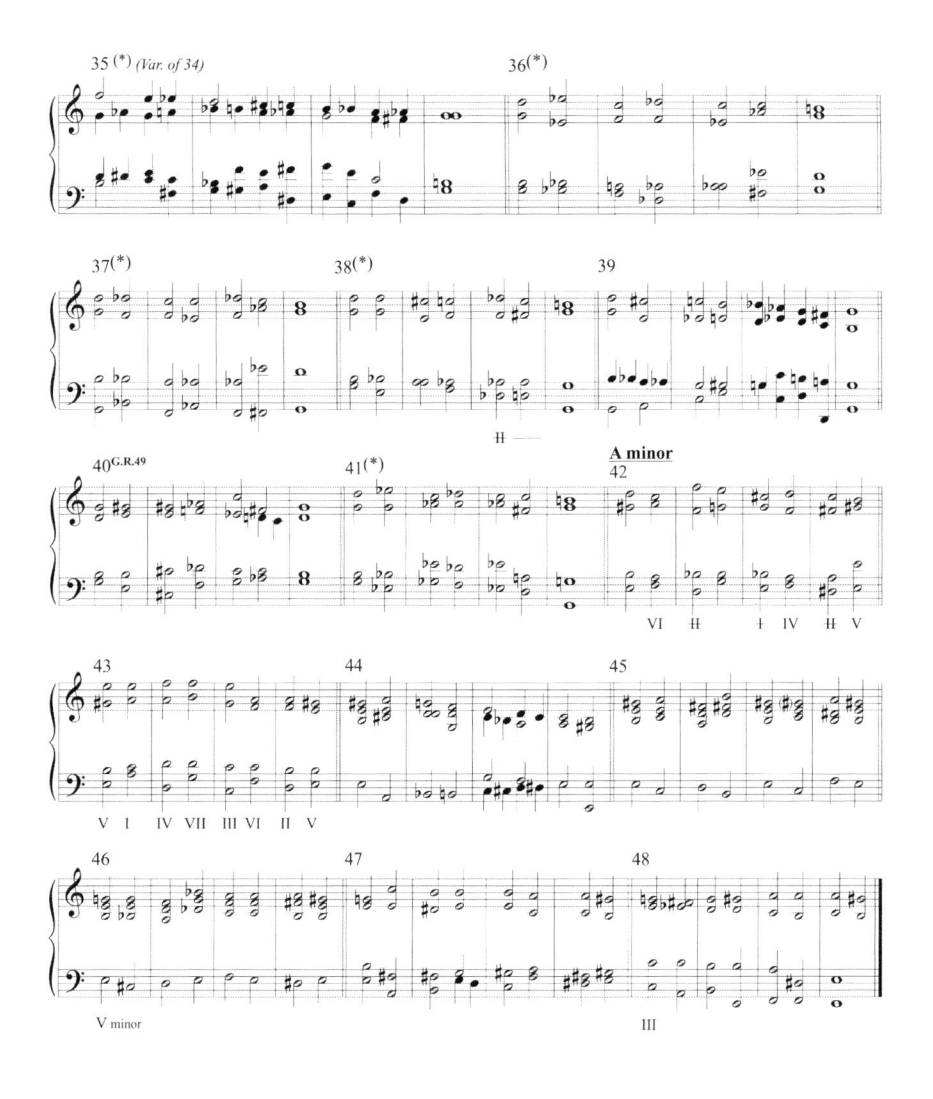

VI. RECAPITULATION (a¹)
of "a" after the Contrasting Middle Section

VII. MINUET^{G.R.50}

VIII. SCHERZO

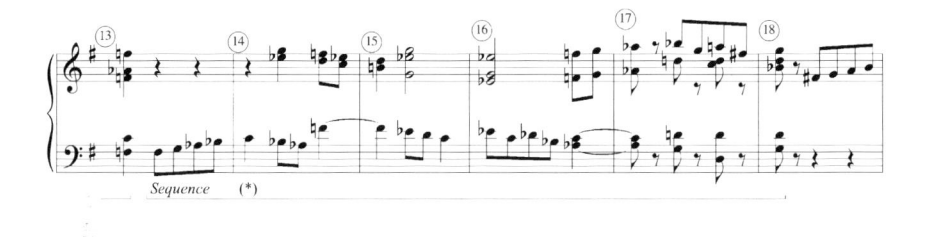

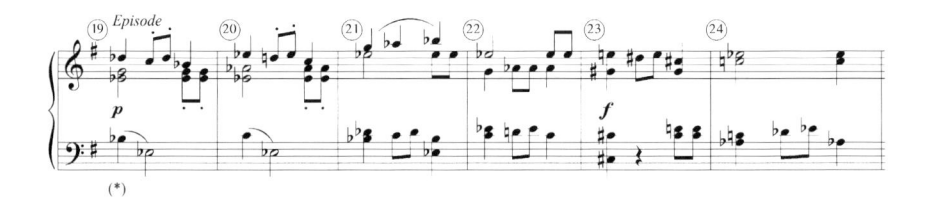

247 "a" section

Recapitulation follows

Extension

249　*Elaboration to 247*

(*) Tonic minor

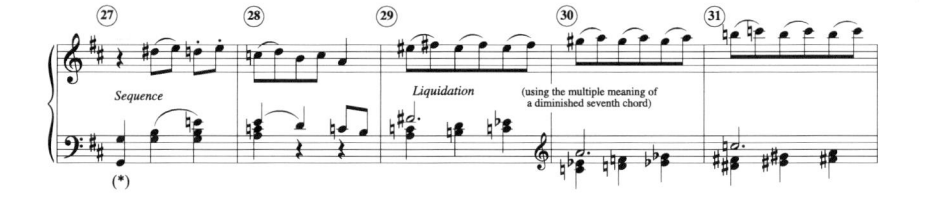

IX. PHRASES, HALF SENTENCES, ANTECEDENTS, AND
"a" SECTIONS OF TERNARY FORMS

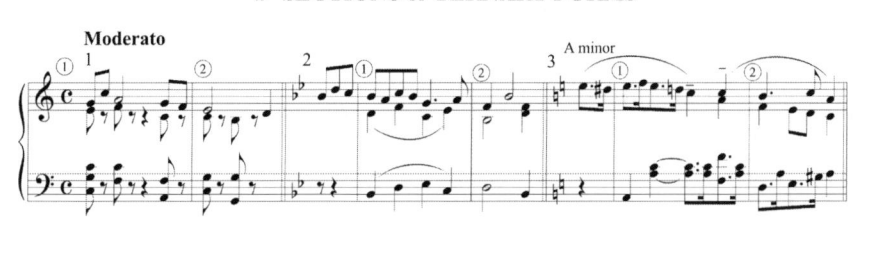

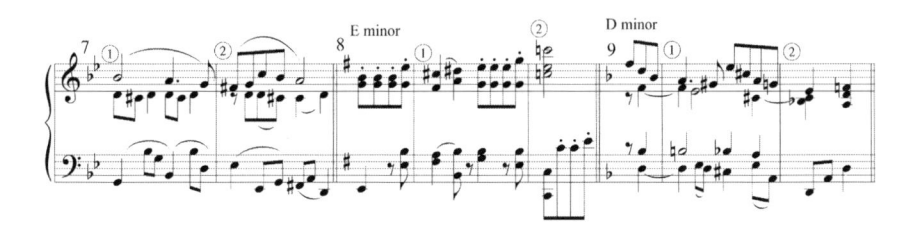

Glossary

In this syllabus a number of terms are used which require explanation, some because they are often used in a vague manner or with a meaning different from that here employed, others because they are not commonly used at all, partly owing to the fact that they have been introduced by this author. In a forthcoming text-book, "Fundamentals of Musical Composition," and a syllabus, "Structural Functions of Harmony," one will find more and more thorough explanations.[†]

Root is the tone upon which a triad (or a seventh or ninth chord) is built by superimposition of a third and a fifth (or a seventh or a ninth). The root **can** be identical with the bass; but, in case of inversions, while the root remains the same, the bass uses a different tone. The difference between the bass and the root can be seen in the following example:

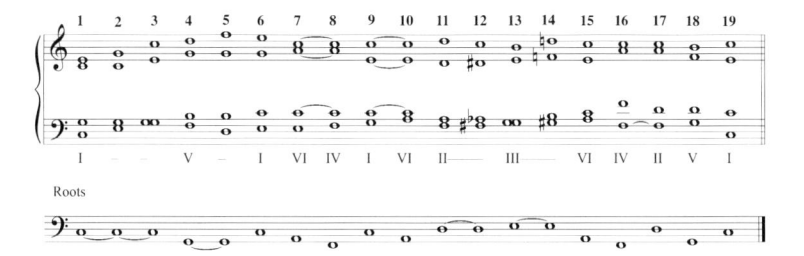

Degrees are marked by Roman numerals, and the first six of them also bear names: I, tonic; II, supertonic; III, mediant; IV, subdominant; V,

---

[†] *Structural Functions of Harmony*, revised ed. (New York: W. W. Norton, 1969); *Fundamentals of Musical Composition* (London: Faber & Faber, 1967).

dominant; VI, submediant; VII has not here been given a name.[54] These numbers refer to the place within the scale and determine the functional relations of the triads (or seventh or ninth chords, etc.) built on them.

To be conscious of these functional meanings is especially important because of the wide-spread misuse of calling a harmony C–E–G C major and D–F–A D minor etc. C–E–G is I in C major, but IV in G major, V in F major, III in A minor, VII in D minor, and even II (as Neapolitan sixth) in B major and minor. And these are decisive functional differences. Replacement of natural tones with substitute tones will generally not change the functional quality of the degree (see also under *Substitute tones*).

Root-progression is the movement from one root to another root. Such a movement produces structural changes in the harmony and its functional meaning, as can be seen in the example. Between 1–2–3 no such change occurs, as these are mere inversions of one triad. The same is true in 4–5. The root also does not move in 11–12 and 13–14, in spite of the chromatic alterations in the upper voices. But in 7–8 and 9–10 there are root-progressions, though the upper voices do not move. And in 16–17, though the bass does not move, there is also a root-progression.

There are three different kinds of root-progressions:

(1) **Strong** or **ascending**:
   (a) a leap of the root a fourth up: I–IV, II–V, III–VI, IV–VII, V–I, VI–II, VII–III.
   (b) a leap of the root a third down: I–VI, II–VII, III–I, IV–II, V–III, VI–IV, VII–V (the latter of questionable value).

Ascending root-progressions are the most effective.

(2) **Weak,** or better called **descending:**
   (a) a leap of the root a fifth up: I–V, II–VI, III–VII (?), IV–I, V–II, VI–III, VII–IV (?).
   (b) a leap of the root a third up: I–III, II–IV, III–V, IV–VI, V–VII (?), VI–I, VII–II (?).

Descending root-progressions are best used in such combinations as finally produce an ascent: I–V–VI (I–VI), or I–V–IV (I–IV), or I–III–VI (I–VI), or I–III–IV (I–IV), etc.

(3) **Super-strong:**
   (a) a step of the root a second up: I–II, II–III, III–IV, IV–V, V–VI, VI–VII.
   (b) a step of the root a second down: I–VII, II–I, III–II, IV–III, V–IV, VI–V, VII–VI.

Super-strong root-progressions produce "deceptive" cadences and half-cadences. If they are not used for a cadence, they should be called "deceptive progressions."

Cadence is a progression of harmonies, selected and arranged to produce a movement towards an ending on a definite degree. Cadences (usually in cooperation with the melody) are designed to mark endings of pieces, or divisions, sections, and even segments. A cadence generally ends on that degree towards which the progression aims. But sometimes, especially in deceptive cadences, endings of segments and sections of any size—occur on different degrees.[55]

Region is a term which was introduced by this author in order to sharpen the discrimination between extended tonality and modulation. One should speak of a **modulation** only if (a) the key has been abandoned distinctly and for a considerable time, and (b) if another key with all its characteristic functions has been established. If such a definite establishment is not present, i.e., if the harmony fails to settle down to a definite key, but rather uses chords which through their multiple meaning can be understood as belonging to several keys, one should speak of **roving harmony.**

The concept of regions derives from a principle of **"monotonality,"** which aims at a unified apprehension of the whole movement of the harmony within one piece of music. Extended tonality not only permits the inclusion in a key of everything which formerly appeared in six independent modes, because they are interrelated by using the same tones of the diatonic scale; but in more modern practice it also permits the inclusion of many other and even more remote relations, which are based on the **functions of the degrees.**

Thus a region—even if it is "carried out like a key"—is considered a related product of a tonic. If, accordingly, a period ends in its eighth measure on V or III of C major, one must not call this a modulation to G major or E minor, but a change or movement to the dominant region or to the region of the mediant.

These are the regions of a major key:

(a) derived from the six modes:

Dorian region (minor) II
Supertonic region (major) II
Mediant region III
Subdominant region IV
Dominant region V
Submediant region VI

(b) based on the relation of a tonic to its subdominant minor:

Neapolitan region ~~II~~
Flat mediant region ~~III~~
Subdominant minor region ~~IV~~
Flat submediant region ~~VI~~

(c) derived from tonic minor:

Tonic minor region ~~I~~
V-minor region ~~V~~

(d) based on the interchangeability of major and minor:

Mediant major region ~~III~~
Submediant major region ~~VI~~

The regions of a minor key can be derived partly from the relative major, partly from the tonic major, and partly from the subdominant minor, excluding some which are too remote. At least in Classical music they have not been considered as related.

(a) from relative major are derived:

Mediant region	III; in C minor, on E♭
Subdominant region	IV " " " " f
V-minor region	V " " " " g (minor!)
Submediant region	VI " " " " A♭

(b) from tonic major can be derived:

Tonic major region	I̶; in C minor, on C
Mediant minor region	I̶I̶I̶ " " " " e (*)
Mediant major region	I̶I̶I̶ " " " " E (*)
Subdominant major region	I̶V̶ " " " " F (*)
Dominant region	V " " " " G
Submediant minor region	V̶I̶ " " " " a (*)
Submediant major region	V̶I̶ " " " " A (*)

(c) from subdominant minor are derived:

Neapolitan region	II; in C minor, on Db
Mediant minor region	I̶I̶I̶ " " " " e♭ (*)
Submediant minor region	V̶I̶ " " " " a♭ (*)

Those starred (*) are more remote, but are more or less often used in Classical music.

The following should be **excluded,** because they are too remote:

a major or minor region on II; in C minor, on D (Dorian and Supertonic)
a major or minor region on VII; "   "   "   "   B♮ and B♭

Changes from one region to another should be based on harmonies common to both regions or on chords with a multiple meaning, e.g. diminished sevenths, augmented triads, augmented $\frac{6}{5}$ or $\frac{4}{3}$ chords, etc.[56]

Substitute tones are tones foreign to the scale, "borrowed" from related regions (or keys). They produce "artificial leading-tones up or down," principally in two ways:

(a) by **chromatically** filling out an interval of a major second up or down in one or more voices;

(b) **quasi-diatonically** by replacing natural tones with such foreign tones as would make a melody similar to the diatonic scale of the region in question.

Generally, when substitute tones are used, the function of the degree is not changed; but sometimes "passing harmonies" assume a form which might be mistaken for a different degree. For instance, the 6-chord on B (marked ?) should not be interpreted as IV of D major but as one of the three transformations of the II of the mediant region.[57]

Tonic reg. I   V   I   III   VI————————————?————————————III
     Mediant reg.   IV   tt   tt   tt   I⁶₄   V   I

Motif is a unit which contains one or more features of interval and rhythm. Its presence is manifested in its constant use throughout a piece. Its usage consists of frequent repetitions, some of them unchanged, most of them varied. The variations of a motif produce new **motif-forms,** which are the material for continuations, contrasts, new segments, new themes, or even new sections within a piece.[58] Not all the features are to be retained in a variation; but some, guaranteeing coherence, will always be present. Sometimes remotely related derivatives of a motif might become independent and then be employed like a motif.

Variation is that kind of repetition which changes some of the features of a unit, motif, phrase, segment, section, or a larger part, but preserves others.

To change everything would prevent there being any repetition at all, and thus might cause incoherence.

Obligations of the motif derive from a tendency or inclination inherent in a motif by which it aims at developing variation. **Obligatory forms** are those in which the tendency of development has not been "neutralized." In meas. 18–20 of Ex. 242, the constant neglect of the interval of this figure of three notes neutralizes the obligations of the basic interval, making the figure finally non-obligatory (see also page 67).

There exists great confusion in the use of the terms **phrase, period,** and **sentence.** In this syllabus, these terms signify the following structural elements:

Phrases are here given as school-forms, limited to two measures. In masterpieces, in rapid tempo, the length is sometimes four measures. They usually contain basic features more than once (see the marks $\wedge$ and ⌐‾‾⌐ in Exx. 58–150). In playing or singing them, one would not consider separating these two measures as if by a breath, but the end would admit the taking of a breath or stopping briefly, as at a comma in punctuation.

Sentences often appear in masterpieces. The opening phrase is repeated at once (with or without variation). This repetition makes further exact repetitions unnecessary, and permits a continuation with either reduced forms of the basic phrase or more remote motif-forms. In the school-form discussed in this syllabus, sentences are restricted to eight measures ending with a cadence. Sentences are usually found at the beginning of a piece or of an independent section of it.[59]

Periods appear in much the same places as do sentences. The school-form is again restricted to eight measures. The period differs from the sentence primarily in the absence of an immediate repetition of the first phrase, instead of which more remote motif-forms appear, which lead (here always in meas. 4), aided by a cadence or half-cadence, to a **caesura.** This caesura is a sharper interruption than that which limits a phrase, and could be compared in its effect to a semicolon. By it the whole section is subdivided into two segments, **antecedent** and **consequent,** the latter producing a (more or less free) repetition of the antecedent, usually concluding this section with a full cadence on I, V, or III.

Codettas are additions after the ending of a section, which are cadences primarily. They are structurally independent, and ordinarily use new and rather more remote motif-forms. Harmonically they are sometimes very simple, occasionally using only the same degree, or a mere interchange of this degree and its dominant, in other cases a full cadence and even richer harmony might appear.

The terms **section, segment,** and **unit** are used for parts of various length. The three parts of every ternary form, including the minuet and scherzo, are called **sections.** The term **segment** refers to the antecedent or consequent of a period, to similar parts of a sentence, and to such parts in the elaboration-section of a scherzo as possess a certain structural independence. Smaller parts, of a lesser degree of independence, are called **units,** if their contents, limitation, or usage justifies their being considered separate.

Elaboration replaces the misleading term "development." In musical composition there is development in every part.

Liquidation, the method of getting rid of the obligations of the motif, is discussed in one example at page 67.[60]

An **up-beat harmony** is a degree that promotes the introduction of the first degree of a new section or segment. Usually the recapitulation of the a-section is introduced by such a harmony. It is the V if this section begins on I, but sometimes III appears instead of V. In the Scherzo of Beethoven's piano sonata Op. 26, the a-section begins on VI. Here the up-beat chord is an artificial dominant on III.

Augmentation, a term known to students who have studied counterpoint, is the repetition of a unit, segment, or section (or even only a part of them) in which the duration of every note (or pause) has been doubled, tripled, quadrupled, etc., while the intervals remain unchanged.

Appendix 1

Manuscript Sources for *Models for Beginners in Composition*

(All manuscripts housed at ASC unless otherwise indicated.)

An Overview of Manuscripts Related to *MBC*

To create the material for the original 1942 self-published edition of *MBC*, Schoenberg and his assistant, Leonard Stein, collected many assignments and materials from Schoenberg's classes at UCLA (see Folder 26 below). Stein then likely typed the preliminary outline summarizing the content of *MBC* (Folder 26).[1] In its completed form, the 1942 edition featured only musical examples, hand-copied by Stein, with no explanatory text or glossary (see p. 111–118). In 1943, Schoenberg created the Schirmer edition of *MBC* by adding many new musical examples to the 1942 edition (see endnote 2 for an itemized list of these additions) and at Schirmer's request, a glossary and explanatory text. Schoenberg began this draft first in German, but then continued it in English (Folder 15). He then revised the text, typing and expanding it with Stein's assistance, a draft contained in Folder 16. It is from this second draft that Schoenberg and the editors at Schirmer created the final version of *MBC*. Their edits are documented throughout the Eastman-Schirmer Manuscripts (see below)—sources that are essentially edited versions of the second draft contained in Folder 16.

TBK 1, Arnold Schönberg Center, Vienna

TBK 1 contains early drafts and various materials related to *Fundamentals of Musical Composition*. Together with these items is an early version of the "Harmonic Schemes for Contrasting Middle Sections" from *MBC*, notable for its omission of the minor-mode progressions (nos. 42–48), which conclude this example in the published edition. Despite this omission, and notwithstanding the lack of roman-numeral analyses in several passages (for example, nos. 22–26), this early draft is nearly identical in its musical content to the finished copy. There are, however, two slight discrepancies in the pitches between this draft and the one in *MBC* (nos. 18, m. 3, alto; and no. 40, m. 3, soprano). These passages are discussed below (See Endnotes to Musical Examples, endnote 49, p. 209).

TBK 5, Arnold Schönberg Center, Vienna

TBK 5, "Textbooks for *Models for Beginners in Composition*," contains manuscripts for the first Schirmer edition of *MBC* (1943).[2] Most of the documents are typescripts or manuscripts handwritten by Schoenberg, but some also appear in the hand of his assistant, Leonard Stein. TBK 5 is divided into seven folders (Folders 15–18, plus three unnumbered folders), as listed below.

Folder 15

Contains loose-leaf first drafts of the preface and table of contents for the first Schirmer edition of MBC (1943). Some sheets at the beginning of the folder are in German; the later ones are in English. Most of the sheets at the start of the folder are single-sided and handwritten by Schoenberg. The only typescript is a double-sided early version of the preface and an abbreviated draft of the explanatory text.

Folder 16

Folder 16 contains an essentially complete second draft of the text of *MBC*, including the Preface, Glossary, and explanatory text for the first Schirmer edition (though these sections are found out of order in the folder). The manuscripts are primarily typescript, single-sided, loose-leaf pages. Although they are typed, these are preedited manuscripts, not yet sent out for proofing by the Schirmer staff. Therefore there are many differences in wording between this version of the preface and the explanatory text, and the published edition. For example, the opening paragraph of the introduction in this draft reads: "This is the second, revised and extended version of a syllabus which I made because I had to teach beginners in composition in a summer session of six weeks." In the published 1943 edition, this passage is rewritten as: "This is the second, revised and enlarged version of a syllabus which I prepared for beginners in composition in a summer session of six weeks at the University of California at Los Angeles."

Differences of this kind are found in nearly every paragraph of the draft in Folder 16 when compared to the published edition. In general, editing was focused on language and writing rather than on content. Folder 16 consists almost exclusively of text, but it does contain four versions of the progression for the definition of "Root" in the Glossary—one draft, one original, and two copies.

Folder 17

Folder 17, labeled "Musical Examples," contains early drafts of examples for *MBC*—probably versions used in Schoenberg's classes. It consists of the following examples:

> Six copies of an early version of "Phrases, Half-Sentences, Antecedents, and 'a' Sections of Ternary Forms"; and
>
> A single copy of the complete Minuet and the untitled scherzo (Example 247) together on the same large sheet of paper.

Folder 18

Folder 18 contains twenty-three copies of the abbreviated typescript draft of the text for *MBC*, identical to the one in Folder 15, as well as thirteen copies of a key for abbreviations and motivic symbols in typescript not contained in the final version of *MBC* (see Appendix 4).

"Introduction"

Contains the same abbreviated version of the text as that found in Folders 15 and 18.

Unnumbered Folder *a*

Folder *a* is labeled "Models for Beginners in Comp 2nd version" in Schoenberg's hand. It is a handcrafted green book with homemade binding consisting of brown paper tape and a foldout paper bag (now empty) designed to hold manuscripts for the drafts related to the initial Schirmer edition described by Schoenberg as the "2nd version" in order to distinguish it from the self-published 1942 edition.

Unnumbered Folder *b*

Folder *b* contains musical examples for *MBC*, including the original copy of the Minuet written on onionskin paper, used for making carbon copies; the Scherzo, which eventually became Example 245, written directly beneath it; and also the untitled scherzo (Example 247) in Schoenberg's hand.

"Models for Beginners in Composition": Arnold Schönberg Center, Vienna

"Models for Beginners in Composition" in the Leonard Stein Satellite Collection includes three folders containing many musical examples used in *MBC* as well as various copies of the syllabus with and without annotations (with remarks in Stein's hand), listed below.

Folder 26: This folder contains a draft of *MBC*, much of it in outline form, for the 1942 edition of *MBC*. At this early stage, *MBC* was still conceived as a book within *FMC*, as evinced by colonic descriptor of its title page: "A

Supplement to Textbook: Fundamentals of Musical Composition." This descriptor was eventually dropped, and the two books (*FMC* and *MBC*), though similar in many respects, developed distinct identities: *FMC* as a *Formenlehre/ Kompositionslehre* and *MBC* as a practical composition manual, documenting the contents and basic mode of presentation specific to Schoenberg's Composition 105 course at UCLA.

Folder 26 also contains the largest number of musical examples from *MBC* of any folder at the ASC. Most are extensive examples, such as the complete sentences that would eventually become Examples 217–32 in *MBC* in Schoenberg's hand. Some of them, such as the two-measure phrases that would be used for Examples 180–88, are notated in Stein's hand—although not necessarily *composed* by him. The neatness of the manuscript containing these passages, with its tightly spaced musical examples and organized formatting, marks this as a transcription rather than an original draft.

Folder 27: This contains the self-published, 1942 edition of *MBC*.

Unnumbered Folder: This contains two copies of *MBC* with Stein's transcriptions of Schoenberg's edits from S141.C1:

> 1943, 1st printing, w/errata sheet pasted to inner cover. This copy is noteworthy for its inclusion of the dedication by Schoenberg, thanking Stein for assisting with *MBC* (see Facsimile 4.1).
>
> 1943, corrected 2nd printing, with errata sheet no longer pasted on inner cover.[3]

TBK 8, Arnold Schönberg Center, Vienna

TBK 8 contains themes used for assignments in Schoenberg's composition class from 1940 to 1941. These assigned melodies were later used as "Phrases, Half Sentences, Antecedents, and A-Sections of Ternary Forms," in *MBC*. Thirty-two of the thirty-nine themes used in the 1943 edition of *MBC* are found in this collection of assignments (missing are melodies nos. 3, 5–9, and 27). One melody, no. 35, was edited for the 1943 edition, but most appear in TBK 8 in their final form. The instructions for many of the assignments in TBK 8 seem to have been written by Schoenberg, with a few by Stein. The music seems to have been consistently copied by an assistant. In correspondence with the author,

ARNOLD SCHOENBERG

MODELS

FOR

BEGINNERS IN COMPOSITION

MUSIC EXAMPLES

To my pupil and assistant Mr Leonard Stein who was helpful to me by arranging and collecting the materials to this booklet Cordially Arnold Schoenberg May 1943

G. SCHIRMER, INC.   NEW YORK

FACSIMILE 4.1
Schoenberg's dedication to Stein on the front cover of the 1943 edition of MBC. Courtesy Arnold Schönberg Center.

Therese Muxeneder from the ASC has positively matched at least some of the notation in these manuscripts with Stein's writing. The neatness of the notation suggests that these are fair copies rather than drafts, likely copied from originals by Schoenberg. For reproductions of a limited selection of the manuscripts in TBK 8, see Appendix 3: Models in Context (127–37).

Schoenberg's Annotated Copies of *Models for Beginners in Composition*: S141.C1–S141.C4; S142.C1–S142.C4, Arnold Schönberg Center, Vienna

S141 and S142 are annotated copies of finished editions of *MBC*. The manuscripts in S141 are copies of Schoenberg's edition of *MBC*, self-published in 1942, which Schoenberg annotated to create Schirmer's 1943 edition. S141 contains these annotations. The manuscripts in S142 are copies of Schirmer's 1943 edition with Schoenberg's annotations. Some of them were used to create the second printing of the book; others were intended for a second edition of the book, which was published posthumously in 1972, edited by Stein. Most of Schoenberg's annotations were incorporated in the 1972 edition; however, several have only now been added. For a list of recent changes based on these annotations, see Example 2.1.

S141.C1

S141.C1 is a self-published 1942 edition of *MBC* with corrections, and with annotations in Schoenberg's hand, including many foldout musical examples attached to the body of the text with glue and brown paper tape (see Facsimile 4.2). Like those shown in Facsimile 4.2, the annotations in the foldout attachment to S141.C1 are often quite elaborate.

This version of *MBC* was sent to Schirmer to create the musical examples for the 1943 edition—one created by adding the pasted examples from S141.C1 to the examples of the 1942 edition and then, later, by adding a preface and explanatory text. By tracing the examples added in S141.C1 and studying the preface and explanatory text, it is possible to gain a fairly clear picture of the evolution of the 1943 version of *MBC* from Schoenberg's original self-published syllabus.[4]

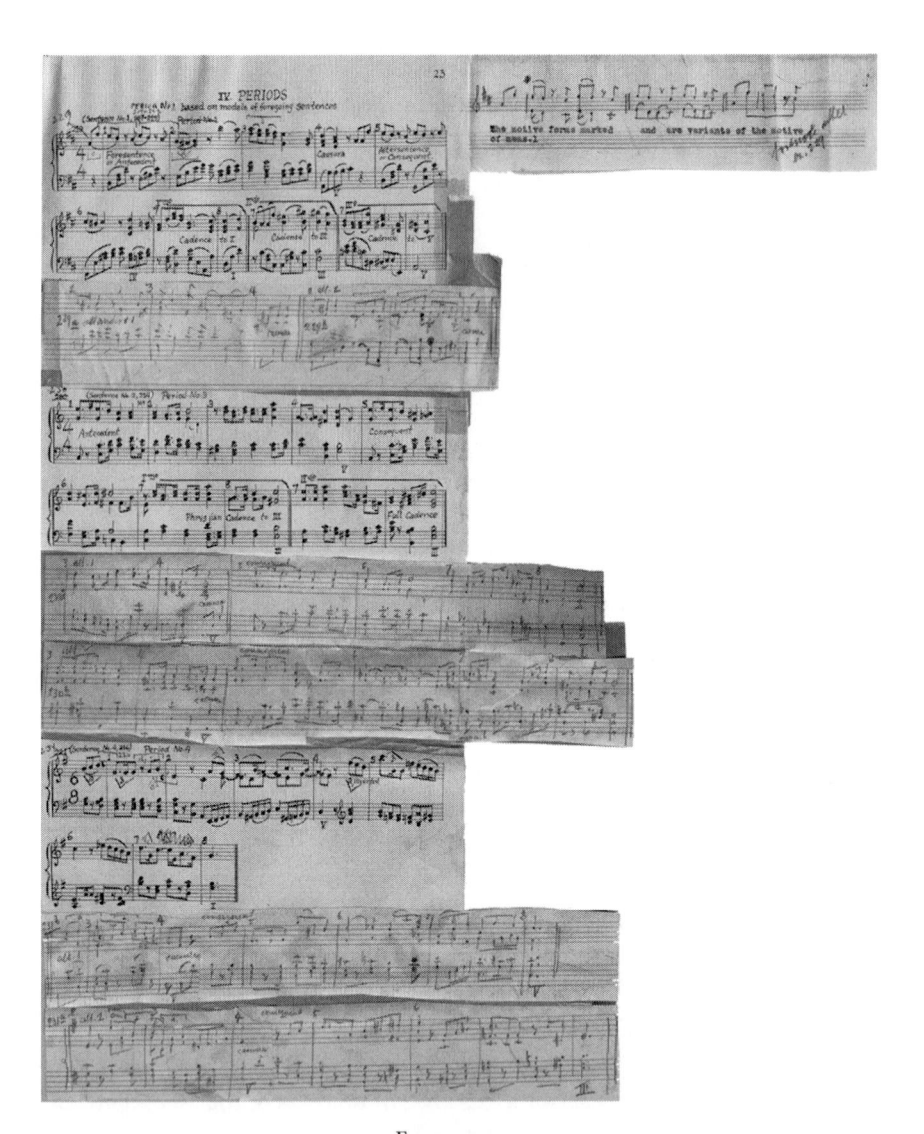

FACSIMILE 4.2

Sample of Schoenberg's foldout attachments to S141.C1. Courtesy Arnold Schönberg Center.

S141.C2–S141.C4

S141.C2 and S141.C4 feature slight annotations to copies of the 1942 self-published edition in the form of harmonic and motivic analyses. S141.C4 is devoid of annotations.

S142.C1–4

S142.C1–S142.C4 are Schoenberg's copies of the Schirmer 1943 edition, first printing. The text came as a removable booklet, which included the glossary and explanatory text. The copies contain Schoenberg's corrections, in characteristic red pencil, for a new edition of *MBC*, many of which made their way into the 1972 edition.

S142.C1: This has no annotations.

S142.C2: This features several corrections made by hand. At the end of the book, attached with brown paper tape and glue, are five fugues from advanced classes in counterpoint. Severine Neff has discovered a sheet containing the title "Models for Contrapuntal Exercises," which suggests Schoenberg might have been planning a practical book based along the lines of *MBC*, for contrapuntal study.[5*]

S142.C3: This contains several handwritten corrections by Schoenberg. There is a discrepancy between the outer folder, which reads "S143.C3," and the inner slip, which reads "S142.C3." The latter seems to be the logical catalog number. Included in this folder is an advertisement for *MBC* (see Example 1.3, xviii).

S142.C4: Features only two manual corrections, both in Schoenberg's hand: "e minor" and "Transforms of II," both added to p. 56 (1943 edition). In addition to this copy of *MBC*, the folder also contains one double-sided sheet of manuscript paper with handwritten harmonic progressions, most of them closely related to those in *SFH*.

Eastman-Schirmer Manuscripts

G. Schirmer Deposit, box 14/8, M2A 2,1—Ruth T. Watanabe Special Collections/Eastman School of Music Archives, Sibley Music Library

The Eastman-Schirmer Manuscripts contain copies of early drafts of the text for *MBC*, including the preface and explanatory text (grouped together) and the glossary. Because they were mailed back and forth for editing, these early drafts feature annotations by both Schoenberg and his many editors at

Schirmer, who included Gustave Reese, Willis Wager, Nathan Broder, Walter Boelke, and Schoenberg's son-in-law Felix Greissle.[6] Previously catalogued as one document, the Eastman-Schirmer Manuscripts actually contain seven separate manuscripts grouped in folder M2A 2, 1.

Typed Manuscript 1 (Preface and Explanatory Text)

Version of the manuscript from TBK5, Folder 16 (described above), after it had been sent to Schirmer for editing. Contains annotations in blue, red, and black pencil, as well as in black and green pen, by several writers, including Schoenberg and his Schirmer editors. The manuscript ends with a dated and signed note in Schoenberg's hand: "May they [i.e., the models] also be helpful to the students of this syllabus! September 12, 1942."

Typed Manuscript 2 (Preface and Explanatory Text)

Typed Manuscript 2 is a later version of Typed Manuscript 1 with the edits from the latter now incorporated in typed form. Thus, the handwritten note that concluded the manuscript is now typed, as are most of the other previously handwritten annotations. However, what survives is not a clean copy, but an annotated version of Manuscript 2, a document that offers insight into this important stage of the editing process. As in Typed Manuscript 1, annotations are in several hands, including those of Schoenberg and the editors at Schirmer: the literary editor, Willis Wager; Nathan Broder; and possibly Gustav Reese, one of the editors to whom Schoenberg later attributed the improved English of his syllabus (see "Preface: On the History of MBC," ix–xx). This version evinces a slight increase in the frequency of Schoenberg's annotations, in the form of both handwritten corrections and typed comments, either pasted to the typescript over existing text or attached to margins in the manner of the foldout additions described in connection with S141.C1.

Glossary (Copy No. 1)

This is an early draft of the glossary for *MBC*. However, since it is already heavily edited with Schoenberg's and Schirmer's annotations, this is clearly not a first draft. It also contains many of Schoenberg's pasted annotations, similar to those in S141.C1. Similar handwriting to that in Typed Manuscripts 1 and 2, even identical writing utensils (red pencil for Schoenberg, green pen and black pencil for Schirmer editors) indicate that this was edited by the same authors as Typed Manuscripts 1 and 2, and at about the same time.

Glossary (Copy No. 2)

First two pages only. Incorporates the edits from Copy No. 1 of the Glossary, but only for these pages. This may indicate a concentrated effort to work on these pages in isolation, or it may simply be an incomplete document.

"Schoenberg's Manuscripts"

The materials in this bundle may be more accurately described as a collection of miscellaneous papers, labeled with a small card and fastened together by a paper clip. The bundle contains several documents, including a note from Schoenberg to his editors regarding his notation for figured bass, two copies of his example for root progressions for the glossary, a cut-out for the definition of "degree," a Western Union telegram dated December 16, 1942, and addressed to Willis Wager in which Schoenberg accepts the font for *MBC*, and an errata sheet with comments by both Wager and Schoenberg, dated December 3, 1942.

Revised Glossary (Copy No. 3)

This features a small square green card, attached with a paper clip, which reads "revised typescript." This is the edited typescript of the glossary, incorporating the edits from Copies Nos. 1 and 2. Like all previous manuscripts, it contains annotations by both Schoenberg and his editors.

Galley Proof 1 (12–2–42)

Galley Proof 1, initialed by Willis Wager and dated 12–2–42, was mailed to Schoenberg during the final stage of editing. This galley proof is printed without illustrations on long sheets of paper. It contains corrections by both Schoenberg and his editors and features many foldout, typewritten annotations by Schoenberg only, glued into the text as in S141.C1 and elsewhere.

Appendix 2

Schoenberg's Teaching Schedule at UCLA

Example 5.1 shows Schoenberg's schedule for each semester that he taught at UCLA.[1] I am grateful to the staff at the UCLA Library, Special Collections, for providing the 1930s and '40s course catalogs and schedules.

1936-37		
Fall		
14A	Counterpoint	TTh 1
104A	Form and Analysis	TTh 2
105A	Composition	MF 1
Spring		
14B	Counterpoint	TTh 1
14B	Counterpoint, Quiz	TTh 3
104B	Form and Analysis	TTh 2
105B	Composition	MF 1
122B	Double Counterpoint, Canon, and Fugue	MF 3
1937-1938		
Fall		
14A	Counterpoint	TTh2
104A	Form and Analysis	MF 1
105A	Composition	MF 3
122A	Double Counterpoint, Canon, and Fugue	TTh 3
Spring		TTh 2
14B	Counterpoint	MF 1
104B	Form and Analysis	MF 3
105B	Composition	TTh 3
122B	Double Counterpoint, Canon, and Fugue	

EXAMPLE 5.1

Schoenberg's teaching schedule at UCLA as documented in the UCLA General Catalogue and Schedule of Classes for each semester taught. Courtesy UCLA Special Collections.

1938-1939		
Fall		
14A	Counterpoint	TTh2
104A	Form and Analysis	MF 1
105A	Composition	MF 3
122A	Double Counterpoint, Canon and Fugue	T 3,4
123A	Advanced Form and Composition	Th 3,4
199	Special Studies in Music	To be arranged
Spring[1]		
14B	Counterpoint	TTh2
104B	Form and Analysis	MF 1
105B	Composition	MF 3
122B	Double Counterpoint, Canon and Fugue	T 3,4
123B	Advanced Form and Composition	Th 3,4
199	Special Studies in Music	To be arranged
1939-1940		
Fall[2]		
105A	Composition	MF 1
106A	Harmonic Construction	MW 3
122A	Double Counterpoint, Canon and Fugue	F 3,4
201A[3]	Advanced Form and Composition	MWF 2
199	Special Studies in Music	To be arranged
Spring		
105B	Composition	MF 1
106B	Harmonic Construction	MW 3
122B	Double Counterpoint, Canon and Fugue	F 3,4
201B	Advanced Form and Composition	MWF 2
199	Special Studies in Music	To be arranged

EXAMPLE 5.1

(Continued)

1. Nelson teaching section 2 of Counterpoint, 14A, and section 2
of Compostion105B.
2. Nelson now teaching both sections of Counterpoint 14A.
3. Formerly listed as 123A.

1940-41		
Fall		
105A	Composition	MF 1
106A	Structural Functions of Harmony	MW 3
122A	Double Counterpoint, Canon and Fugue	F 10, 11
201A	Advanced Form and Composition	MWF 2
199	Special Studies in Music	To be arranged
Spring		
105B	Composition	MF 1
106B	Structural Functions of Harmony	MW 3
122B	Double Counterpoint, Canon and Fugue	F 10, 11
201B	Advanced Composition[4]	MWF 2
199	Special Studies in Music	To be arranged
261	Special Studies for Composers	To be arranged
1941-42		
Fall		
14A	Counterpoint	MF 10
104A	Form and Analysis	MF 11
105A	Composition	MF 1
106A	Structural Functions of Harmony	MW 3
201A	Advanced Composition	MWF 2
199	Special Studies in Music	To be arranged
Spring		
14B	Counterpoint	MF 10
104B	Form and Analysis	MF 11
105B	Composition	MF 1
106A	Structural Functions of Harmony	MW 3
201A	Advanced Composition	MWF 2
261	Special Studies for Composers	To be arranged
Summer		
S105A	Composition	TTh 2–4

EXAMPLE 5.1

(*Continued*)

4. Formerly called "Advanced Form and Composition."

1942-1943 Fall		
104A	Form and Analysis	MF 11
105A	Composition	MF 1
122A	Advanced Counterpoint	W10–11
261	Seminar: Special Studies for Composers	To be arranged
Spring	Spring	MF 11
104B	Form and Analysis	MF 1
105B	Composition	MF 1
122B	Advanced Counterpoint	To be arranged
261	Seminar: Special Studies for Composers	
1943-1944 Fall		
14B	Counterpoint	MF 10
105B	Composition	MF 1
106B	Structural Functions of Harmony	MF 2
261	Special Studies for Composers	To be arranged
Spring	Schoenberg on sabbatical Spring 1944	

EXAMPLE 5.1
(Continued)

Appendix 3

Models in Context: Assignments from
Schoenberg's Beginning Composition
Class, Composition 105, UCLA

The following assignments, contained in the Leonard Stein Satellite Collection (ASC) and in boxes such as TBK 8, are related to the materials of Schoenberg's courses and to the preparation of *MBC*. These assignments provide the rare opportunity to experience the models of Schoenberg's syllabus in context, and to imagine what it may have been like as a student in Schoenberg's beginning composition class at UCLA. What were the topics of the assignments? What did the final project entail? If the assignments below can offer some insight into these questions, they may help to reanimate a book that was once naturally enlivened by its function as a practical teaching manual.

Composition of Two-Measure Phrases Using Broken Chords

Like *MBC*, Schoenberg's composition class began with assignments based on two-measure phrases using broken chords (see Facsimile 6.1, recto). As Stein's notes indicate, Schoenberg taught "phrases first, motives later."[1] That is, it was the two-measure phrase rather than the motive that was primary. As in Example 6.1 (verso) from the same course, motives in Schoenberg's composition

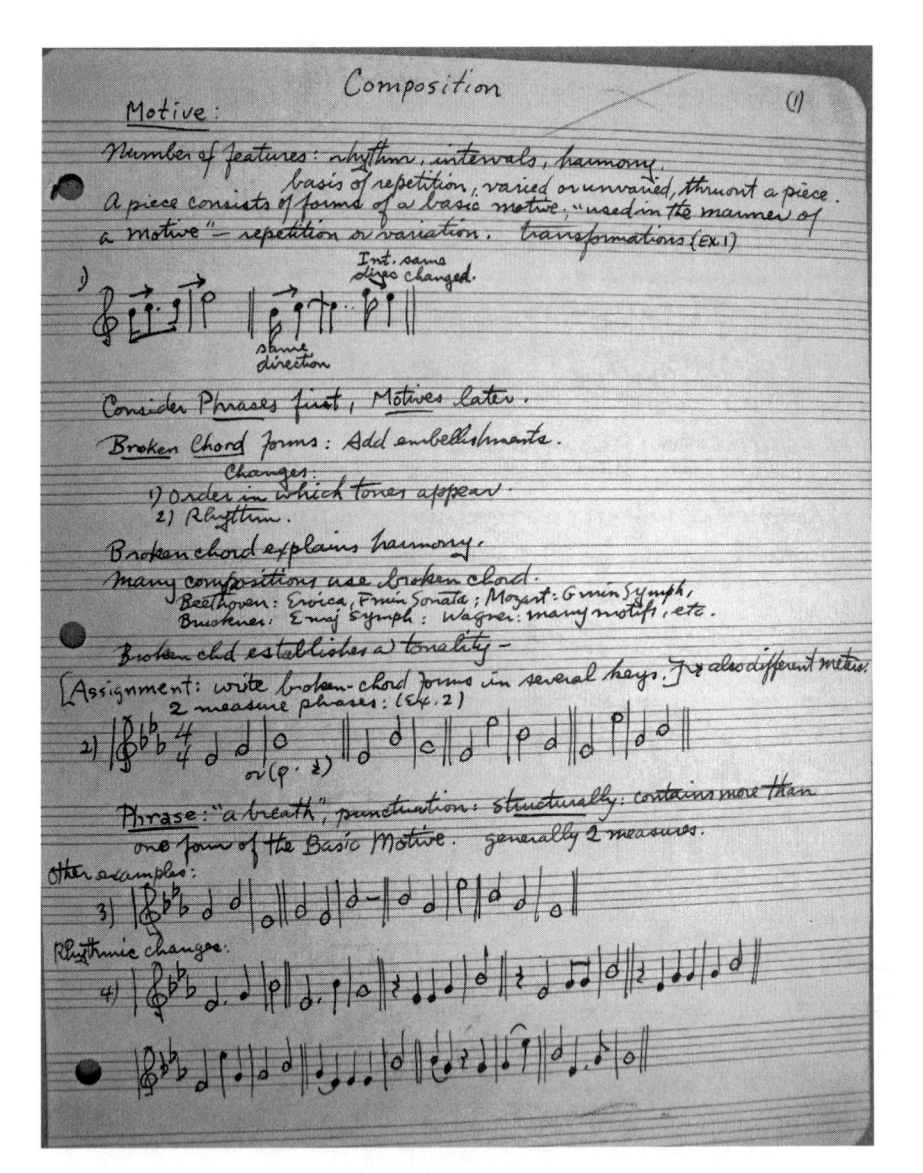

FACSIMILE 6.1 RECTO

Assignment: Compose two-measure phrases using broken chords (Leonard Stein Satellite Collection, UCLA Notes, Folders 103–17, Folder 103, p. 6, recto, ASC). Courtesy Arnold Schönberg Center.

FACSIMILE 6.1. VERSO

Assignment: Compose motives by inserting passing tones between the broken chord forms of two-measure phrases (Leonard Stein Satellite Collection, Folder 103, p. 6 verso, ASC). Courtesy Arnold Schönberg Center.

class were taught by "inserting" embellishing tones between the chord tones of the basic two-measure phrase in the broken chord forms.

Motives Derived from Broken Chord Forms

Sentences

After mastering two-measure phrases with motives, students would learn to vary the harmonies and motives of these phrases. This was followed by composing sentences and periods, which would later function as the themes of scherzos and minuets, the final projects of Composition 105. Though they contain many errors, the sentences shown in Facsimile 6.2, written by a student in Schoenberg's 1941 composition class, illustrate the kinds of assignments students would have written in preparation for the final project. Particularly interesting is Schoenberg's comment that the opening four measures of the first sentence in G major sounds like a "period in 2/4." Because m. 4 ends with a half-cadence, the final cadence of this hypothetical period is no more conclusive than the initial one in m. 2. Thus, a literal period structure is not viable here. However, what Schoenberg seems to dislike about the theme is the ambiguity that arises from the exaggerated caesura at the end of m. 2, a pause that makes it sound like an antecedent phrase, and which therefore causes the goal harmony (II) to sound awkward and out of place. This problem with unwanted caesuras continues in m. 4. Schoenberg also notes that the theme should modulate to V, a feature that will later be required in the opening theme of the small ternary form for the final project.

Themes for the Openings of Small Ternary Forms

The themes shown in Facsimile 6.3a and b, from TBK 8 (ASC), were assigned to the students of Schoenberg's composition class in 1940–41 (three of the manuscripts are stamped and dated 1940). As discussed in the commentary, there are many such assignments contained in TBK 8 (thirty-two in all), which were eventually used for the "Phrases, Half Sentences, Antecedents, and 'a' Sections of Ternary Forms" to conclude the example section of *MBC*. These assignments, carefully tailored to each individual student (with names

FACSIMILE 6.2

Composing sentences for Composition 105 (Leonard Stein Satellite Collection, Folder 108, ASC). Courtesy Arnold Schönberg Center.

included), provide instructions, (either typed or handwritten), explaining how the student should proceed. For instance, in the final example (Facsimile 6.3b), the student is asked to add an accompaniment and repeat the phrase, ending in m. 16 on V. This theme is also noteworthy in that it offers a variation

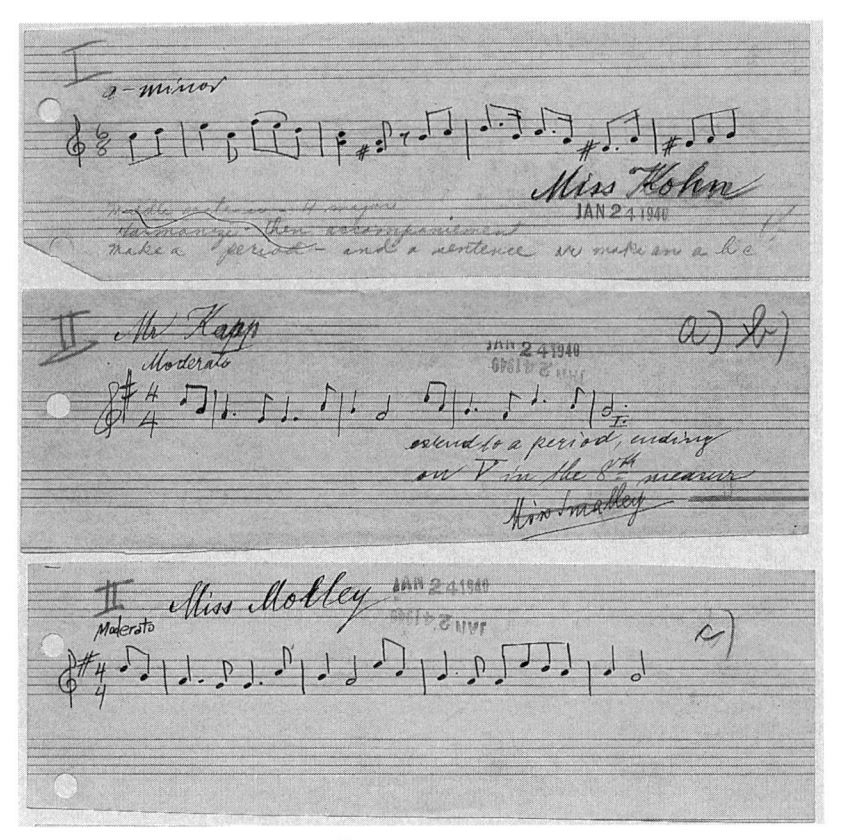

FACSIMILE 6.3A
Themes for the openings of small ternary forms (TBK 8, ASC).
Courtesy Arnold Schönberg Center.

on theme 35 not included in the final version of "Phrases, Half Sentences, Antecedents, and 'a' Sections of Ternary Forms" in *MBC*.

The Final Project

Among the extant archival materials in Stein's notes for Composition 105, 1941, is a little minuet (see Example 6.1) by the future Pulitzer Prize–winning composer Leon Kirchner (1919–2009).[2] Similar to the empirical approach of Berg's lessons, Schoenberg's course in beginning composition had as its

FACSIMILE 6.3 B
(Continued)

goal the creation of what Schoenberg called "small ternary" forms. Kirchner's minuet reads as a virtual model of the course's pertinent topics and techniques. Not surprisingly, these topics also closely follow those presented in *MBC*, the eventual syllabus for this course. Like many of the "a" sections offered in *MBC*, Kirchner's minuet begins with a sentence consisting of a two-bar motive and its sequential repetition, followed by a continuation leading to a cadence in the dominant region. Following the dictates of Schoenberg's famous 1947 essay "Brahms the Progressive," we might imagine the teacher to have admired the slightly asymmetrical 4 + 6 grouping of Kirchner's theme.

The "contrasting middle section" which follows this theme in mm. 11–28 also features many of the characteristics Schoenberg suggests for such sections. For example, the development of the opening phrase of the sentence in mm. 11–14, which begins with a verbatim statement of the initial motive

FACSIMILE 6.4 RECTO
Kirchner's minuet for Composition 105, 1941 (Leonard Stein Satellite Collection, Folder 108, ASC). Courtesy Kirchner Heirs. 6.4 Recto, 6.4 Verso

Note: Although Folder 108 in the Leonard Stein Satellite Collection is labeled "Structural Functions of Harmony," it contains many notes and papers from Beginning Composition 105a, 1941. Properly situating some of these materials is possible through an examination of the subject matter, but in many cases there is little ambiguity in any event, since the papers are clearly labeled by students or by Stein himself as "105a" or "Composition."

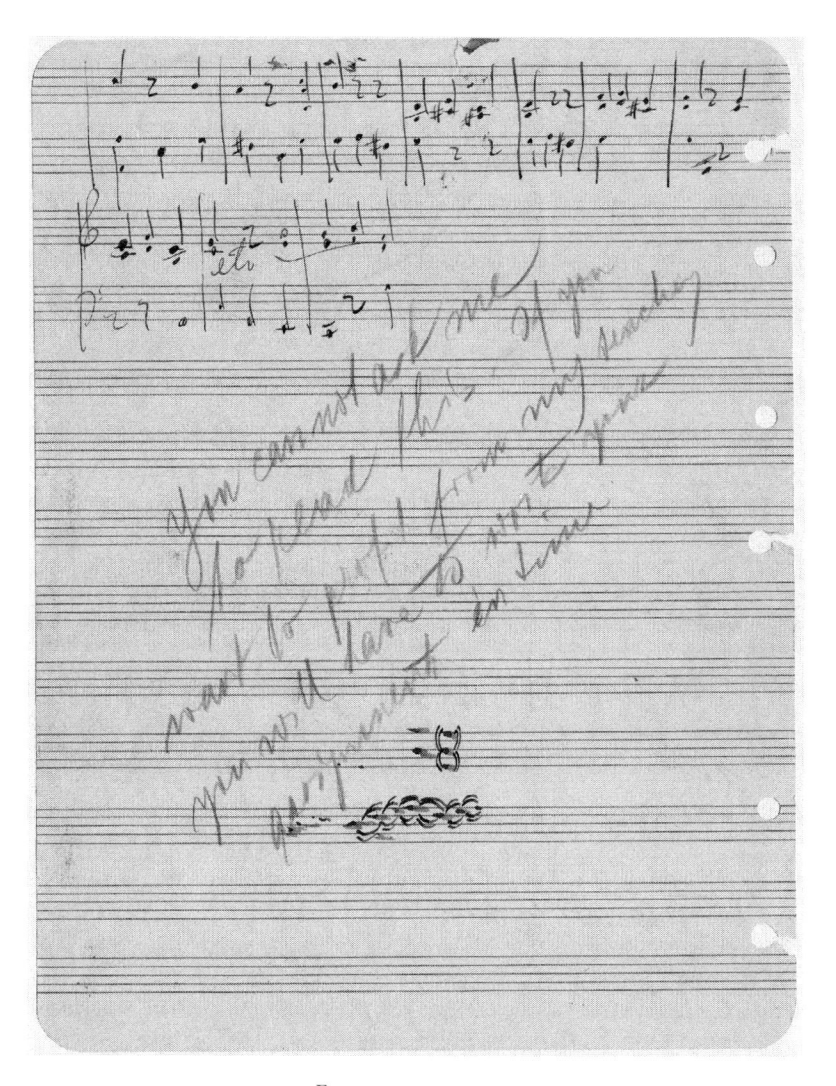

FACSIMILE 6.4 VERSO
(Continued)

immediately followed by a retrograde inversion of its original contour, would
seem to encapsulate the developmental spirit of the "middle section," whose
"contrast," Schoenberg explains in *MBC*, is achieved through similar methods of variation. Likewise, the sequential structure of Kirchner's melodic
development and the quasi-sequential treatment of the harmonies in this

EXAMPLE 6.1
Transcription of Kirchner's minuet

Note: Several pitches in Kirchner's Minuet are difficult to verify with certainty. In mm. 15–16, the bass is particularly unclear. In Example 6.1, I have interpreted this line as G♯–G–F (in support of a descending-fifths progression leading to II). In m. 25, I have notated only B in the upper voice. It is possible that there is also a G5 above this—though, given the voicing of the previous chord (a dominant seventh with an anticipatory tonic in the bass), the mark near this spot seems more likely to be a smudge on the page.

section satisfy the imperatives of Schoenberg's examples in *MBC* concerning contrasting middle sections.

Further reminiscent of Schoenberg's discussion in *MBC* is the imitative texture of Kirchner's motivic work in mm. 18–22, a design Schoenberg describes as "semi-contrapuntal imitations of a prominent rhythm in the accompanying voices." Finally, the expansion of the dominant concluding the retransition section of Kirchner's minuet in mm. 25–28 corresponds with

Schoenberg's famous notion of "standing" or "dwelling" on the dominant—a concept he had incorporated into his composition courses as early as 1936, one famously referenced in his discussion of "the small ternary form" in *FMC*, and even earlier than this, in the *TH* of 1911.[3]

We might expect Kirchner's thorough presentation of these procedures to have garnered the praise of his teacher, but the tardiness of his poorly notated minuet seems to have overshadowed its structural merits. At the bottom of the page is a note in red pencil not of encouragement, but of admonition. "You cannot expect me to read this," his perturbed teacher lectured. "If you want to profit from my teaching you will have to [submit] your assignments [on] time" (see Facsimile 6.4a and b, and Example 6.1).

Appendix 4

Key to Schoenberg's Symbols
and Abbreviations in *MBC*

In order to clarify the meaning of his analytic notation, Schoenberg provided his students with the following key of abbreviations and symbols, now contained in Folder 18 of TBK 5 at the ASC. Of the abbreviations used both in Schoenberg's handout and *MBC*, many, such as "neap." (which also appears as "Neap." and "np."), "rep.," "recap.," and "var." are understandable without Schoenberg's key. Others may be less self-evident and may therefore require reference to it. These would include the abbreviation "str.," which stands not for the conventional "strings," but rather for the contrapuntal technique of stretto. This would also likely include "rov.," which refers to "roving harmony," Schoenberg's term for the highly chromatic, unstable harmony typical in the elaboration sections of sonatas and scherzos.

Schoenberg's key may also be helpful for its explanation of motivic symbols (see p. 2 of Schoenberg's key). As indicated, the angled brackets ("carets and letters") designate rhythmic motives, while the square brackets refer to intervallic motives; Schoenberg differentiates the latter from purely rhythmic motives only somewhat vaguely in his key of abbreviations, describing them merely as "motives" (rather than "rhythmic motives"). Both varieties of motivic symbols are used extensively in *MBC*.

In addition to the motive and phrase symbols found in Schoenberg's key of abbreviations, *MBC* also makes use of two important performance signs not shown in this key: ⊠ and ⬦. They have to do with alternative passages of musical examples. Following these signs entails the same basic procedure involved in following a coda symbol, with the fundamental difference that in *MBC*, passages referred to by such signs are entirely optional. For instance, when arriving at the sign ⊠ in m. 8 of Example 247 (103), the performer may either finish the example as written, or examine the alternative to this passage. To do the latter, simply peruse the music until the cross-symbol [⊠] is reached (in this case, the ⊠ sign appears again as Example 248 on the following page), and then perform the passage following the symbol. In situations such as mm. 5–8 of the Scherzo in G, Example 245, in which Schoenberg has composed more than one alternative passage, a single symbol covers all alternative passages pertaining to a particular example. To apply these alternative passages in context, simply read the original example and, after reaching the sign, skip ahead to the alternative passages. Once there, you may choose which alternative passage to read. For instance, if you wish to examine the alternate passages of Example 245 (101), simply play this example until reaching the ⊠ sign in m. 5, then skip ahead to the next ⊠ sign on p. 102. There you will find two alternatives (the second is labeled Example 246) from which to choose. The first offers four possible endings, each of which varies somewhat harmonically and motivically from the others. Like the harmonic and motivic variations found throughout *MBC*, the larger significance of Schoenberg's alternative endings is found in the wealth of instruction and insight they offer into the strategies and techniques of variation. (Facsimile 7.1)

ABBREVIATIONS

a-b-a	three-part song form	f. cad.	full cadence
A-B-A	rondo form	Fg.	bassoon
acc.	accompaniment	fig.	figure
add.	addition	fign.	figuration
alt	alto	Fl.	flute
ant.	antecedent	Fl. son.	flute sonata
appog.	appogiatura	funct.	functional
art. dom.	artificial dominant	functls.	functionless
aug.	augmentation		
auth.	authentic	germ. m.	germ motive
aux.	auxiliary	gr. n.	grace note
B. Cl.	bass clarinet	har.	harmony
br.	bridge	h. cad.	half cadence
br. ch.	broken chord	hem.	hemiolia
bs.	bass		
		imit.	imitation
cad.	cadence	ins.	insertion
cam.	cambiata	int.	interval
canon	canon	intro.	introduction
C. Bs.	contra bass	inv.	inversion
C. Fg.	contra bassoon		
circum.	circumscribing	liq.	liquidation
Cl.	clarinet		
Cl. son.	clarinet sonata	m.	measure
Cl. tr.	clarinet trio	m. acc.	motive of accompaniment
coda	coda		
con.	consequent	maj.	major
cons.	consonance	mel.	melody
cont.	continuation	min.	minor
contr.	contrast	mod.	modulation
contr.sec.	contrasting middle sec.	mot.	motive
conv.form.	conventionalized formulas	m. var.	" of the variation
crab f.	crab form		
cpt.	counterpoint	neap. 6.	neapolitan 6th
c-ta.	codetta	neut.	neutral, neutralization
char.	character	non-oblig.	non-obligatory
O 5ths.	circle of 5ths		
		pass. h.	passing harmony
I, II, III,	degrees	pass. n.	passing note
dev.	development	ped.	pedal
dim.	diminution	per.	period
dimin.	diminished	phr.	phrase
diss.	dissonance	Pic.	piccolo
div.	division	Pio.	piano
dom.	dominant	plag.	plagal
Durch.A.	Durchbrochene-Arbeit	P. Qu.	piano quartet
		P. Qnt.	piano quintet
E.H.	English Horn	prep.	preparation
elab.	elaboration	prog.	progression
embell	embellishing	P. son.	piano sonata
ep.	episode	p. tone	principal tone(s)
est.	establishing	P. tr.	piano trio
ext.	extension	p. u.	pick up

FACSIMILE 7.1

Schoenberg's abbreviation key. Courtesy Arnold Schönberg Center.

ABBREVIATIONS

recap.	recapitulation	t.	theme
reduc.	reduction	ten.	tenor
rep.	repetitions	tie	tie
res.	resolution	ton.	tonic
retr.	retrograde	tone rep.	tone repetition
retran.	retransition	Tr.	trumpet
rh.	rhythm	trans.	transition
rh. shift	rhythmical shift	Trn.	trombone
rov.	roving		
		upb. ch.	upbeat chord
sbst.	substitute		
sc.	scale-line	Va.	viola
sec.	section	var.	variation
sect.	sector	Vcl.	violincello
segm.	segment	Vcl.son.	" sonata
sent.	sentence	Vi.	violin
sept.	septet	Vi. son.	violin sonata
seq.	sequence		
sl.	slur		
sop.	soprano		
S. T.	subsidiary theme		
str.	stretto		
Str. Qu.	string quartet		
Str. Qnt.	string quintet		
Str. Tr.	string trio		
subd.	subdominant		
subdiv.	subdivision		
subd. reg.	subdominant region		
subsid.	subsidiary		
succ.	succession		
susp.	suspension		
sxt.	sextet		
sync.	syncopation		

- - - - - - - - - - - - - -

To indicate points quoted in the text use:

brackets and letters	⌐a⌐ ⌐b⌐ ⌐c⌐	for motives and motive-forms
carets and letters	⌃a ⌃b ⌃c	for rhythms
braces and letters	⌢a ⌢b	for phrases and small segments
slurs and letters	⌢a	for sequences, sections, antec., conseq., etc.

FACSIMILE 7.1

(Continued)

Appendix 5

Primer in Regions

This primer in regions is a supplement to the material in *MBC*. Not only is a basic understanding of regions needed to follow the analysis of harmonic progressions in *MBC*, it is also crucial for comprehending form in *MBC*'s school compositions. Much research has been devoted to this topic since the posthumous publication of Schoenberg's landmark harmony text, *Structural Functions of Harmony* (1954). The present overview is offered as a convenience to the reader by situating Schoenberg's theory of regions within the specific context and topics of *MBC*.

Survey of Literature on Schoenberg's Regions, Transformations, and Substitute Tones

In his seminal 1968 article "Inversional Balance as an Organizing Force in Schoenberg's Music and Thought," David Lewin uncovers many instances of inversional balance in Schoenberg's music and theoretical works.[1] The Chart of the Regions is one of several concepts he examines, a structure he describes as a tonal network, "a fulcrum about which all else [is] balanced."[2] Lewin offers the symmetrical regional design in Schoenberg's First String Quartet as an application of such inversional balance.

Dieter Rexroth's 1971 dissertation, "Arnold Schönberg als Theoretiker der tonalen Harmonik," traces both the similarities with and differences between Schoenberg's harmonic theories and the earlier ideas of Simon Sechter and Hugo Riemann.[3] His study considers the ideas in Schoenberg's *TH* at length while examining concepts such as regions and monotonality. Rexroth's work was influential for later studies such as Phillip Murray Dineen's 1989 dissertation on Schoenberg's harmonic theories (discussed later) and Robert Wason's 1985 staple, *Viennese Harmonic Theory from Albrechtsberger to Schenker and Schoenberg*.[4] Wason's work remains useful for its outline of the Viennese harmonic tradition, which influenced Schoenberg's theories, and for its explanation of the ways in which they both continued and diverged from this tradition. Without Wason's work, it would be difficult to imagine the historically oriented studies of Bernstein and Dudeque.

Patricia Carpenter, who studied with Schoenberg both at UCLA and privately from 1944 to 1949, authored a number of important papers and articles on Schoenberg's tonal theories.[5] She focused particularly on the related concepts of the *Grundgestalt*, the musical idea, and the tonal problem. In addition to her edition and translation of *MI* with Severine Neff, perhaps her best-known article on Schoenberg's tonal theories is the 1983 "*Grundgestalt* as Tonal Function."[6] In this essay, Carpenter not only analyzes the workings of the *Grundgestalt* and the presentation of the musical idea in Beethoven's "Appassionata" Sonata, applying many of Schoenberg's harmonic theories in the process, she also discusses the substitute tones, transformations, and structure of Schoenberg's Chart of the Regions.

In many ways, Neff, Carpenter's student, has continued in the tradition of her teacher, exploring the vast array of issues related to Schoenberg's theories of harmony, form, counterpoint, and the musical idea. In her 1984 article "Aspects of *Grundgestalt* in Schoenberg's First String Quartet, Op. 7," Neff analyzes the musical idea and its presentation in this work through the interaction of motive, harmony and theme.[7] As an introduction to her analysis, she discusses many of Schoenberg's harmonic theories, including monotonality, transformation, substitute tones, vagrant chords, the five classifications of regional relationships, and the structure of the Chart of the Regions.

In her 1993 essay, "Schoenberg and Goethe: Organicism and Analysis," Neff returns to some of these topics from a new perspective.[8] Here, she examines the influence of Goethe's scientific writing on Schoenberg's concepts of monotonality and the *Grundgestalt*, which, as in her other essays, she treats as interconnected and interdependent phenomena. Within this discussion, she reviews the Chart of the Regions and Schoenberg's classifications of their relationship.

In "Schoenberg as Theorist" (1999), Neff examines Schoenberg's three forms of motivic presentation: developing variation, juxtaposition, and contrapuntal combination.[9] As she demonstrates, the first of these, associated primarily with the repertory of the Classical and Romantic eras, works within Schoenberg's larger framework of monotonality. Neff describes the interconnection between developing variation and monotonality:

> The statement of a theme introduces the relationships of the *Grundgestalt* and sets up the "tonal problem." This "problem" demands expansion and continuation in regions away from the tonic, eventually including the most tonally distant reinterpretation of the opening material, the climax of centrifugal force. But in an organically tonal piece, this leads to a retransition as the centripetal force begins to overcome the centrifugal one. The final section or coda eliminates all centrifugal tendencies of the "tonal problem," reinterpreting both the material of the *Grundgestalt* and the "tonal problem" in the tonic. Thus, in a truly organic work, the opening already presents the tonal form of the whole.[10]

When explaining these concepts, Neff discusses the concept of monotonality and the structure of the Chart of the Regions. In her 2011 article, "Editing Schoenberg's Music-Theoretical Manuscripts: Problems of Incompleteness and Authorship," Neff returns to the regions once again, this time with an examination of the origins of Schoenberg's thoughts on the topic by defining an early chronology of manuscripts related to the first draft of Chart of the Regions.[11]

Another of Carpenter's students, Phillip Murray Dineen, has written extensively on Schoenberg's tonal theories, contributing many articles, papers, and a dissertation on these topics.[12] He begins his 1989 dissertation, "Problems of Tonality: Schoenberg and the Concept of Tonal Expression," by examining Schoenberg's derivation of the tonal system in *TH* and exploring each of the major concepts related to Schoenberg's theories of harmony and tonality, including regions, vagrant chords, substitute tones and transformation.[13] He also discusses at length the concept of transference, the process by which Schoenberg applies the transformation of one degree to all others in a scale. In this way, a half-diminished chord on II, for example, derived through the minor subdominant (see *SFH*), is first isolated as an abstract chord type and then "transferred" to other scale degrees, so that any degree of the scale can theoretically be harmonized using a half-diminished seventh chord. Following the analytic tradition of Carpenter, Dineen concludes his study with a consideration of the tonal problem in Schoenberg's song "Erwartung," Op. 2 No. 1, and Beethoven's Op. 2 No. 1.[14]

Continuing in the historical tradition of Wason, David Bernstein notes the possible influence of Hermann Erpf's 1920s *Tonnetz* on Schoenberg's Chart of the Regions.[15] Playing on the dialectical theories of his study, Bernstein argues that Schoenberg's harmonic theories "synthesize," on the one hand, the ideas of Sechter and *Stufentheorie* and, on the other, the doctrines of Riemann and *Funktionstheorie*. Schoenberg's fixed-degree-based roman-numeral approach provides evidence of the former, while his emphasis on "symmetrical arrangements," in particular his description of the dominant and subdominant, his devotion of an entire chapter to the minor subdominant, and the symmetrical design of the Chart of the Regions, evinces the latter. Schoenberg's own notion of dialectical opposition is later captured in terminology such as centrifugal and centripetal motion from *SFH*.

In his 2005 study *Music Theory and Analysis in the Writings of Arnold Schoenberg*, Norton Dudeque devotes considerable attention to Schoenberg's theories of harmony.[16] Influenced by the seminal work of John Spratt, Dudeque distinguishes between certain "speculative" or philosophical theories in Schoenberg's writings and other practical or pedagogically oriented ones.[17]

Among the former, he scrutinizes concepts such as "the rejection of tonality as a natural law" and Schoenberg's famous "emancipation of dissonance," while among the latter he includes the categorization of root progressions, transformations, the interchangeability of major and minor, and most of the concepts covered in *SFH*. Dudeque's summary of Schoenberg's harmonic theories is thorough, covering not only the presentation of these concepts in *TH* and *SFH*, but also their use in many secondary analytical sources.

Primer in Schoenberg's Regions

As shown above, the ultimate goal for students working through *MBC* was to write school compositions that incorporated their knowledge of motives, thematic structures, diatonic and extended tonality, and finally form. Central to Schoenberg's conception of form in tonal music was his notion of monotonality, the framework of which is most comprehensively shown by his Chart of the Regions. First published posthumously in *SFH*, it measures relatedness between a tonic and its twenty-three regions (see Example 8.1).[18] Like the exhaustive harmonic and motivic charts from Berg's 1907 lessons mentioned earlier, Schoenberg's Chart of the Regions presents potential structures for both original and school compositions.

   Along the vertical plane, Schoenberg's Chart of the Regions is organized by fifths (reading from bottom to top), with the tonic in Example 8.1b located in the center, surrounded by its two most closely related regions: dominant and subdominant.[19] Each of these regions holds a maximum number of pitches in common (six each). Moreover, the dominant and subdominant balance symmetrically around the tonic key, highlighting its central position (the dominant a fifth above, and the subdominant a fifth below).[20] The relations of these keys to the tonic are termed "direct and close."[21]

   If we combine each region along the horizontal plane (reading left to right) with its parallel partner, temporarily to allow for nine "modally ambiguous" regions (rather than eighteen separate major and minor ones), as in Example 8.2a, a symmetrical design in the horizontal plane comes to the foreground.[22] In this arrangement, the tonic region is clearly balanced by the

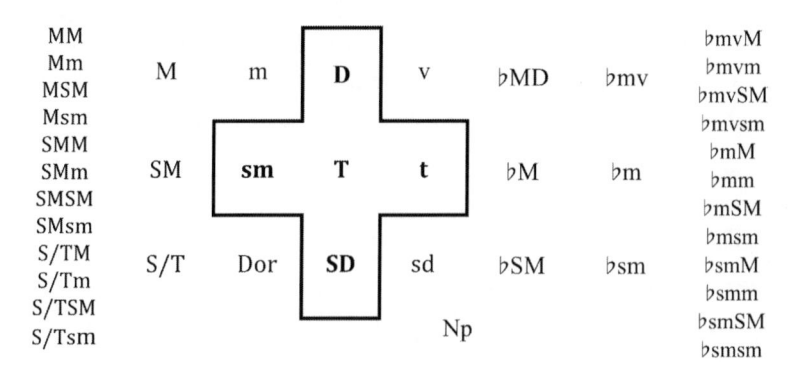

MM							♭mvM
Mm	M	m	**D**	v	♭MD	♭mv	♭mvm
MSM							♭mvSM
Msm							♭mvsm
SMM							♭mM
SMm	SM	**sm**	**T**	**t**	♭M	♭m	♭mm
SMSM							♭mSM
SMsm							♭msm
S/TM	S/T	Dor	**SD**	sd	♭SM	♭sm	♭smM
S/Tm							♭smm
S/TSM							♭smSM
S/Tsm			Np				♭smsm

T	Tonic	**Np**	Neapolitan
D	Dominant	**Dor**	Dorian
SD	Subdominant	**S/T**	Supertonic
t	tonic minor	♭**M**	Flat mediant major
sd	subdominant minor	♭**SM**	Flat submediant major
v	Five-minor	♭**MD**	Flat mediant major's dominant
sm	submediant minor	♭**m**	Flat mediant minor
m	mediant minor	♭**sm**	Flat submediant minor
SM	submediant major	♭**mv**	Flat mediant minor's five
M	mediant major		

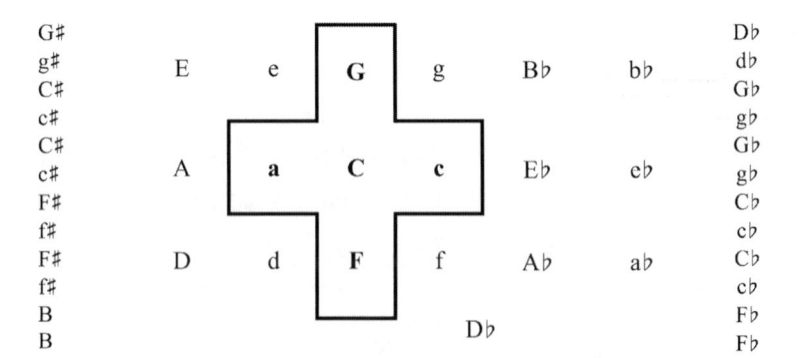

G♯							D♭
g♯	E	e	**G**	g	B♭	b♭	d♭
C♯							G♭
c♯							g♭
C♯							G♭
c♯	A	**a**	**C**	**c**	E♭	e♭	g♭
F♯							C♭
f♯							c♭
F♯	D	d	**F**	f	A♭	a♭	C♭
f♯							c♭
B			D♭				F♭
B							F♭

Example 8.1

Reproduction of Schoenberg's Chart of the Regions from SFH, 20.
Courtesy Faber and Faber.

Note: The meaning of most of Schoenberg's labels in the Chart of the Regions is fairly self-evident, but there are a few which might require brief explanation. One of these is the region of the second degree, here labeled as "Dor" for Dorian, when minor, and "S/T," for supertonic, when major.

E   G   B♭
A   C   E♭
D   F   A♭

T_{-3} (D)   **D** = T_7 (T) T_3 (D)
T_{-3} (T)   **T** T_3 (T)
T_{-3} (SD)   **SD** =T_{-7} (T) T_3 (SD)

EXAMPLE 8.2A
Underlying structure of the Chart of Regions.

flatted mediant region (E♭ to the right and the submediant region (A) to the left. Similarly, the subdominant region (F) is balanced by the flatted submediant region (A♭) and the supertonic (D). Within this symmetrical design, Schoenberg categorizes the tonic minor, flat mediant, and major submediant as "indirect but close" relations to the tonic.[23]

This idea stems from Schoenberg's earlier theory of substitute tones. Schoenberg claimed that the Dorian region gradually evolved into D minor, by borrowing characteristics from the Aeolian mode (after having been altered through musica ficta), incorporating C♯ when ascending, and B♭ when descending. Unlike the other regions, D minor retains its original modal designation (Dor) in Schoenberg's labeling of regions. The others, of course, also directly correspond to Schoenberg's normalized modes; the mediant region corresponds to the normalized Phrygian mode, the subdominant to the Lydian, and so on. In general, in his chart of the regions, Schoenberg gives preference to these functional labels, rather than to their original modal designations. The rationale for retaining the original modal designation "Dor" in connection with the supertonic remains unexplored in *SFH*. For secondary relationships, in the chart of regions, such as "mediant of the mediant," the leftmost label always corresponds to the most immediate derivation of a particular region, while the right-hand one refers to a secondary function. For instance, in the label ♭**MD** (in the top right-hand portion of the chart), ♭**M** indicates that this region derives from the flatted mediant, while the letter **D** shows that the region itself is the dominant of ♭M. The complete label, then, is understood as "the dominant of the flatted mediant." Symbols involving tertiary relationships can be somewhat unwieldy, but the principle is the same. For example, the symbol ♭**mvM**, at the top of the leftmost column, refers to a region which functions as "the major mediant of the minor dominant of the flatted minor mediant." If the global key is C major, this is a key enharmonically equivalent to the Neapolitan region, but reached through the dominant of the flatted minor mediant. A flat sign, as in the final column of Schoenberg's Chart of the Regions, affects only the region immediately adjacent to it, after which all other regions are calculated diatonically. For example, ♭mvSM is read as "the major *submediant* of the minor dominant of the flatted minor mediant." Schoenberg's C major–oriented version of the Chart of the Regions confirms that G♭ is indeed the intended key for ♭mvSM, and that this same logic for the use of the flat symbol applies throughout the right-hand column.

Inversional balance by perfect 5th

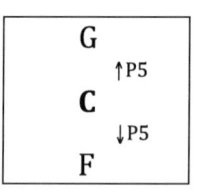

Inversional balance by minor 3rd

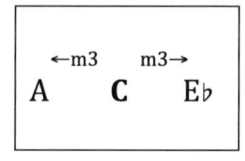

EXAMPLE 8.2B
Inversional balancing around tonic.

Schoenberg's original chart in Example 8.1 is flanked on either side by a list of additional regions in parallel relationships. For example, at the top of the leftmost column, we find MM (the major mediant of the major mediant) and Mm (the minor mediant of the major mediant). These relationships simply continue the transpositional sequence by minor thirds in each row and by perfect fifths in each column, so that if these additional regions were integrated into the chart proper, it would become extended by two new columns on each side. Example 8.3a provides a more visually comprehensible version of this extended chart, Example 8.3b converts these relationships to pitch-class letters, and Example 8.3c omits all pitch-class duplications to accentuate the basic structure of Schoenberg's design.

These relations (MM and Mm) are considered "indirect" relations to the tonic, while many of the remaining regions in the left-hand column and the one to the right are either "indirect and remote" or "distant." Example 8.4 summarizes Schoenberg's "Classification of Relationship" and includes his rationale for these categorizations from *SFH*.

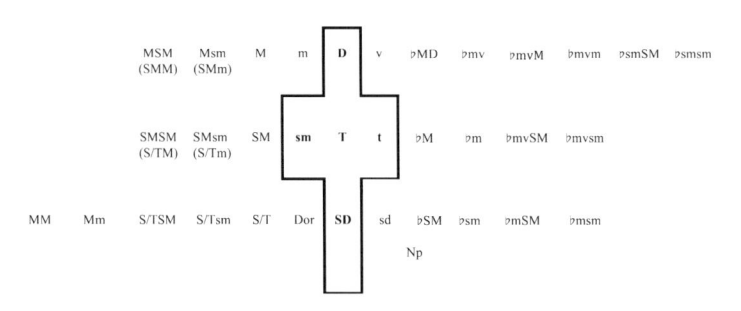

EXAMPLE 8.3A
Extended Chart of the Regions.

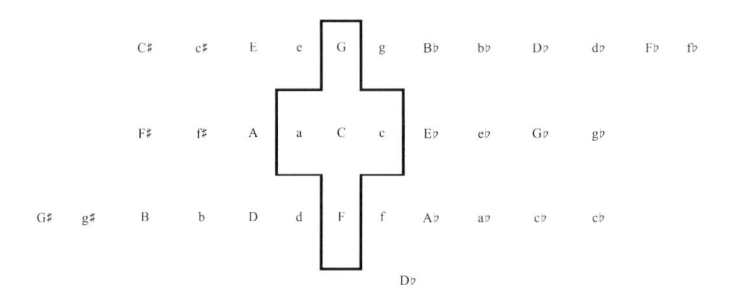

EXAMPLE 8.3B
*Extended Chart of the Regions with pitch-class letters substituting for functional
designations.*

C♯	E	G	B♭	D♭	F♭
F♯	A	C	E♭	G♭	
G♯	B	D	F	A♭	C♭

EXAMPLE 8.3C
Simplification of extended chart with letter names in C major.

As Example 8.4 illustrates, Schoenberg's rationale for the categorization
of each region is based primarily on the number of common tones shared with
the tonic, a property that figures into his explanation for classes 1, 2, and 3.
The common-tone rationale also explains several of the classifications of distant relations in class 5. This would certainly be true of the tritone relations
SMSM and ♭mvSM (F♯ and G♭, respectively), which naturally share the least
possible number of common tones (six) with the tonic.[24]

Class	Regions [as related to T]	Rationale for Relationship
1. Direct and Close	SD, D, sm, m	Five or six tones in common with T

2. Indirect *but* Close	A. Through Common Dominant
	    i) t, sd, v
	    ii) SM, M
	B. Through Proportional Transposition
	    bM, bSM
		Regions in Class 2 are either related to the regions in Class 1, or to the tonic minor, and have three or four tones in common with T. Schoenberg explains that t, sd, v, SM, and M relate to regions in Class 1 through a "Common Dominant." In other words, t shares a common dominant with T, sd with SD, v with V, and so on. This allows for interchangeability of major and minor, in which, the dominant of one of these keys might appear, followed by either the major or minor version of the region.

3. Indirect	bm, bsm, MM, Mm, bsmSM, bsmsm (Ebm, Abm, G#, G#m, Fb, Fbm)	"All regions in Class 3 are more distant than class 2, and the number of tones in common with T is negligible" SFH, 68. Schoenberg also explains that these regions may be easily replaced by their enharmonic equivalents (i.e. instead of G#, Ab, instead of Fb, E, etc.), so that the relationships to Class 1 and 2 are much closer than they first appear. The parallel relationships here would also seem notable (see the interchangeability of major and minor in Class 2).
4. Indirect and Remote	Np, dor, S/T, bMD, bmv	Schoenberg's rationale for the relative "remoteness" of the regions in Class 4 is unclear. Rather than offering general principles, he points only to specific relationships. "Class 4 is called INDIRECT AND REMOTE because these five regions are connected in the following manner: Dorian **(dor)** is subdominant's submediant minor **(SDsm)**; Supertonic **(S/T)** is subdominant's submediant major **(SDSM)**; Neapolitan **(NP)** is subdominant minor's submediant major **(sdSM)**; Flat major mediant's dominant **(bMD)** is subdominant's subdominant **(SDSD)**; Flat minor mediant's "five-minor" **(bmv)** is subdominant minor's subdominant minor **(sdsd)**." (SFH, 69)
5. Distant	MSM, Msm, SMM, SMm, SMSM, SMsm, S/TM, S/Tm, S/TSM, S/Tsm, bmvM, bmvm, bmvSM, bmvsm, bmM, bmm, bmSM, bmsm, bsmM, bsmm	Schoenberg provides no rationale for the distant relationships in Class 5, but several of the relationships including the tritone relationships discussed above, would seem to draw their classification as distant relations from their lack of common tones, as well as from their derivation as secondary relationships of non-diatonic regions.

EXAMPLE 8.4

Summary of Schoenberg's "Classification of Relationship."

Example 8.5 shows Schoenberg's Chart of Regions in Minor from *SFH*. Like the chart in major, the minor version features the same symmetrical balancing of regions about the tonic. The vertical plane is characterized by fifth relations with the dominant above and the subdominant below, while the horizontal plane alternates in third and parallel relations (tonic minor–tonic major–sharp submediant minor, reading left to right; and tonic minor–relative major–mediant minor, reading right to left). The design of the minor chart differs only in the regional labels from the major version (shown in Example 8.5b).

a.

CHART OF THE REGIONS IN MINOR

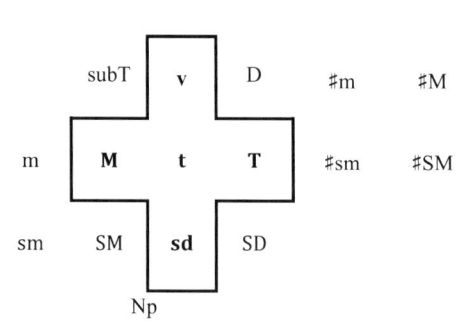

	subT	**v**	D	♯m	♯M
m	**M**	t	**T**	♯sm	♯SM
sm	SM	**sd**	SD		
		Np			

ABBREVIATIONS

t	tonic minor	**Np**	Neapolitan
v	five-minor	**sm**	submediant minor
sd	subdominant minor	**m**	mediant minor
M	relative major	**SD**	subdominant major
SM	submediant major	**D**	dominant major
subT	subtonic	**♯sm**	sharp submediant minor
T	Tonic major	**♯m**	sharp mediant minor
		♯SM	sharp submediant major
		♯M	sharp median major

b.

CHART OF THE REGIONS IN MINOR

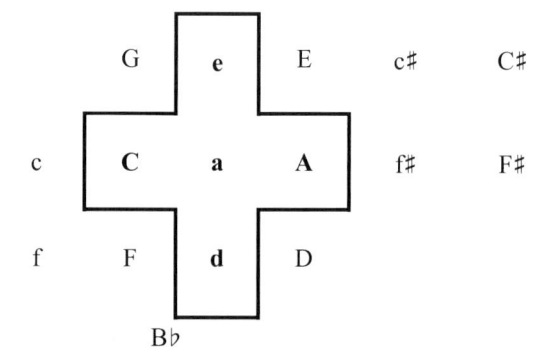

	G	**e**	E	c♯	C♯
c	**C**	a	**A**	f♯	F♯
f	F	**d**	D		
		B♭			

EXAMPLE 8.5

Reproduction of Schoenberg's Chart of the Regions in Minor from SFH, 30. Courtesy Faber and Faber.

Note: The key of abbreviations is given here for convenience only. It is not included in the minor version of Schoenberg's original Chart of the Regions. See *SFH*, 30.

Although the concept and presentation of the Chart of the Regions were fully developed during the 1930s, this useful construct remains strangely absent from 1942's *MBC*. In precisely the place where it would most likely appear, Schoenberg's chart is replaced by a noticeably less serviceable list of regions—a design having none of the visual elegance and little of the precision of the former.[25] For ease of discussion, Example 8.6 recasts this list as a table. Each of the requisite regions appears in this simplification, yet any sense of the symmetry, relative proximity, or distance of these regions from the central tonic is lacking. In place of a "yardstick" for measuring relatedness—clearly the most attractive feature of the chart of the regions—we find a somewhat unsatisfactory summary of their derivation.

Diatonic scale degrees of chord roots	Regions derived from the modes	Regions derived from the subdominant minor	Regions derived from the tonic minor	Regions derived through the interchangeability of major and minor
$\hat{1}$			tonic minor	
$\hat{2}$	Dorian or Supertonic	Neapolitan		
$\hat{3}$	mediant	flat mediant		mediant major
$\hat{4}$	subdominant	subdominant minor		
$\hat{5}$	dominant		V-minor	
$\hat{6}$	submediant	flat submediant		submediant major

EXAMPLE 8.6
Schoenberg's list of regions from MBC *(presented here as a table for ease of discussion).*
Courtesy Belmont Music Publishers.

The omission of Schoenberg's Chart of the Regions from *MBC* is mysterious. Perhaps there was some pedagogical rationale for its absence. Maybe Schoenberg considered its contents to be overly theoretical for his summer class—or perhaps he wished his students to work within a more limited sphere of closely related tonalities and thus deemed the vastness of the chart too overwhelming for the task at hand. However, if this were the case, Schoenberg could have easily constructed a simplified version of his Chart of the Regions, one similar to Facsimile 8.1, from Stein's course notes for Structural Functions of Harmony (UCLA, 1941–42).[26]

If needed, we can imagine further simplifications, involving the deletion of all chromatic mediants, leaving only close and direct relations. Considering

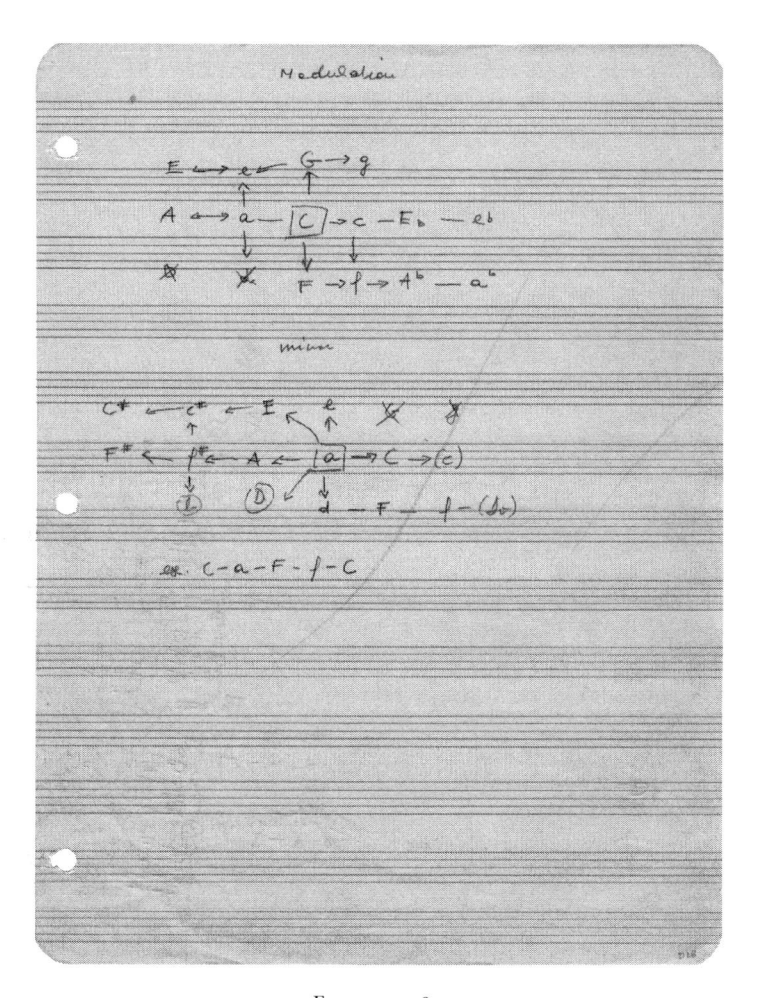

FACSIMILE 8.1
Simplified Chart of the Regions from Leonard Stein's Notes for Structural Functions of Harmony, UCLA, 1941–42 (Leonard Stein Satellite Collections, Folder 111, Notes for Structural Functions of Harmony).

such expedient pedagogical solutions, it is doubtful that these simplifications would account for the chart's omission. A more likely explanation would be that Schoenberg might have wanted to save his Chart of the Regions for his larger composition text. To include the main attraction of his theory before the book was published would have prematurely revealed a significant aspect of its allure, a compromise Schoenberg may have been reluctant to make.

Appendix 6

Primer in Transformations

Introduction

The following primer in Schoenberg's theory of transformation introduces readers to the harmonic vocabulary and notation in *MBC*. As explained in Appendix 5: Primer in Regions (153–165), many scholars, including Patricia Carpenter, Phillip Murray Dineen, Norton Dudeque, and Severine Neff have explored Schoenberg's theory of transformation and substitution. The present overview is offered as a convenience for elucidating issues related to Schoenberg's harmonic notation and interpretation. Some of them, such as subposition applied to the diminished seventh and augmented-sixth chords, may cause confusion for readers, and they are not explained in the more substantial studies outlined in Appendix 5. Beginning with a discussion of notational issues related to Schoenberg's roman-numeral analyses of transformations in *MBC*, the primer simultaneously covers the evolution of transformation from Schoenberg's substitute tones and examines the structure of his unique harmonic system. Wherever possible, each transformation is scrutinized within the context of the exercises used in *MBC*. In order to facilitate understanding, descriptive labels are added to Schoenberg's transformations.

Schoenberg's Harmonic Notation in *MBC*

Example 9.1 (Example 10, 95, *MBC*) illustrates some of the idiosyncrasies setting Schoenberg's harmonic notation apart from current North American conventions. A few of these features may make his analyses in *MBC* difficult for contemporary readers to follow. First, all chords, regardless of quality, are labeled with uppercase roman numerals.[1] Thus, the diminished chord in m. 1 is labeled simply as Ⅲ, the minor chord in m. 2 as VI (with no change to a lower case roman numeral), and the artificial dominant in m. 4 (beat 3) simply as Ⅱ, with no secondary function specified. Secondly, although the root of Ⅲ in m. 1 is absent, many readers will recognize the implied E as a concept derived from the theories of Rameau.[2] With this interpretation (more closely examined later), all fully diminished seventh chords are considered to be ninth chords with the fundamental omitted. In this case, the mediant triad would be (E)–G#–B–D–F.

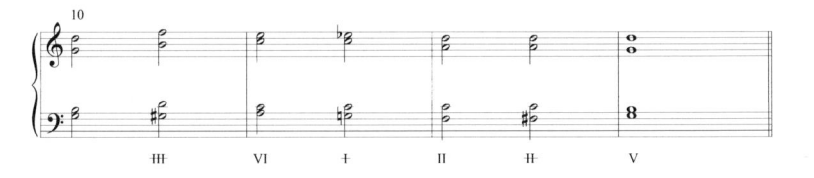

EXAMPLE 9.1

Schoenberg's fixed-roman-numeral analysis for minor chords, artificial dominants, and chords with implied roots. Courtesy Belmont Music Publishers.

Although the roman numeral under the second chord in m. 2 specifies no secondary function, the strikethrough symbol indicates that it has been chromatically altered—or, in Schoenberg's terminology, that it is a *transformation* of the original diatonic harmony. Despite this lack of specificity regarding "secondary dominants," Schoenberg's notation accurately reflects the inclusive nature of his theory of monotonality, a system in which all chromaticism is incorporated into a main tonality, one in which the chromatic rather than the diatonic scale is ultimately responsible for all pitch resources in a key. In this system, each scale degree contains potential for both altered and unaltered versions, and even the former maintain integrity as members of the original degree—not as unnecessary ornamentations of an a priori diatonic structure, but more accurately as members of a kind of scale-degree class.[3]

Substitution

For Schoenberg, this expansion of the concept of scale degree was part of a larger claim founded on the belief that "the many laws" of harmony which "purport to be natural laws" could be more accurately attributed to human creativity in composition. In fact, Schoenberg believed that the tonal system had been "produced" by the "manipulation" of particular "devices" and that its language had been molded only through the painstaking "struggle of craftsmanship to shape the material." For him, tonality, though a perfectly valid medium for artistic expression, was one forged not by nature but by *individuals*.[4] Thus, Schoenberg saw the rise of the tonal system as a process of historical evolution wedded to practice—and this Hegelian view of such practice in music history was idiosyncratically his own.[5] He generally described the High Renaissance as an era of diatonic harmony and counterpoint (no Gesualdo here!) that, through the standardization of its use of musica ficta, pointed forward to the establishment of the major/minor system in the Baroque era and beyond. The use of the major and minor keys in turn led to the extension of diatonic relations and the chromatic tonality of the Classical and Romantic eras. This process finally culminated in the extended tonality of the late Romantic and early Modernist periods. Schoenberg writes:

> [The] transition from twelve major and twelve minor keys to twelve chromatic keys ... is fully accomplished in the music of Wagner, the harmonic significance of which has not yet by any means been theoretically formulated.[6]

Following this logic, Schoenberg would eventually propose a theory of the chromatic scale as the ultimate expression of tonality, and this idea guided many of his harmonic principles as it developed.[7]

In his definition of the term "Region" in *MBC* (113), Schoenberg outlined this view (albeit in abbreviated form) regarding the chromatic nature of tonality. More substantial elaboration is found in *TH* and *SFH*, texts that trace the source of chromatic tonality back to the Renaissance. According to Schoenberg, the process of chromaticism begins with substitution, or the gradual tendency to alter certain degrees of the modes in order to emulate the sound of the major scale. Accordingly, the Aeolian mode was first, with musica ficta applied to its sixth and seventh degrees in an attempt to recreate, in minor, the pull toward the tonic that was so characteristic of the Ionian mode, or major scale. Subsequently, this altered Aeolian mode became the model for all others containing a minor tonic. In each case, Schoenberg explains, the characteristic modal degrees—the Lydian fourth, the Dorian sixth, the Mixolydian seventh, and so on—were thus altered through a process that rendered them indistinguishable from their Ionian and Aeolian counterparts—a homogenization that eventually led to the demise of the modal system. In the Dorian mode, for example, lowering the sixth degree when descending and raising the seventh when ascending emulated the alterations typically applied to the Aeolian mode. Similarly, lowering the fourth degree in the Lydian mode simulated the Ionian (the major scale). Example 9.2 from *SFH* shows the complete process applied to the modes based "in C major."

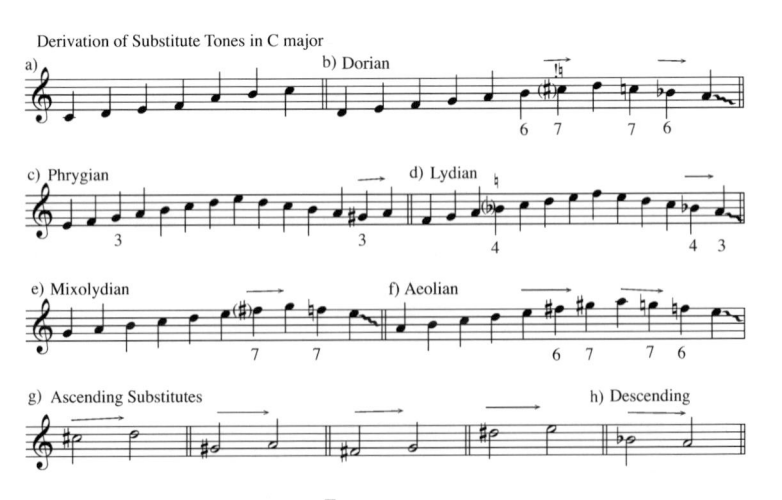

EXAMPLE 9.2

Derivation of the substitute tones and the resultant homogenization of mode (adapted from SFH, 15). Courtesy Faber and Faber.

Schoenberg understood the ficta of modes as contributing the first chromatic alterations, or "substitute tones," to the original diatonic collection of C major. He thus conceptualized these pitch classes as added components to the C scale. D-Dorian contributed C♯ to the scale; G-Mixolydian, F♯; A-Aeolian, G♯; E-Phrygian, D♯; and F-Lydian, B♭.[8]

In this way, chromatic pitch classes originally resulting from musica ficta through substitution become *incorporated into* C major. Through this process, C major inherited the collection of chromatic pitch classes shown in Example 9.3. Taken together, these substitute tones, combined with the C major scale, create a complete chromatic collection. Schoenberg argued on the basis of this idea that the chromatic scale, rather than the diatonic one, was the true basis of tonality.[9]

Chromatic Tetrachord: 8 T 1 3 6 = Complement of "white-note" diatonic set (0 2 4 5 7 9 E)

8 T 1 3 6 ∪ 0 2 4 5 7 9 E = 0 1 2 3 4 5 6 7 8 9 T E

EXAMPLE 9.3
Substitute tones in union with the diatonic set to complete the chromatic collection.

Schoenberg would eventually account for most of the enharmonic equivalents (i.e., A♯, D♭, E♭, G♭, and A♭) of the substitutes by applying a later historical phenomenon: the parallel minor, a region heard most frequently in the elaboration sections of Classical works, and even commonly in expository passages of Romantic ones. The subdominant minor, inherent in the parallel minor, was the region emphasized in Schoenberg's writings as a sort of gateway to contemporary extended tonality. The former contributes E♭ to this enharmonic design, while the latter offers A♭, D♭, and even G♭ (derived from the Neapolitan of this region). Unfortunately, no rationale for A♯ is provided in *SFH*, and this pitch class is mentioned in *TH* only to explain that the raised artificial dominant on VI (F♯–A♯–C♯–E) in A minor will not be usable in the exercises he is writing "at the moment." In this case, the qualification points to an ambiguous future use for this chord.

Transformations

For Schoenberg, substitution and the resultant chromatic scale (see the lower part of Example 9.3) would generate new altered harmonies, or "transformations," to use his terminology, when they appeared in *MBC*, and later *SFH*, designated by a struck-through roman numeral.[10] Such harmonies "transform" a diatonic harmony in the tonic into one of several of possible altered harmonies affiliated by or sharing a common root (the exception being the Neapolitan transformation), yet having a unique chromatic content and an often inherent multiple functionality. The notion of a scale degree as associated with an inclusive class or category of such chromatic chords was made explicit only in *SFH*. However, the inclusivity of each scale degree is clearly illustrated in the following diagram from Schoenberg's landmark chapter in *TH*, "The Chromatic Scale as a Basis for Tonality" (Example 9.4).

EXAMPLE 9.4
Scale degrees as inclusive classes from TH, p. 387.
Courtesy The University of California Press and Faber and Faber.

Combining the methods outlined in *TH* and *SFH*, each degree is expanded by borrowing tones from the three sources that historically generated the chromatic scale: the substitute tones, the parallel minor, and the subdominant minor. Example 9.5 provides a summary of the harmonies in C major resulting from these borrowings. The top row of Example 9.5 lists the diatonic roman numerals in C major; the first row beneath it lists the chords appearing diatonically in this key, the second shows chords available via the parallel minor, the third lists the chords available to C through its

	I	**II**	**III**	**IV**	**V**	**VI**	**VII**
C major	C	Dm(7)	Em(7)	F	G7	Am(7)	B°7
C minor	Cm	Dø7	E♭	Fm	Gm	A♭	B♭
F minor	Cm	D♭	E♭	Fm	Gø7	A♭	B♭m
		Ger. 6					
		Fr. 6					
Substitute Tones	C7	D7	E7		Gm(7)	A7	B7
	or	or	or			or	or
	E°7	F♯°7	G♯°7			C♯°7	D♯°7

EXAMPLE 9.5

Expansion of degrees in C major resulting from substitution and borrowings from tonic and subdominant minor.

minor subdominant, and the fourth features chords available to C through the substitute tones of Example 9.3.[11]

As Example 9.5 illustrates, seven transformational chord types are made available via substitution and borrowing from the parallel minor and subdominant minor modes, as follows: Mm7, mm7, °7, Fr. 6 (or Mm7[♭5]), °7, Ger. 6, and a major chord functioning as the Neapolitan. Because it contained the greatest variety of these harmonies (six in all, summarized in Ex. 9.6) and because it explained both the French sixth and German sixth transformations, II became the model for all chromatic transformations (see column 2 of Example 9.5). As Example 9.5 shows, the common-practice usage of French and German augmented-sixth chords had naturally given this degree two extra harmonies compared to the others, so that II was capable of supporting six transformations: Mm7, °7, Fr. 6, °7, Ger. 6, and Neap., shown in Schoenberg's transformations of II, adapted from *SFH* (Example 9.6).

Crucial to understanding the concept of transformation is the way in which Schoenberg transfers the complete set of transformations, originally culled from the alteration of II, to each scale degree in C major.[12] In this way, each of the six transformations becomes available, not through any literal

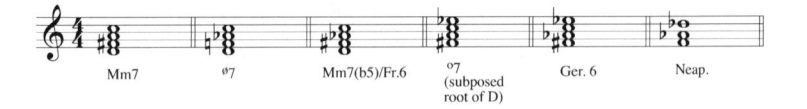

EXAMPLE 9.6
*Schoenberg's transformations of II, adapted from SFH (chord labels added,
and process simplified to show only seventh chords).*

derivation of pitch but through a conceptual borrowing of the transformational *process* itself. Schoenberg described this process as "transference," in
which each scale degree, like II, now contains six possible transformations.
Once the chromatic scale as a foundation for tonality had been achieved
through the admission of substitute tones and major/minor interchangeability, this model of transformation *transferred* to each degree amounted to a
rearrangement of internal chromatic elements.

Schoenberg's Chart of Transformations

Several points must be clarified in the following overview of Schoenberg's
chart of transformations and each of its individual harmonic types. First,
in *SFH* it is understood that the transformations need not always appear
as seventh chords; many, such as the Mm7 transformation and °7, might
be used in triadic form.[13] Secondly, although theoretically possible, transformations such as MM7 or Mm7(♯5) remain absent from the chart of
transformations. Because the former fails to play a significant role in
Schoenberg's tonal vocabulary, its omission from the chart of transformations is understandable. However, the latter (Mm7♯5) *is* heard occasionally in the *SFH* exercises; Schoenberg mentions it in both *SFH* (45) and
TH. He considered this chord to be an extension of the augmented triad,
one derived from the whole-tone scale rather than from substitution or
modal borrowing. Thus, it did not belong with the set of harmonies given
above.[14]

When applied to certain degrees, several of the transformations, including the ø7 transformation on VII; the Mm7 transformation on V; and
the mm7 transformation on II, III and VI, are omitted from the Chart of

Transformations, seemingly because of the resulting identity relations (II transformed by mm7 remains a mm7 chord, as do III and VI). However, Schoenberg also avoided the latter transformation on I and VII, without explanation.[15] One of his final statements on this chart in *SFH* makes clear that he viewed it as somewhat incomplete: "Transformations like the preceding can be built on all degrees of all regions. Many of these forms might duplicate forms of less remote regions. Even so the number of cases would be immense. This excludes a thorough evaluation of them; some might be impossible, others might be "dangerous but passable [*recte*: possible]."[16]

The Mm7 Transformation

EXAMPLE 9.7
Transcription of Schoenberg's chart of transformations from SFH, p. 38.
Courtesy Faber and Faber.

The first column of Example 9.7 contains the familiar sound of an artificial-dominant chord, henceforth labeled a Mm7 transformation, which, in *MBC*, is *applied* to chords or regions within a key—usually in order to create harmonic variation. For example, in IID, Example 47a, the Mm7 transformation is transferred to III, creating an artificial dominant of VI (Example 9.8a, m. 2). Again, no secondary function is specified; only a strikethrough symbol is applied, indicating that the chord has been transformed. Example 9.8 illustrates the use of the Mm7 transformation in Examples 47a and 167 from *MBC*.

EXAMPLE 9.8

Mm7 transformation used as an artificial dominant in Examples 47a and 167 (system 5, m. 2) from MBC. Courtesy Belmont Music Publishers.

The ø7 Transformation

The °7 transformation in the third column of Example 9.7 is rare in *MBC*; when it does occur, it is generally used as an altered pre-dominant harmony (rather than as a transformation leading to a full-fledged modulation to the minor mode). Example 9.9a (Example 175) shows the °7 transformation applied to III, with VI following as an artificial dominant; Example 9.9b (Example 176), a variation of 9.9a, features this same transformation applied to II as an altered supertonic leading to V. This coloristic use of the °7 transformation is common in passages making use of modal mixture, or what Schoenberg described as the "interchangeability of major and minor."[17] In each case, the success of the example is due in large part to the smooth chromatic descent of the bass—a factor Schoenberg does not acknowledge in his discussion.

EXAMPLE 9.9

The ⁰7 transformation used as an altered second degree in Examples 175 and 176 from MBC. Courtesy Belmont Music Publishers.

Implied Roots and the ⁰7 Transformation

Facsimile 9.1 shows an excerpt from Stein's notes for Schoenberg's Structural Functions of Harmony, Music 106. In the top left-hand corner of this manuscript is a diagram of transformations with C sustained throughout, a notation marking this pitch, although not literally present, as the fundamental for each of these transformations.

FACSIMILE 9.1

Leonard Stein's notes for Schoenberg's SFH Course (106B, 1941–42) featuring transformations in C with implied fundamental written below (top left-hand corner) (Leonard Stein Collection, Folder 111, 1941–42, verso). Courtesy Arnold Schönberg Center.

Moreover, the understanding of the chord no. 4 in Strang's notes, a fully diminished seventh chord, as an incomplete ninth chord, derives from Rameau's theory of subposition.[18] According to this principle,

Rameau attempted to explain all progressions in a manner that would theoretically allow for the strict preparation and resolution of chordal sevenths. Thus, with the help of an implied bass below a seventh chord, any progression could be rationalized as a descending fifth, descending third, or ascending second (any of which fulfills Rameau's goal of potentially preparing or resolving the seventh). A bass positioned at the interval of a third below a seventh chord results in a ninth chord, while one at the interval of a fifth below results in an eleventh chord. As Joel Lester explains in *Compositional Theory in the Eighteenth Century*, although the placement of the implied fundamental a third below the root of the diminished seventh chord belongs generally within the theory of subposition, its rationale represents something of a special circumstance. Lester describes this circumstance:

> Rameau explains that the diminished seventh chord arises *by borrowing* (*par emprunt*) when the sixth scale-degree in minor replaces the root of a dominant seventh chord (*F–G♯–B–D* instead of E–G♯–B–D). He calls it the chord of the augmented second, not a type of "diminished chord," reflecting the fact that E, not G♯, is the fundamental bass. By deriving the diminished seventh from the dominant seventh, Rameau formalized observations other theorists had made about the interchangeability of these chords.[19]

Despite Rameau's rationale for the implied root of the fully diminished seventh chord a third below the leading tone, in *TH* Schoenberg explained this concept squarely in terms of subposition, preferring root motion—notwithstanding the perfectly allowable progression of an ascending second when this chord continues to the tonic.

> In the manner of a deceptive cadence, the root goes up a step (VII–I). It is most frequently found in this function. Theory, however, which has recognized the root progression a fourth upward to be the simplest and most natural, cannot admit here the progression of a second upward. ... Hence,

it will do better to trace the resolution of this chord too, back to the root progression [of] a fourth upward by assuming that the diminished seventh chord is a ninth chord with the root omitted. That means, for example, on the tone d (as root) a (secondary) dominant is constructed, d–f♯–a–c and a minor ninth, e♭, is added.[20]

Schoenberg perhaps comes closer to Rameau's rationale above when he describes the fully diminished seventh chord in *SFH* as an incomplete V9, "enforc[ing] the consciousness of the structural functions of the root progression."[21] In this way, his modernized explanation implies a slightly shifted point of view in which the rationale for the implied root now stems from its dominant function rather than from any preference for root motion by fourth or fifth (Example 9.10).[22]

EXAMPLE 9.10
Diminished seventh chord built on VII, analyzed as V in MBC *(Example 225, m. 6, beat 4). Courtesy Belmont Music Publishers.*

Just as the diminished seventh chord built on $\hat{7}$ is analyzed by Schoenberg as V, so too is the diminished seventh chord in *MBC* similarly understood as a "dominant" with an implied root a third below the sounding one. Example 9.11 (originally Example 167, *MBC*) illustrates this concept as it pertains to artificial leading-tone chords and their use to "enrich" the harmony of the two-measure phrase. In Example 9.11a, the chord on beat 4 of m. 2 (vii°7 of V, or E°7) is analyzed as Ħ, indicating the implied root of C, so that the chord is understood as an artificial dominant of V. Analogously, in Example 9.11b, vii°7 of vi (f♯°7) (m. 2, beat 2) is analyzed as Ħ to indicate its implied root D, and its function as an artificial "dominant" of VI (D9). In the larger context, the chords in Example 167, like those in Examples 147–49, are heard as harmonic variations on the basic I–II–V progression presented at the start of IID, which is in turn a harmonic variation on the I–V model for the two-measure phrases in IB.[23]

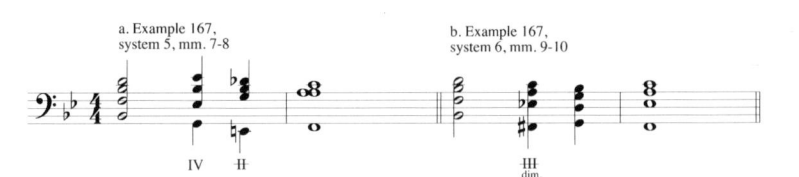

EXAMPLE 9.11

Schoenberg's analysis of applied diminished seventh chords (artificial dominants) in MBC *in Example 167 [II. D) Models of Harmonies for Two-Measure Phrases enriched by one or more harmonies] (*MBC*, Example 167, p. 21). Courtesy Belmont Music Publishers.*

The diminished seventh chord with the implied or understood bass C in Facsimile 9.1 may be a familiar concept to many readers; however, the implied tonic bass under the fifth chord of Stein's notes is somewhat puzzling (see again Facsimile 9.1). Spelled as an augmented-sixth chord in B♭, this harmony would seem to have only a distant relationship to the initial C major harmony at the start of the example. How can this chord be understood to have C as a root?

The German Sixth Transformation

In a well-known chapter from *TH* entitled "At the Frontiers of Tonality," Schoenberg discusses what he describes as the "augmented six-five, four-three, two, and sixth chords," each of which is a particular inversion of the "German sixth" chord. Whereas many current texts analyze this chord with a root of $\hat{4}$, Schoenberg proposes $\hat{2}$ as the fundamental, the same one that contemporary authors such as Aldwell and Schachter reserve for the French sixth. Example 9.12a shows Schoenberg's original rationale for this analysis as it appears in *TH*, while Example 9.12b provides a slightly annotated version of this excerpt, including figured-bass symbols and a brief description of the derivation process at each stage of his illustration.

EXAMPLE 9.12A
Schoenberg's derivation of the German augmented sixth in the Harmonielehre (Example 183, TH, p. 246). Courtesy The University of California Press and Faber and Faber.

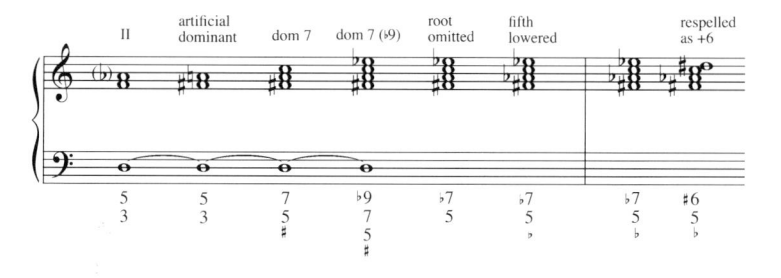

EXAMPLE 9.12B
Schoenberg's diagram annotated to include information regarding function and figured bass.

Example 9.12b begins with II in major or minor (the parenthetical ♭ before the A allows for either possibility), which is then transformed from a triad into a dominant ninth chord. The root of this chord is then omitted (see the fifth chord from the left) and its fifth is lowered (see the sixth chord from the left). This results in a "German sixth chord" with the raised fourth degree in the bass. Finally, in m. 2 of Example 9.12b, the flatted third degree is enharmonically respelled as a raised second degree (D♯).[24]

Although it is more common to hear this chord with the lowered sixth degree in the bass, for Schoenberg the inversion with the raised fourth degree in the bass (shown in Example 9.12a) is the primary one, heard throughout *SFH* and *MBC*.[25] Because of this, and because the flatted third degree (E♭) is respelled as a raised second (D♯) in his example, it is possible to use a figured-bass symbol for this chord identical to the one found in most harmony text-books today, although for very different reasons. Example 9.13 shows a typical analysis of this chord as an altered subdominant in first inversion, resulting in a familiar augmented-sixth sonority. Here, the chord derives its defining adjective, "augmented," from the sixth above its lowest pitch.

IV 6
   5

EXAMPLE 9.13
*Typical North American analysis of the augmented sixth
as an altered IV chord in first inversion.*

The annotated version of Schoenberg's interpretation of the German sixth in Example 9.12b illustrates how he was able to arrive at the same "$^6_5$" figure used in many twenty-first-century harmony texts, despite the use of an entirely different inversion of the chord. This seems to have been pos-sible because of the combination of his inversion with F♯ in the bass and his (enharmonic) respelling of the E♭ here as D♯. Further, because of the im-plied bass D, Schoenberg's chord may indeed retain its defining adjective, "augmented;" however, in this case, the interval in question is no longer a sixth, but an augmented octave (D–D♯)! The immediate result of this deri-vation is that all German augmented sixths are analyzed with an implicit root a third below the bass of Schoenberg's characteristic $^6_5$ inversion (i.e., a third below the raised fourth scale degree).

Example 9.14 applies the augmented-sixth transformation to each dia-tonic degree in C major. As in the original example, the implied root, as Schoenberg would have it, is notated as a filled-in note head. Row 1 gives the roman numeral for each chord, while row 2 shows the transformation to each degree in the scale and row 3 the primary referential region in which each transformation would likely function in C major. For example, this transformation applied to IV is shown to function as a German sixth in the lowered-mediant region (flat mediant), the same transformation applied to VII functions as a German sixth in the submediant region, and so on.

Moreover, the familiar enharmonic transformation of the German sixth to a dominant seventh allows either chord to function potentially in more than one region, a potential Schoenberg explores in both *TH* and *SFH*, and one that led him to describe these harmonies as *vagierend*, or "vagrant" in *TH*. Later, in *SFH*, he would devote an entire chapter to vagrant harmonies.[26] As he explains in this text: "Many of the transformations are vagrant harmonies because of their constitution ... and also because of their *multiple meaning*."[27] Included in his list of vagrant chords are diminished sevenths, augmented triads, augmented sixths, *and* dominant seventh chords—though he explains the inclusion of the last only in a subsequent paragraph: "By an enharmonic change in their notation, augmented $_5^6$ and $_3^4$ chords can become dominant seventh chords, and vice versa."[28]

Applied to the transformation in column 1 of Example 9.14, an enharmonic interpretation of the Ger. 6 as a dominant seventh (G♭7) would lead to C♭, so that a secondary region could be added below the primary one; this same logic could be applied throughout, with each Ger. 6 reinterpreted as a dominant seventh in a secondary region. Further, if Schoenberg's implied root is taken literally, an even more remote interpretation would be applicable as the altered dominant in a third region, lying a fifth above

Roman numeral	I	II	III	IV	V	VI	VII
Ger. 6 Trans.							
Primary referential region	subtonic (B♭)	tonic (C)	dor (D min)	flat mediant (E♭)	subdominant (F)	submediant (G)	submediant (A min)

EXAMPLE 9.14

The German sixth transformation applied to each degree in C major.

the primary one. Not counting the interchangeability of major and minor, the chord in column 1 has at least four possible interpretations as a dominant or augmented sixth chord (each altered): an augmented sixth in B-flat, a dominant in F, a dominant in C-flat, or an augmented sixth in F-flat. The same logic applies to the Fr6 transformation. Admittedly, not all of these transformations are pursued equally in *SFH*, but this potential for multiple interpretation certainly supports Schoenberg's view of the chord as a vagrant harmony.

The French Sixth Transformation

Returning briefly to Example 9.7, the fourth chord in Schoenberg's transformations applied to the tonic, notated as C7(♭5), or V7 (♭5) in the subdominant region, is enharmonically equivalent to the French sixth in E minor (the mediant region). Because of this potential for dual interpretation, it is labeled in Example 9.15 as the Mm7(♭5)/Fr. 6 transformation. This duality is continued in each column so that the Mm7(♭5)/Fr. 6 transformation transferred to III, for example, is shown to potentially function as a dominant in the submediant region, or as a French sixth in the Dorian region.[29]

Roman numeral	I	II	III	IV	V	VI	VII
Fr. 6							
Referential region(s)	subdominant (F)	Dominant (G)	submediant (A min)	subtonic (B♭)	tonic (C)	dor (D min)	mediant (E)
	subtonic (B♭)	Tonic (C)	dor (D min)	flat mediant (E♭)	subdominant (F)	dominant (G)	submediant (A min)

EXAMPLE 9.15
The Mm7(♭5)/Fr. 6 transformation applied to each degree in C major.

Moreover, Example 9.16 shows that when applied to II, the French sixth transformation yields either "V7(♭5) of V" or a French sixth in C, depending upon the voicing of the chord and the voice leading surrounding it. If the transformation progresses as in Example 9.16a (with scale degree 5 ornamented by neighbors ♯4 and ♭6, and scale degree 7 by neighbor 1, with 2 held as a common tone), then it is heard as a traditional French sixth transformation

a. Example 40 from MBC (standardFr6 usage)

b. Example 38 from *MBC* (inversion of Mm7(♭5)/ Fr. 6, with "cadential" descending-fifth emphasizing Mm7(♭5) sound.
Courtesy Belmont Music Publishers.

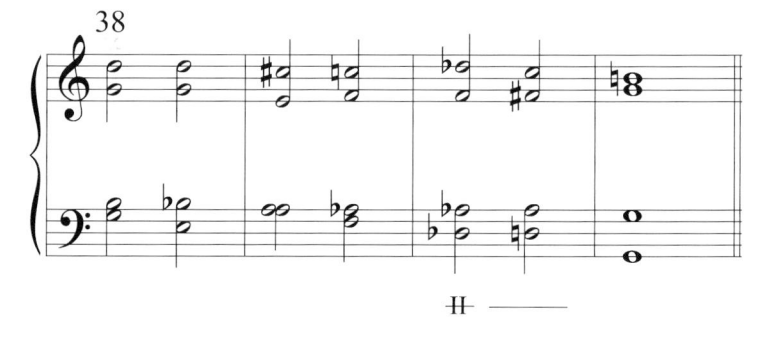

c. Example 59 from SFH, featuring Mm7(♭5) progressing directly to I and functioning as artificial dominant (SFH, 40). Courtesy Faber and Faber.

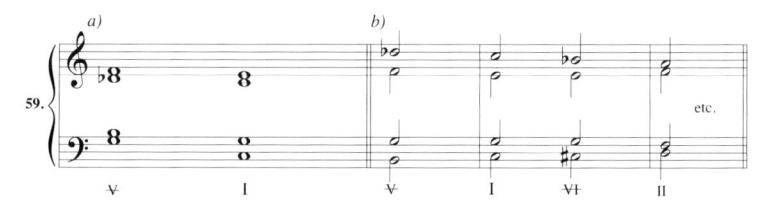

EXAMPLE 9.16
The Mm7(♭5)/Fr. 6 transformation in SFH and MBC

(mm. 3–4). However, if the chord is voiced with a cadential descending-fifths bass, as in Example 9.16b (mm. 3–4), then it may be heard as an Mm7(♭5) chord—an artificial dominant of the dominant. Finally, as in Example 9.16c, this chord is *most* likely heard as an Mm7(♭5) transformation when it progresses directly to a local tonic, with the characteristic cadential bass descending by fifth (m. 1).

The Neapolitan Transformation

The final chord of Schoenberg's transformations applied to the tonic in Facsimile 9.1 is best described as the "Neapolitan" transformation ("Np." or sometimes "Neap." in Schoenberg's writings). In *TH*, Schoenberg posits the theoretical use of this transformation on each degree of the diatonic scale, resulting in a flatted version of the original scale degree. Just as II may be transformed to become ♭II, III can become ♭III, IV, ♭IV, and so on—though the flat sign is not generally included in the labels of the chords. Each of these degrees may then function as a Neapolitan applied to a particular region, either in the manner of a local, intensified II or as an agent of a more extensive establishment of the Neapolitan region. In C major, Ⅲ (E♭) can function as Ⅱ "in" the Dorian region (D), Ⅴ (G♭) as Ⅱ "in" the subdominant, and so on. Like the more typical Neapolitan based on the second scale degree, these artificial Neapolitan chords progress to a dominant harmony or, expressed more accurately in such cases, to an artificial dominant.[30] Example 9.17 illustrates the Neapolitan transformation applied to V.

$$\text{Ⅴ} \qquad \text{Ⅰ} \qquad \text{IV} \qquad \text{V} \qquad \text{I}$$

EXAMPLE 9.17
The Neapolitan transformation applied to V.

In Example 9.17, V is lowered to become G♭, which is then applied to IV as a Neapolitan. The chord then progresses to a dominant transformation of Ⅰ, which functions as an artificial dominant applied to IV. Although Schoenberg notes in *SFH* that the Neapolitan transformation can be applied to any diatonic degree, he acknowledges that some of these applications may have limited use owing to their "remoteness" from the tonic.[31] The Neapolitan transformation applied to I, resulting in a flatted tonic (appearing in both

Roman numeral	I	II	III	IV	V	VI	VII
Np trans.							
Referential region	subtonic (B♭)	Tonic (C)	dor (D min)	flat mediant (E♭)	subdominant (F)	dominant (G)	submediant (A min)

EXAMPLE 9.18

The Neapolitan transformation applied to each degree in C major.

Schoenberg's chart and Stein's notes above), would certainly qualify as one of these remote harmonies; the C♭ harmony in this example would typically function as ♭II in B♭ (the subtonic).[32] Example 9.18 shows the Neapolitan transformation applied to each degree in C major. Each artificial Neapolitan is shown in its characteristic first inversion.

Notes

Preface, Editorial Notes, and Commentary

1. Carl Engel to Arnold Schoenberg, February 9, 1942, Library of Congress. *Models for Beginners in Composition* is henceforth referred to as *MBC*.

2. In its earliest stages, *MBC* was meant as a supplement to *Fundamentals of Musical Composition* (henceforth referred to as *FMC*). This intent is clear in the subtitle "A Supplement to Textbook: Fundamentals of Musical Composition" typed on the title page of an early draft of the 1942 edition. Later the two texts developed distinct identities, with *MBC* focused almost entirely on composition and *FMC* emphasizing formal analysis. See also Appendix 1, 119–30.

3. Arnold Schoenberg to Carl Engel, August 8, 1942, Library of Congress.

4. Carl Engel to Arnold Schoenberg, August 26, 1942, Library of Congress.

5. Arnold Schoenberg to Carl Engel, September 12, 1942, Library of Congress.

6. Carl Engel to Arnold Schoenberg, September 21, 1942, Library of Congress.

7. Arnold Schoenberg to Willis Wager, October 14, 1942, Library of Congress.

8. Like his teacher, Josef Rufer also refers to the opening four bars of the sentence as the antecedent or *Vordersatz* and the second half as the consequent or *Nachsatz*. See Josef Rufer, *Composition with Twelve Tones*, trans. Humphrey Searle (Westport, CT: Greenwood Press, 1979), 28–32.

9. Arnold Schoenberg to Felix Greissle, October 13, 1942, Library of Congress. Schoenberg writes: "I do not agree that, the terms foresentence etc., are misleading. But as it is not important to use them, I agree to use only antecedent and consequent."

10. Arnold Schoenberg to Felix Greissle, October 9, 1942, Library of Congress.

11. Arnold Schoenberg to Felix Greissle, October 13, 1942, Library of Congress.

12. Arnold Schoenberg to Carl Engel, September 12, 1942, Library of Congress.

13. Schoenberg requested that the syllabus be completed by October 10, but according to the UCLA Academic Calendar for 1942, the fall term actually began on October 12. This and all subsequent information related to the dates of courses derives from the UCLA Academic Calendars, accessed through the Special Collections Department of the university's library; see Appendix 2, 131–35.

14. Arnold Schoenberg to Carl Engel, December 9, 1942, Library of Congress.

15. Arnold Schoenberg to Carl Engel, February 1, 1943, Library of Congress.

16. UCLA Academic Calendar, 1942.

17. Arnold Schoenberg to Carl Engel, February 9, 1943, Library of Congress: "There are quite a number of errors to the greater part due to the imperfect manuscript that I delivered, because I did it in such a hurry. I think it will be necessary to add a list of errata, perhaps a page."

18. Later in 1943 Schirmer reprinted *MBC* with Schoenberg's corrections. First editions of *MBC* with the errata sheet are occasionally found (one was purchased for the present project), but the corrected second printing is more widely available.

19. Arnold Schoenberg to Carl Engel, October 23, 1943, Library of Congress. In a subsequent letter (April 10, 1944), Schoenberg attributes the failed revision of *MBC* to a combination of poor health (the onset of diabetes) and a prioritization of his counterpoint text, which was subsequently edited by Leonard Stein and posthumously published as *Preliminary Exercises in Counterpoint* (henceforth referred to as *PEC*). For a discussion of the disintegrating relationship between Schoenberg and Schirmer, see Sabine Feisst, *Schoenberg's New World* (New York: Oxford University Press, 2011), 184–91.

20. Ibid.

21. Alexander Goehr, "The Theoretical Writings of Arnold Schoenberg," *Perspectives of New Music* 13, no. 2 (Spring–Summer 1975): 3–16.

22. Editorial footnotes are distinguished from those of Schoenberg by the initials G. R.

23. See Appendix 1 for a comprehensive account of manuscripts related to *MBC*.

24. Schoenberg's initial courses in the United States (documented in Stein's 1935 notes for Composition 108 at USC) are more philosophically oriented in content than Berg's notes or Stein's teaching notes for courses in the 1940s. See endnote 45.

25. In *MBC* Schoenberg uses the term "model" to describe the many musical structures in the syllabus, which he intended for students to study for possible inclusion in school compositions. When proposing his syllabus to Carl Engel, Schoenberg alluded to the centralized role of models in his teaching: "I used to ask students: 'If you wanted to build an airplane, would you disregard what others have achieved before you?'" Arnold Schoenberg to Carl Engel, August 8, 1942, Library of Congress.

26. Ulrich Krämer confirms the handwriting of the motivic chart in Example 3.1 as Schoenberg's. He also attributes the examples from folio 2 to Schoenberg (transcribed here as Examples 3.2–3.6), whereas he attributes the C major themes from folio 3 to Berg (transcribed here as Examples 3.7–3.8); see Ulrich Krämer, *Alban Berg als Schüler Arnold Schönbergs: Quellenstudien und Analysen zum Frühwerk* (Vienna: Universal Edition, 1996), 21.

27. The set of guiding principles given here is derived from the left-hand portion of Schoenberg's matrix—the only portion of which is interpretable as a self-contained example. Of course, the rules of this matrix would change if the isolated motivic sequence, *baab*, to the right of this had been followed through all of its logical permutations. As it stands, Schoenberg chose not to continue the permutations of this sequence. Perhaps this decision is attributable to the focus on thematic structures in this lesson. Themes in Schoenberg's texts tend to be labeled with motives beginning with *a*, while phrases beginning with *b* imply a developmental function—one more typical of a contrasting middle section than an opening thematic gesture. For instance, see the contrasting middle section in Example 105 from *FMC* (Example 105f, p. 134), which begins with two statements of motive *b*. This distinct function granted for motivic sequences beginning with non-*a* motives may warrant consideration of *baab* as the start of a separate matrix, a chart having little to do with Schoenberg's demonstration on expository design in Berg's 1907 lesson.

28. In Facsimile 3.1, Schoenberg acknowledges this similarity by underlining successions 1–7. In a general sense, the upper half of Schoenberg's grouping unites all successions involving the repetition of two distinct motives; the lower half groups all successions using the repetition of only one distinct motive.

29. Schoenberg's matrix exhausts all the combinations.

MOTIVE SUCCESSIONS 1–3

Successions 1–3 exhaust possibilities given one *a* motive and one contrasting element—under Rule 3, this contrasting element must be *b*. Under Rules 1 and 3, *b* may occupy positions 4, 3, or 2, as shown in the portion of the matrix below.

Motive Successions 1-3

1)	a	a	a	b
2)	a	a	b	a
3)	a	b	a	a

MOTIVE SUCCESSIONS 4–6

Successions 4–6 exhaust possibilities given *two* identical contrasting elements and two *a* motives. Under Rule 3, in a two-motive succession, these contrasting elements must be *b* motives. Under Rule 1, the two *b* motives must occupy positions 2, 3; 3, 4; or 2, 4—combinations which are exhausted in motivic successions 4–6 (although not in a systematic order).

Motive Successions 4–6

4)	a	b	a	b
5)	a	b	b	a
6)	a	a	b	b

MOTIVIC SUCCESSION 7

Succession 7 exhausts possibilities given *three* identical, contrasting elements—these must be *b* motives under Rule 3. Under Rule 1, this is the only possible ordering of a succession with three identical contrasting elements (since *a* must begin the succession).

Motivic Succession 7

7)	a	b	b	b

MOTIVE SUCCESSIONS 8–14

Successions 8–14 exhaust the possibilities with three distinct elements (a, b, c) in a four-motive succession under Rules 1–3.

For explanatory purposes, the diagram presents these successions more systematically than does Schoenberg's original arrangement:

Motive Successions 8, 11, and 14

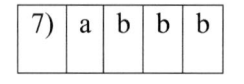

11)	a	a	b	c
14)	a	b	a	c
8)	a	b	c	a

Successions 8, 11, and 14 explore all possibilities given a three-motive succession *a, b, c*, with *a* as the returning or repeating component (following Rules 1–3). The returning *a* is heard initially as the second component, the third, and finally the fourth.

Motive Succession 9 and 12

12)	a	b	b	c
9)	a	b	c	b

In successions 9 and 12, *b* is the returning element. Under Rule 3, this exhausts all the possibilities with *b* as the returning element. Under Rule 3, *b* must be heard initially as the second element. This leaves only positions 3 and 4, which are exhausted in successions 9 and 12.

Motive Successions 10 and 13

10)	a	b	c	c
13)	a	b	e	e

In succession 10, *c* is the returning element. Under Rule 3, c must first appear as the third element. As succession 10 shows, this leaves only position 4 for the repetition of *c*. The strikethrough in succession 13 indicates that it is a duplicate of 10 (perhaps attributable to hasty notation).

30. In its systematic exploration of all possible relationships given the two-chord tonic-dominant model, it is analogous to the chart in the *Theory of Harmony*, which is equally systematic in its examination of common-tone properties for triads on each diatonic degree (*Theory of Harmony* [henceforth referred to as *TH*], 39).

31. A tonic or dominant pair in this arrangement must occupy one of the following position pairs: 1, 2; 1, 3; 1, 4; 2, 3; 2, 4; or 3, 4. Schoenberg's matrix satisfies each of these combinations.

32. Schoenberg described all progressions by a second (ascending or descending) as "superstrong." He viewed these progressions not as a single root progression, but as "the sum of two root progressions" (*TH*, 119). Schoenberg urges the student to use "superstrong" progressions sparingly (*TH*, 123). See also *Structural Functions of Harmony* (henceforth referred to as *SFH*), 6–8. Progressions by second were "excessively strong," because they added together "two strong progressions." For example, Schoenberg viewed IV–V as a truncated version of the progression IV–II–V in which the middle chord, II, had been omitted. Both root motions that make up this progression are "ascending" progressions: IV–II is

a descending-third progression, and II–IV is an ascending fourth (Schoenberg described this motion as an ascending fourth, rather than a descending fifth). Although he likely derived this idea of the compound progression from Simon Sechter, the concept is traceable back to Rameau (compare Appendix 6 167–87). Sechter describes the middle, implied chord of such progressions, as "concealed" (*verschwiegen*), while the process itself is described as "concealment" (*Verschweigung*). See Simon Sechter. *Die Grundsätze der musikalischen Komposition, Erste Abtheilung* (Leipzig: Breitkopf und Härtel, 1853), 35.

33. In Schoenberg's pre-1930s writings we find only infrequently terms such as "period," and "sentence." See *Zusammenhang, Kontrapunkt, Instrumentation, Formenlehre* (henceforth referred to as *ZKIF*), 17. In *ZKIF* (1917) Schoenberg's mention of these terms is brief and without explanation. His use of the term *Satz* in *ZKIF* is similar to the broad sense in which it is used in traditional German theory of the nineteenth century (see for example Marx, endnote 60). Schoenberg's description of a *Satz* in *ZKIF* generally refers to a phrase, although it is vague enough in its translation (e.g., sentence, movement) to raise questions about its specific meaning. In *The Musical Idea and the Logic, Technique, and Art of Its Presentation* (henceforth referred to as *MI*), Schoenberg elaborates on the characteristics of this thematic type. His analyses of specific themes such as Beethoven's Op. 2 No. 3 and the "liquidation" in Mozart's String Quartet K. 465 are instructive (*MI*, 163–77). However, Schoenberg clarifies his descriptions of the sentence in general terms in later texts such as *MBC* and *FMC*. Compare *MBC*, 7–8; *FMC*, 58–59; and *MI*, 131.

34. Above the melody in Facsimile 3.2, Schoenberg demonstrates how to write two- and four-bar motives. All of them may be set to the tonic–dominant or tonic–dominant–subdominant combinations of the preceding matrices. However, here the principal topic is the variation of a motive rather than that of harmonic design.

35. In his 1932 talk for Frankfurt Radio, Schoenberg discusses intervallic expansion as a method of variation. The lecture was subsequently translated by Claudio Spies. See Arnold Schoenberg, "Analysis of the Four Orchestral Songs, Op. 22," in *Perspectives on Schoenberg and Stravinsky*, ed. Benjamin Boretz and Edward T. Cone (New York: W. W. Norton, 1972), 33. Also compare Jack Boss's excellent discussion of this lecture and its ramifications for the analysis of Schoenberg's music in "Schoenberg's Op. 22 Radio Talk and Developing Variation in Atonal Music," *Music Theory Spectrum* 14, no. 2 (Fall 1992): 125–49. See also J. Daniel Jenkins, ed., *Arnold Schoenberg: Program Notes and Analyses (1902–1951)* (New York: Oxford University Press, 2016).

36. In *ZKIF* Schoenberg posits the idea of a single pitch, such as the final *c* motive in m. 8 of Example 3.3, as a motive. He writes: "*First of all*: even *the smallest musical event* can become a motive if [it is] permitted to have an effect, even an individual tone can carry consequences. Under certain circumstances, each *single tone* can be a motive." See *ZKIF*, 27.

37. Schoenberg seems to have been unsure of how to categorize motive *b* (m. 7). Facsimile 3.2 shows that he initially labeled this motive *a* before subsequently changing it to *b*.

38. In his 1934 *Gedanke* manuscript, Schoenberg includes the contraction of an interval as one possible method of variation (*MI*, 167).

39. The quotation is from Schoenberg's definition of complementary rhythm in *FMC*, 84: "Complementary rhythm is that relation between voices or groups of voices in which one voice fills out the gaps in the movement of the others, thus maintaining the *motus*, i.e., the regular subdivision of the measure. The accompaniment is often added as a complement to the basic rhythm of the principal part." Schoenberg omits this term altogether from his discussion of accompaniments in *MBC*, opting instead to describe the phenomenon more generally as the "independent movement of one or more voices" (*MBC*, 7). However, Stein's notes for Composition 105a, dated September 26, 1941, show a similar passage to the one in Example 3.5, with the words "complementary rhythm" scribbled above it. This confirms that Schoenberg was still using the term in his courses when he was writing *MBC* (Leonard Stein Collection, Box 5 of 6, Folder 103, p. 2, verso).

40. Two of the pitches, the second pitch of the soprano (m. 7) and the second eighth note of the tenor (m.7), are illegible in Facsimile 3.2, fol. 2 verso. The former may either be G^5 or F^5, and the latter may either be B♭ or A. Alternate versions are shown in Example 3.5b.

41. In *ZKIF* Schoenberg describes two types of variation: one that merely ornaments a motive, and a second that allows "new ideas to arise." "This second method," he explains, "can be termed developing variation" (*ZKIF*, 39). For a catalog of Schoenberg's other statements about developing variation, see *MI* 113, 167, and 247; see also Walter Frisch, *Brahms and the Principle of Developing Variation* (Berkeley and Los Angeles: University of California Press, 1984). In general, developing variation is created by preserving the characteristic pitch relations of a motive while altering those of rhythm, or, alternatively, by keeping the characteristic rhythmic relations of a motive and changing those of pitch. The pitch motive is also frequently varied through the permutation, expansion, contraction, or omission of intervallic relationships.

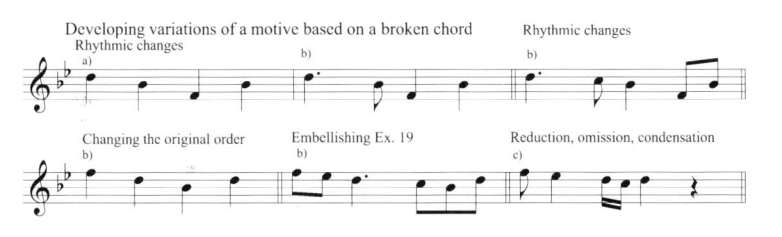

EXAMPLE EN 41
Illustration adapted from Examples 17–21 of FMC, pp. 12–13.

42. Berg's example shows F♯ as the final pitch of m. 4. The sound of this incomplete neighbor in the context of the G major harmony, along with the cross-relation resulting in combination with the subsequent G $\frac{4}{6}$ (m. 5), creates an awkward effect. In writing rapidly (perhaps during the lesson), Berg may have neglected to cancel the previous F♯. For this reason, Example 3.7b offers an alternate version with F♮ as the final pitch of m. 4.

43. Berg's stemming is problematic in mm. 7– 8 (e.g., A– G– F faces downward, and B up). His original notation has been preserved throughout.

44. Gerald Strang Satellite Collection, Folder 51, ASC, Vienna. Strang's notes for Composition 108s offer a remarkably complete record of Schoenberg's class. In fact, although the individual papers are out of order, the collection is missing only one class meeting (Friday, June 10) for the period of June 22 to July 27, 1936.

45. In its philosophical orientation, the Composition 108a course Schoenberg taught in 1935 seems to have been different from the one he gave in 1936. As demonstrated in Murray Dineen's 2002 article "Gerald Strang's Manuscripts to Arnold Schönberg's Classes (1935–37)," the notes for the 1935 summer version of Composition 108a are perhaps closer in content to the *Gedanke* manuscripts than *MBC*. See Phillip Murray Dineen, "Gerald Strang's Manuscript Notes to Arnold Schönberg's Classes (1935–37): Construction and the Two Learnings," in *Arnold Schoenberg in America: Report of the Symposium, May 2–4, 2001*, ed. Christian Meyer, *Journal of the Arnold Schönberg Center* 4 (2002), 104–18.

46. It is also possible that Strang simply stopped taking notes during Schoenberg's lecture. Even so, Schoenberg's treatment of motives in *MBC* and elsewhere had clearly become too nuanced to accommodate the limited motivic matrix from the era of his early European pedagogy.

47. Schoenberg explains the function of angled versus horizontal brackets in a manuscript titled "Abbreviations," reproduced in Appendix 4, 149–52.

48. Schoenberg had mentioned the sentence in *ZKIF* (1917), and with more substantial explanation in the *Gedanke* manuscripts (1934–36; see *ZKIF*, 17, and *MI*, 113). In a recent paper entitled "Schoenberg's Sentence," delivered at the Society for Music Theory's annual meeting in Milwaukee (2014), Áine Heneghan has explored this history as well as other aspects of Schoenberg's development of the sentence. Her edition of *Schoenberg on Form* (New York: Oxford University Press) is forthcoming.

49. Throughout Schoenberg's course materials and in *MBC*, the two-measure phrase is treated as a flexible grouping. Although there are many regular two-measure phrases in *MBC*, they need not always remain confined to the bar line. Many examples, such as Examples 8 and 10 of IA (Building Two-Measure Motives or Phrases on a Single Harmony in Broken Chord Forms), begin with an anacrusis. The upbeat remains possible in all of *MBC*'s sections involving two-measure phrases, and occasionally, as in Example 55, the anacrusis extends for up to half a measure (see Example 228). In such cases, the "two-measure" phrase may be longer than two bars.

50. Although no bar lines appear between the tonic–dominant successions in Example 3.10, each brace is intended to parse a two-measure unit.

51. A symmetrical 2 + 2 grouping structure as in Schoenberg's theme would have been possible using the motivic permutations of Berg's lessons. For example, motivic groupings 6 (*aabb*) and 4 (*abab*) both have the potential to pair into "two-measure phrases." Whereas in Berg's lessons the parallel 2 + 2 grouping is merely one possible configuration, in Schoenberg's California classes it becomes the preferred mode of organization.

52. For Schoenberg's interpretation of thematic and formal symmetry in his own music (the Serenade, Op. 24 [1920–23]), see the section "On Wilhelm Werker's *Studies of Fugal Symmetry*, etc. in *BACH*" in Leonard Stein, "Five Statements," *Perspectives of New Music* 14, no. 1 (Fall–Winter1975): 169–72. The manuscript Stein studies in "Five Statements" is also included in J. Daniel Jenkins, ed., *Arnold Schoenberg: Program Notes and Analyses (1902–1951)* (New York: Oxford University Press, 2016). See also Neff's discussion of this manuscript in Severine Neff, ed., *Preliminary Exercises in Counterpoint* (New York: Oxford University Press, forthcoming).

53. The musicologist Ulrich Krämer similarly notes the shift in pedagogical emphasis from the four-bar phrase model of Berg's lessons (compare pp. 2–12) with one motive per measure, to the "zweitakige Phrasen" of Schoenberg's California classes. He touches on Schoenberg's use in his American teaching of the two-measure phrase as a modular unit, one that could be used to create either a sentence or period, depending upon its continuation. Krämer, *Alban Berg als Schüler*, 41.

54. In *TH*, Schoenberg uses the term *liquidieren* to describe the gradual elimination not of motivic characteristics, but rather of those scale degrees distinguishing the modes of two parallel-related major and minor keys (*TH*, 208). In the commentary to *MI*, Patricia Carpenter and Severine Neff describe the motivic aspect of liquidation: "Liquidation is mainly a motivic procedure. Its function is to 'neutralize the obligations' of previous motivic material, by gradually depriving the motive forms of their characteristic features and dissolving them into uncharacteristic forms, such as scales and broken chords. It may combine with a cadential harmonic progression to delimit a theme or section, or with a modulatory progression to function independently as a transition" (*MI*, 53). Although liquidation is commonly associated with the sentence, Schoenberg sometimes used this concept to describe the same process during the consequent phrase of the period; see *FMC*, 30.

55. See Waltzes for String Orchestra, in Arnold Schönberg, *Sämtliche Werke*, ed. Joseph Rufer et al. (Mainz: B. Schott's Söhne and Vienna: Universal Edition, 1966), ser. A, vol. 9, 125–29. See also "Erwartung," Op. 2 No. 1, where the repetition of the opening motive in the sentence form (mm. 1–2) creates a sense of suspense appropriate for the narrative and imagery of the text.

56. The writings of Schoenberg's students Erwin Ratz and Josef Rufer, both of whom discuss the sentence in some detail, indicate that Schoenberg may have introduced this concept during his

classes given in the 1920s at the Prussian Academy of Art in Berlin. However, since both of their texts were written *after MBC*, it is at least possible that one or more than one of these authors may have derived portions of their explanation of the sentence from Schoenberg's later writings rather than directly from his classes. In *Schoenberg and His School*, René Leibowitz, who studied with Schoenberg in the 1940s, specifically cites *MBC* when discussing the sentence. See René Leibowitz, *Schoenberg and His School: The Contemporary Stage of the Language of Music*, trans. Dika Newlin (New York: Philosophical Library, 1949). See also Josef Rufer, *Composition with Twelve Tones Related Only to One Another*, trans. Humphrey Searle (Westport, CT: Greenwood Press, 1979), 32–33 (originally published as *Die Komposition mit zwölf Tönen* [Berlin: Max Hesses Verlag, 1952]). Finally, see Erwin Ratz, *Einführung in die musikalische Formenlehre* (Vienna: Universal Edition, 1968), 21–28, in which individual examples of sentences abound. The earliest reference to sentences in the materials from Schoenberg's American courses—and one contemporaneous with his discussion of this concept in the *Gedanke* manuscripts (see endnote 45)—seems to be Gerald Strang's USC notes for the "Construction of Themes," dated December 10, 1935. On one key page, below the word "SENTENCE," Strang listed Schoenberg's favorite examples: the opening themes to Op. 2 No. 1 and Op. 2 No. 3 (The Gerald Strang Satellite Collection, Folder 51, ASC).

57. Although Berg's notes are remarkably comprehensive, they remain incomplete. According to Krämer, pages are missing from at least one folder, F 21 Berg 27 (dated 1907). However, because this folder contains complete compositions rather than a pedagogical study of themes, it is a less probable source than F 21 Berg 55/I for an introduction to the two-measure phrase. Given the absence of the sentence in the demonstrations of F 21 Berg 55/I, it seems unlikely that Schoenberg emphasized this grouping in Berg's 1907 lessons. For a discussion of the missing contents of F 21 Berg 27, see Krämer, *Alban Berg als Schüler*, 34.

58. Like Schoenberg's *MBC*, Marx's *Die Lehre von der musikalischen Komposition* is thematically driven. However, the four- or eight-bar *Satz* takes precedence in his discussions.

59. With its repeated *Einschnitt* above a varied harmonic framework, Koch's *zusammen geschobener Satz*, or compound phrase, is identical to Schoenberg's two-measure phrase. Several of Koch's examples even create sentences, ending with the classic cadential phrase that Schoenberg would later describe as a continuation (see figs. 1–4, section 122). See Heinrich Christoph Koch, *Versuch einer Anleitung zur Composition, II* (Hildeshelm: Georg Olms Verlag, 1969), 456–460. See also, William Rothstein, *Phrase Rhythm in Tonal Music* (Ann Arbor: Musicalia Press, 2007), 150–151. In the nineteenth century, the two-measure phrase also figures prominently in A.B. Marx's *Die Lehre von der musikalischen Komposition*, a text that Schoenberg owned and annotated (Arnold Schönberg Center, M32v1). Only vols. 1 and 3 are extant. In a brief foreword to Erwin Stein's 1923 practical guide to the *Harmonielehre*, Schoenberg cited Marx's *Kompositionslehre* as an influence on his thought:

> Brehm's *Tierleben* [*Life of Animals*], Heyse's *Grammatik* [*Grammar*], Marx's *Kompositionslehre* [*Theory and Practice of Musical Composition*], and all these good books from which we have learned, are no longer available. Though they only convey the viewpoint of a specific time, each reflects the level of a personality, which does not hide an opinion, but which emerges from the work as an ethically important document.

Erwin Stein, *Praktischer Leitfaden zu Schönbergs Harmonielehre: Ein Hilfsbuch für Lehrer und Schüler* (Vienna: Universal Edition, 1923), 1.

60. A. B. Marx, *Die Lehre von der musikalischen Komposition, Praktisch-theoretisch*, vol. 1 (Leipzig: Breitkopf und Härtel, 1863), 43. For a discussion of Marx's *Satz*, see Adolf Bernhard Marx, *Musical Form in the Age of Beethoven: Selected Writings on Theory and Method*, ed. and trans. Scott Burnham (New York: Cambridge University Press, 1997). A *Satz* in Marx's writings is essentially a phrase, ending with a half-cadence or authentic cadence (ibid., 42). However, as Burnham notes in his

introduction, "Marx uses the word *Satz* to denote a coherent musical utterance at any level of musical form: a phrase, a theme, or an entire movement" (14).

61. In his discussion of period forms in *Katechismus der Musik*, Johann Christian Lobe similarly remarks on the two-measure phrase, which perhaps coming closest to Koch he describes as an *Abschnitt*—a grouping that comprises two one-measure motives. Two *Abschnitte* grouped together create a *Satz* or phrase, and two *Sätze* create a period. See Johann Christian Lobe, *Katechismus der Musik* (Leipzig: J. J. Weber, 1881), 89–91. Krehl's *kleine Satz*, discussed below, may have been influenced by Koch's *Einschnitt* and/or Lobe's *Abschnitt*. There is no evidence that Schoenberg was directly familiar with Lobe's writings. However, he did own a copy of Koch's *Musikalisches Lexicon* (1865), now held at the ASC.

62. Krehl held a prominent post as a professor of piano and music theory at the Leipzig Conservatory from 1902 until his death in 1924; he became the school's director in 1921. Although he failed to match the international fame of his colleague Max Reger as a composer, Krehl enjoyed some regional success. Among his most highly regarded compositions are the String Quartet Op. 17, the Sonata for Cello and Piano Op. 20, and the cantata *Tröstung*, all of which evince the influence of Johannes Brahms. Krehl was more influential as a theorist than as a composer. His theoretical writings have been reprinted in several editions and translated into Spanish and Japanese. They include: *Musikalische Formenlehre (Kompositionslehre)* (1902; henceforth referred to as *MFK*), *Allgemeine Musiklehre* (1906), *Fuge, Erläuterung und Anleitung für Kompositionslehre* (1908), *Kontrapunkt* (1908), and *Harmonielehre* (1921). Throughout his life, Krehl embraced the dualistic Leipzig tradition of Moritz Hauptmann and Arthur von Oettingen.

63. "Jemnitz, Sándor [Alexander]," in *The New Grove Dictionary of Music and Musicians*, 2nd ed., ed. Stanley Sadie and John Tyrell (London: Macmillan, 2001).

64. When working as a film composer, Zmigrod used the pseudonym Allan Gray, a name inspired by the dandy antihero of Oscar Wilde's novel *The Picture of Dorian Gray*. See Peter Gradenwitz, *Arnold Schönberg und seine Meisterschüler: Berlin 1925–1933* (Vienna: Paul Zsolnay Verlag, 1998), 128. For specific information regarding Zmigrod's studies with Schoenberg see ibid., 127–42. Under the name of Allan Gray, Zmigrod went on to score many successful films, including Michael Powell and Emeric Pressburger's romantic fantasy *A Matter of Life and Death* (1946), Peter Brook's *Love's Labour's Lost* (1946), and John Huston's American classic *The African Queen* (1951). For an accessible biography on Gray from a film-historical perspective, see "Allan Gray," www.powell-pressburger. org/Reviews/Gray/Gleason.html (accessed December 21, 2014).

65. Julia Bungardt and Eike Fess, email message to the author, June 2013.

66. *MFK*, 28.

67. *MFK*, 22–23.

68. For illustration and discussion of Schoenberg's dominant and tonic forms, see *MBC*, 7–8 and 25–27; and *FMC*, 20–24.

69. *MFK*, 28.

70. Ibid.

71. In a letter to Carl Engel, Schoenberg explains to his friend: "I doubt whether I can now make the revised version of the 'models.' I have so much to do on account of my illness, and I would prefer to finish the first book of my Counterpoint." Arnold Schoenberg to Carl Engel, April 10, 1944, Library of Congress. Although Schoenberg mentions poor health, Sabine Feisst has cautioned against taking such comments at face value. She cites the many compositions and numerous writings Schoenberg completed during the 1940s, as well as the vibrant social and academic life that he enjoyed during this period, as evidence that health may have been less of a factor in hampering Schoenberg's productivity

than is typically acknowledged. Perhaps other projects, such as the counterpoint text (*PEC*) that Schoenberg mentions in his letter, simply took precedence. See Feisst, *Schoenberg's New World*, 6.

72. Several tenets of Schoenberg's harmonic theories, including his concepts of regions and transformations, are discussed in Appendices 5 (153–65) and 6 (167–87) respectively.

73. *SFH*, 19.

74. Ibid., 68. See Appendix 5 for a discussion of these relationships.

75. *SFH*, 19.

76. *TH*, 271.

77. See Appendix 6, 167–87. See also Phillip Murray Dineen, "Schoenberg on the Modes: Characteristics, Substitutes, and Tonal Orientation," *College Music Symposium* 33–34 (1993–94): 140–54.

78. In *FMC*, 58–62, Schoenberg preferred the term "continuation," while in the main body of *MBC* he described such passages as the "completion" of the sentence—a term he also employed in the subtitle of his discussion of this topic in *FMC*, 58. In the Glossary of *MBC*, under the definition of "sentences," he mentions the term "continuation" only briefly, offering little discussion of the topic.

79. Schoenberg mentions the similar treatment of the end of a sentence and consequent of a period in *FMC*, 59.

80. Each of these topics—Schoenberg's treatment of VII and his theories on chromaticism—is discussed below and in Appendices 5 and 6 (153–65 and 167–87 respectively).

81. In the essay "The Constructive Function of Harmony," Schoenberg describes the five formal functions of a work as "introductory, establishing, transitional, connecting, [and] closing" (*MI*, 210).

82. Contemporary accounts of sentence structure such as Caplin (2013) refer to *reductions of the principle motive* as fragmentation. For a discussion of liquidation, see endnote 54.

83. *TH*, 200, 286, and 380. The corresponding passages appear in *HL* (1922), 243, 342, and 456. As in *TH*, Schoenberg also uses the term "harmonic variation" in *MBC* (Examples 147–49 and 130a). Harmonic variation is illustrated in many examples throughout Schoenberg's syllabus. However, the clearest instances, because they are labeled as such, appear in Examples 147–49. Example 147 features a two-measure phrase harmonized as I–V varied in Example 148 through the insertion (m. 1) and substitution (m. 2) of diatonic harmonies—the latter resulting from Schoenberg's reharmonization of the melody with II rather than V.

84. See Examples 147–49. There is a more traditional sense in which *a3* can be heard as a variation of the harmony in *a*: VI in *a3* substitutes for the opening tonic of *a*, and the original descending-fifth progression (I–IV) now accelerates with a half-note harmonic rhythm, so that VI–II occupies only one measure (m. 5). This basic root motion is then sequenced by step *upward* as VII–III (m. 6).

85. See *MBC*, Example 167.

86. When illustrating variation technique, Schoenberg seldom excluded any musical possibility absolutely (the idea being that even an awkward passage in one setting might find appropriate use in another). This spirit is succinctly captured in his discussion of Example 314 in *TH*. "Perhaps no one will have much interest in putting these four figures, as they are here, directly next to one another," he explains, "but that it could be done admits their use for something better: for harmonic variation, which opens up another route along which a phrase [or composition] may continue"; *TH*, 380.

87. For Schoenberg's explanation of the constructive functions of harmony, see *MI*, 203–14. Schoenberg's "Constructive Functions of Harmony" illustrates connections between various kinds of harmonic progressions and the specific formal functions of a work, which he later described as "progressions for various compositional purposes." In *SFH* he offers these specific kinds of

progressions for periods, contrasting middle sections, and elaboration sections—each tailored to fit its particular "compositional purpose." See *SFH*, 114–91.

88. Dineen, "Gerald Strang's Manuscript," 104–18.

89. *MI*, 210. For Schoenberg's description of the continuation as developmental, see *FMC*, 58

90. *FMC*, 59.

91. For a discussion of Schoenberg's alternate endings, see Appendix 4, 149–52.

92. This school composition was originally given the simple title of "Scherzo" in the 1942 self-published edition of *MBC* (S141.C2, ASC). Like the other full-length school compositions, in the 1942 edition it was separated from the surrounding examples. The reason for the lack of a title in the published 1943 Schirmer edition is unknown.

93. Schoenberg described the minuets and scherzos in *MBC* as "small ternary" forms rather than "rounded binary," the more typical designation. For a discussion of this issue, see endnote 14 under "Endnotes to Schoenberg's Text."

94. The symbol "smdor" is used to designate the region of C$\sharp$, which arises here as the "Dorian" region of the submediant.

95. For a more thorough discussion of symmetry in Schoenberg's harmonic designs, see the analysis of the Minuet below. Here, the indices of 1+5 and e+7 are each 6 or 18. The axis of symmetry is thus 9. The other axis, 3 is not emphasized.

96. The fair copy of Op. 43a is dated August 24, 1943, and signed by Schoenberg on its final page. See www.schönberg.at: Originalfassung für Orchester op. 43b, Lichtpausreinschrift, Seite 45, 1820.

97. For a discussion of the Chart of the Regions, see Appendix 5 (153–66). Schoenberg's penchant for inversionally symmetrical key relationships is well documented. In his 2010 article "Schoenberg and The Tradition of Chamber Music for Strings," Michael Cherlin explores this characteristic in *Verklärte Nacht*. As he reads it, the work is a "double sonata," with two complete expositions (see also Richard Swift, "Tonal Relations in Schoenberg's *Verklärte Nacht*," *19th-Century Music* 1, no. 1 [July 1997]: 3–14). Cherlin discusses the way in which the two "second themes" in this design, in B$\flat$ minor (50–99) and F$\sharp$ major (249–65) respectively, balance about the tonic axis, D. Later, in two passages, one just before the second closing theme (266–76), and the other, once the closing theme has begun, E$\flat$ and D$\flat$ similarly balance about the tonic. Schoenberg had used the first of these inversional designs (B$\flat$–D–F$\sharp$) for the movements of his D Major String Quartet (1897). The first and fourth movements bookend the work in D major; the second movement is in F$\sharp$ minor, and the third is in B$\flat$ minor. See Michael Cherlin, "Schoenberg and Chamber Music for Strings," in *The Cambridge Companion to Arnold Schoenberg*, ed. Jennifer Shaw and Joseph Auner (New York: Cambridge University Press, 2010), 30–52.

Schoenberg's First Quartet, Op. 7, also shows some evidence of inversional tonal planning in its large sections. After a troubled exposition in D minor (mm. 1–13) the next large section, an animated Scherzo, begins with a main theme in G$\flat$ (rehearsal numbers E–E50). The axis of symmetry of these keys, E (in this case E major), enters with the principle theme of the adagio section (rehearsal numbers K–K51). Arriving immediately after the recapitulation of the principle thematic material, this literal tonal balance complements the sense of formal balance engendered through the thematic return. Earlier, the opening section's subordinate themes, in E$\flat$ and F respectively (rehearsal numbers A56–A70 and A71–A81), had also foreshadowed the E axis. For a chart summarizing the work's form, see Michael Cherlin, *Schoenberg's Musical Imagination* (New York: Cambridge University Press, 2007), 167. Cherlin does not discuss the symmetrical key relationships in Op. 7 particularly, but he points to many similar designs in other works (see endnote 96). For another discussion of tonal design in this work, see: Severine Neff, "Aspects of *Grundgestalt* in Schoenberg's First String Quartet, Op. 7," *Theory and Practice* 9, nos. 1–2 (1984): 24. Neff discusses an important large-scale tonal design in the first movement involving the leading tone (C♯) and Neapolitan regions (E♭), which balance symmetrically about the tonic.

Other examples include Brahms's Symphony No. 3, a work well-known to Schoenberg whose F major tonic is balanced by its upper and lower chromatic mediants during the exposition; first D♭ during the transition (mm. 21–23), then A major for the subordinate theme (mm. 36–44). See Peter Smith, "Brahms and Schenker: A Mutual Response to Sonata Form," *Music Theory Spectrum* 16, no. 4 (1994): 94. Smith begins his discussion with an overview of Felix Salzer's analysis of this same work. See also Appendix 5 (pp. 153–65).

98. Stein's notes for this class, dated October 24 (no year) on the recto of the page of the manuscript, are included with the manuscripts for *MBC* rather than with class notes. Their inclusion with the manuscripts for *MBC* would indicate that at least some of the examples on either the recto or verso of this sheet were at one time considered for inclusion in the syllabus ("Models for Beginners in Composition," Folder 26, Leonard Stein Collection, ASC). Schoenberg's analysis of Op. 31 at the top of Facsimile 3.7 addresses motivic rather than harmonic characteristics of the theme.

99. For Cherlin, Schoenberg's predilection for inversional designs is representative of a pervasive mode of dialectical thinking found throughout his musical language, one attributable to the fin-de-siècle environment in which he spent his formative years. See Michael Cherlin, *Schoenberg's Musical Imagination* (New York: Cambridge University Press, 2007), 44–67. For a thorough and specific treatment of symmetry in Schoenberg's twelve-tone works see Jack Boss, *Schoenberg's Twelve-Tone Music: Symmetry and the Musical Idea* (New York: Cambridge University Press, 2014). In many ways, Cherlin's exploration of inversional balance in Schoenberg's theoretical ideas takes up where his teacher, David Lewin, left off. See David Lewin, "Inversional Balance as an Organizing Force in Schoenberg's Music and Thought," *Perspectives of New Music* 6, no. 2 (Spring–Summer 1968): 1–21.

100. *ZKIF*, 61 and 105.

101. I use the term "tonal problem" here in the sense that Patricia Carpenter and Severine Neff describe it in the Commentary to *MI*. That is, that the *Grundgestalt* of a work generally creates a tonal problem by presenting elements that contradict the tonic. As Carpenter and Neff put it, "The rest of the movement will elaborate and ultimately solve the problem presented by the theme." It does this by making "explicit the relation to the tonic of the conflicting elements" (67). See also Schoenberg's claim that "every musical form can be considered as an attempt to treat . . . unrest either by halting or limiting it, or by solving the problem" (*FMC*, 102). Schoenberg had alluded to this sort of unrest or tonal problem as early as 1911. See *TH*, 130–31.

102. "Construction of Themes," Strang Collection, Folder 51, ASC.

Models for Beginners in Composition

NOTES TO ORIGINAL PREFACE

1. Stein's sources for the corrections in the 1972 edition included Schoenberg's annotated copies of *MBC* (S141.C1–4 and S142.1–4). Stein also owned two copies of the 1943 edition with Schoenberg's edits from S141.C1, now held at the ASC (Leonard Stein Satellite Collection, Folder 27, Unnumbered Folder).

ENDNOTES TO SCHOENBERG'S TEXT

2. Schoenberg's description of Examples 1–19 as "two-measure motives or phrases on a single harmony" may seem odd on two counts. First, rather than one iteration of the motive, many of

Schoenberg's two-measure phrases contain multiple motivic statements. Second, in many contemporary accounts of form, it is likely that each of these examples would be described as a "subphrase" rather than a "phrase." Regarding the latter point, in his "*Gedanke* manuscripts" Schoenberg had described passages similar to those in Examples 1–19 of *MBC* as *Gestalten* rather than "two-measure phrases." Like the later two-measure phrases, Schoenberg's *Gestalten* usually consisted of at least two successive motivic statements, lasting a total of two measures. See Schoenberg's discussion of a *Gestalt* in Beethoven's Op. 2 No. 3 (*MI*, 163–65). To create a theme, one *Gesalt* could easily be followed by another (often a variation of the first)—a repetition resulting in either the four-bar antecedent phrase of a period, or in "the beginning" of a sentence. This symmetrical 2 + 2 unit, a grouping heard in countless themes from the Classical and Romantic eras, figured prominently in Schoenberg's pedagogy at USC and UCLA, and also in his writings of the 1930s and '40s. See Commentary, "The Two-Measure Phrase as a New Model."

3. In the original manuscript of *MBC* (self-published, 1942), Schoenberg's caveat regarding the "unbalanced" sound of certain examples was integrated into the text rather than appended as a footnote. This idea remains unelaborated in *MBC*, but the value placed on even slightly awkward examples illustrates Schoenberg's prioritization of inventiveness above stylistic accuracy. Whether through the hundreds of harmonizations in *TH* or in the numerous contrapuntal combinations of *PEC*, Schoenberg consistently valued possibility above idiomatic precision. It was his goal to instill in his students a sense of both musical imagination and "musical logic." (For Schoenberg's ideas on musical logic, see *MI*, 269–70.) His emphasis on these two ideas is demonstrated in the assignments he created for his composition classes. In one, from Advanced Composition 208, 1936, students composed four or five "new convincing closes for Beethoven's Adagio, b. 4." Gerald Strang Satellite Collection, Folder 51, notes for Advanced Composition 208, 1936, June 26, 1936.

4. Throughout his theoretical writings (including *TH*, *SFH*, and *MBC*), Schoenberg uses fixed roman numerals regardless of chromatic alteration, inversion, or local harmonic function. Thus, despite its function as an "artificial dominant," the F$^\sharp$7 chord in Examples 44–50 is labeled simply as III rather than (V^7/vi). This fixed-scale-degree method stems from the tradition of Viennese *Stufentheorie* and in particular from the teachings of Simon Sechter and Anton Bruckner, a similarity discussed in Appendix 6: A Primer in Transformations, 167–87. See also Robert W. Wason, *Viennese Theory: From Albrechtsberger to Schenker and Schoenberg* (Rochester, NY: University of Rochester Press, 1982).

5. Schoenberg's use of the term "passing harmony" is often idiosyncratic. Although he frequently uses it in the typical sense, as a stepwise bass motion of a third passing between chord tones of a single harmony (such as I–V $^6_4$–I^6), he sometimes uses it more generally to refer to the ornamentation of a basic harmonic framework through the addition of contrapuntal or ornamental chords of *any* kind, including neighboring chords. It is in the latter sense that he employs the term with regard to Examples 86–93 and 167–71. Thus, the basic framework of I–V often used in the opening *Gestalt* of a sentence may be enriched through the insertion of ornamental chords, such as II^6 as a neighbor to V. See Schoenberg's discussion of passing $^6_4$ chords in *SFH*, 5, and *TH*, 78, or his mention of passing seventh chords, *TH*, 139. For a discussion of Schoenberg's ideas on ornamentation in an atonal context, see Jack Boss, "Schoenberg on Ornamentation and Structural Levels," *Journal of Music Theory* 38, no. 2 (Autumn 1994): 187–216.

6. Despite its divergence from the more typical English term "motivic," Schoenberg's idiosyncratic term "motival" is preserved throughout this edition of *MBC*.

7. That is, although Examples 130 and 144 may sound somewhat "overcrowded" by themselves, this effect may be counterbalanced by an accompaniment sufficiently contrapuntal to assert a sense of melodic independence. In Example 130a, this results from imitation at the octave between the bass and soprano, while in Example 144a it is achieved through a more general contrast of contour.

8. See "Region" and "Substitute tones" in the Glossary of *MBC*. Although Schoenberg neglects to examine transformation in detail in *MBC*, he does mention the concept briefly in his discussion of substitute tones. See also Appendix 6: A Primer in Transformations (167–87).

9. Both the 1943 and 1972 editions of *MBC* read: "according to the model ... V–IV." Based on the chord successions in Example 167b (all of which feature the much more typical IV–V), these progressions should be described as ascending by second (IV–V).

10. In his 1934–36 *Gedanke* manuscripts, Schoenberg used the term "sentence" or *Satz* to describe a theme featuring an opening *Gestalt* (usually two measures in length) followed by its varied repetition, and subsequently by a terminative passage leading to a cadence (*MI*, 131–34 and 163–65). Although Schoenberg defines the sentence briefly in the glossary of *MBC*, this concept is perhaps better understood through the many *composed* examples of sentences in his syllabus. For Schoenberg, the quintessential sentence was no doubt the opening theme of Beethoven's Piano Sonata in F Minor, Op. 2 No. 1, reproduced as Example 207 in *MBC*. For a discussion of this sentence, see *FMC*, 20–24 and 58–81. Of the several examples of sentences from the literature featured in *MBC*, most appear also in *FMC*. However, the opening themes of Beethoven's Fifth Symphony and the Rondo Op. 22 are unique to *MBC* (see also Dudeque, *Music Theory and Analysis in the Writings of Arnold Schoenberg* (Burlington, VT: Ashgate, 2005), 143–50. For further discussion of the sentence, see Commentary, "The Two-Measure Phrase as a New Model" and "Models for Harmonizing the Two-Measure Phrase," 28–32.

11. Schoenberg's enigmatic description of a sentence with a dominant whose meaning is merely metaphorical refers to the idea that the "tonic form" of the initial "two-measure phrase" of a sentence, which is usually followed by a "dominant form," may instead be followed by a transposition of the two-measure phrase to some other degree. For example, "Sentence No. 4" features a two-measure phrase on the tonic followed by a transposition of this "phrase" to the subdominant. Rather than referring to this arrangement as a tonic form followed by a subdominant form, Schoenberg simply refers to the second segment as a "dominant form." "Dominant form" is thus used to describe the transposition of the initial two-measure phrase without regard to its literal harmonic setting. In many instances, the "dominant form" of the sentence is simply an untransposed repetition of the original motive. For this kind of literal repetition, see the opening themes of K. 310 and K. 330. The scholarship surrounding sentences is rich and varied. Perhaps the most influential contemporary treatment of this thematic type is found in William Caplin's books on form. See William Caplin, *Classical Form: A Theory of Formal Functions for the Instrumental Music of Haydn, Mozart, and Beethoven* (New York: Oxford University Press, 1998). See also William Caplin, *Analyzing Classical Form: An Approach for the Classroom* (New York: Oxford University Press, 2013). Although Caplin's analyses are often insightful, I have chosen in *MBC* to limit all sentence-related vocabulary to terms used in Schoenberg's writings. For further discussion of the sentence, see David Forrest and Matthew Santa, "A Taxonomy of Sentence Structures," *College Music Symposium* 54 (August 2014): http://symposium.music.org. For pioneering work on the sentence see Walter Frisch, *Brahms and the Principle of Developing Variation* (Berkeley and Los Angeles: University of California Press, 1984); William Rothstein, *Phrase Rhythm in Tonal Music* (New York: Schirmer, 1989); and Patricia Carpenter and Severine Neff, *MI*, "Commentary." Recent discussions may be found in James Hepokoski and Warren Darcy, *Elements of Sonata Theory: Norms, Types, and Deformations in the Late-Eighteenth-Century Sonata* (Oxford: Oxford University Press, 2006); Matthew BaileyShea, "Beyond the Beethoven Model: Sentence Types and Limits," *Current Musicology* 77 (Spring 2004): 5–33; Mark Richards, "Viennese Classicism and the Sentential Idea: Broadening the Sentence Paradigm," *Theory and Practice* 36 (2011): 179–224; and Stephen Rodgers, "Sentences with Words: Text and Theme-Type in Die schöne Müllerin," *Music Theory Spectrum* 36, no. 1 (Spring 2014): 58–85.

12. Although admittedly brief, Schoenberg's definition of condensation in *MBC* is useful in explaining this somewhat elusive term. The description of condensation as an acceleration of harmonic rhythm (the rate of chord changes) at the cadence of a phrase is useful. Elsewhere, however,

Schoenberg also uses this term to refer to a compression of *motivic* content by omitting one or more motivic features of the model (*FMC* 59). Thus, contemporary scholars influenced by Schoenberg have sometimes opted for a more categorical labeling of these phenomena. For example, rather than use two terms (condensation and reduction) to describe a decrease in grouping structure during the continuation, William Caplin uses one: fragmentation. Caplin labels the *increased* rate of harmonic changes as harmonic acceleration. See Caplin, 2013. .

13. Although liquidation is most commonly associated with the sentence, it refers generally to the process by which "characteristic features" of the motive, "which demand continuation," are "reduced" to "uncharacteristic ones," thereby loosening the "motival obligations" in preparation for the cadence (*FMC*, 30). This process may take place not only in the continuation of a sentence, but also during the consequent phrase of a period; and, in fact, the description above is taken from Schoenberg's discussion of the former from *FMC*. See Commentary, "Models for Harmonizing the Two-Measure Phrase." See also Commentary, endnote 54.

14. The form that Schoenberg describes here as "ternary"—or, in *FMC*, 119–36, as "small ternary"—is often called "rounded binary" by other theorists. For Schoenberg, the term "binary" refers only to forms lacking a return of the opening thematic material. The latter, often described by theorists as "simple" binary form, plays only a minor role in Schoenberg's pedagogy. Nevertheless, by way of contrast, Schoenberg's few references to "binary form" in *FMC*, 168, illustrate the distinction between these two forms. Crucially, each of the forms he cites as "binary" lacks a return of the opening thematic material—a list that includes the theme of Beethoven's Twenty-four Variations on Vincenzio Righini's "Venni amore," WoO 65, and the theme from his Twelve Variations on "Ein Mädchen oder Weibchen," Op. 66. In contrast to this, the opening theme of the Adagio from Beethoven's Op. 2 No. 1 (mm. 1–16)—a piece that Schoenberg cites as an example of the quintessential "ternary" form—features a varied return of the opening thematic material (mm. 13–16).

15. Schoenberg's claim that the harmony makes the "decisive contribution" to contrast in the middle section of small ternary forms derives from his concept of the constructive functions of harmony. See Commentary, "Models for Harmonizing the Two-Measure Phrase," 25–32.

16. The page numbers for the "forty-eight schemes" mentioned here are changed in this edition to 94–97. They were incorrectly printed as 30–33 in the 1943 and 1972 versions.

17. The purposeful descent of the bass from D to B♭, the artificial dominant of E♭, in the following measure, no doubt contributes to the "excellent . . . effect" of the harmony changing as the motive is repeated verbatim (Example 244, mm. 13–14).

18. Scherzo, p. 66–67. The scherzo, treated as a steppingstone to the composition of sonata-allegro form, is of central importance in Schoenberg's pedagogy. As Schoenberg explains in *MBC* and *FMC*, its contrasting or "elaboration" section is often modulatory and sequential—a property aligning it with sections of the same name in a sonata-allegro form. According to Schoenberg, an elaboration typically begins with a modulatory sequence followed by a liquidation of the motives thereof and a "standstill on V" (*MBC*, 66–67). This pattern is confirmed in the elaboration of Schoenberg's Scherzo in G major from *MBC*—a passage opening with an imitative five-bar model modulating from B♭ to F minor. This model is then sequenced by ascending second (mm. 13–18) to C minor and G minor. As a whole, the harmonic sequence ascends by fifth (B♭–F minor–C minor–G minor). This is followed by an emphasis of the Neapolitan region (A♭) (mm. 19–26) in conjunction with a liquidation of the motives from the original model. Schoenberg's elaboration culminates with "standstill on the dominant" (mm. 30–36) (preceded by an artificial dominant applied to V, mm. 27–29). The structure of this contrasting middle section is similar to the third movement of Beethoven's Piano Sonata Op. 2 No. 2. Like Schoenberg's elaboration, Beethoven's middle section begins with a model (mm. 9–12) sequenced stepwise upward (mm. 13–19) (F♯ minor to G♯ minor), followed by an "episode" (mm. 19–30) leading to the dominant. Whereas Schoenberg's episode leads to the dominant

via the Neapolitan region, Beethoven's does so through a chain of secondary dominants. Although Beethoven's Scherzo lacks a literal standstill on the dominant, it is similar to Schoenberg's example in its emphasis of the dominant region at the close. Many of Beethoven's elaborations confirm Schoenberg's claims regarding the typical structure of these sections. These include the scherzos in Op. 26; Op. 2 No. 3; Op. 14 No. 2; Op. 28; and Op. 31, several of which are mentioned by Schoenberg in *FMC*.

19. Because it was written before the final publication of *MBC*, as part of a manuscript sent to Schirmer for editing in 1942, Schoenberg's original signature and handwritten postscript given here are dated 1942 instead of 1943. The original signature and handwritten postscript do not appear in the 1943 edition, which instead features the typewritten postscript: "May it also be helpful to the students of this syllabus!" with no signature.

NOTES TO SCHOENBERG'S MUSICAL EXAMPLES

20. Page 69, Example 12, m.1. The symbol + in Schoenberg's theoretical texts refers to embellishing tones (passing or neighbor figures; see Examples 13–19). However, in Examples 189–97, it is used to refer to variations of the motive in the dominant form of the two-measure phrase. In manuscript S143.C3 Schoenberg has also added it to Example 198 in the latter sense.

21. Page 70, Examples 44–48. In the present edition of *MBC* a strikethrough is added to III in order to reflect its alteration—a change that maintains the consistency of Schoenberg's notational system. See Appendix 6: Primer in Transformations.

22. Page 70, Example 48, m. 2. As above, the diminished seventh chord in m. 2, an altered III, is labeled with a strikethrough. See Appendix 6: Primer in Transformations, 167–87.

23. Page 71, Example 85, the 1942 edition in the Leonard Stein Satellite Collection shows a D♯ handwritten correction, creating the major dominant triad shown here (m. 2).

24. Page 72, Example 87, m. 1, beats 2 and 4 (bass). Despite the dramatic appearance of these parallel fifths (A–E; F♯–C♯), the rest on beat 3 significantly softens their effect.

25. Page 72, Example 91, m. 1, beats 3–4. Since they feature transformations, IV and II have strikethrough symbols. The analysis of the chord on beat 4 may cause some confusion here, since it is clearly not II. The idea is that this chord is an artificial dominant of ♯ (Neap.), heard as part of a larger emphasis on this degree in the following measure.

26. Page 73, Example 109. In the 1943 and 1972 editions, Example 109 was presented with its own separate cautionary treble clef.

27. Page 75, Example 149. In Example 149, strikethrough symbols have been added to VI and II in order to indicate that these chords are transformations of their original diatonic degrees.

28. Page 75, Example152, beat 1, bass. Beaming in motives *a* and *a1* has been made identical in order to reflect the relation of motives.

29. Page 77, a strikethrough has been added to II to indicate its transformation.

30. Page 77, Example 167, as in the examples above, strikethrough symbols have been added to Schoenberg's notation wherever transformations are used.

31. Page 77, Example 167, last system, m. 8. Schoenberg's figured-bass symbols sometimes appear in reverse order, e.g., $\frac{4}{6}$ instead of $\frac{6}{4}$—an arrangement common in Austro-German music theory.

32. Page 78, Example 168, system 2, m. 7. Schoenberg states that it is "not very practicable" to let VII as an artificial dominant progress directly to VI in the syntax of common-practice tonality. The

EXAMPLE EN 35
Alternative version of Example 174 from MBC.

chord should be G major, which would be a deceptive substitute for a B minor chord (III). A further substitution of E minor does not sound particularly convincing.

33. Page 78, Example 169, system 2, mm. 1–2. The question mark in Example 169*b* likely refers to the chromatic mediant relation between I (F) and III (A), which, although striking, *does* have precedents, for instance, in the Scherzo of Beethoven's *Spring Sonata* for violin and piano.

34. Page 78, Example 171*d*. The question mark in Example 171*d* asks whether III would make a viable passing chord between I and II. With its retrogressive root motion, I–III–II is certainly not heard often in common-practice harmony, except perhaps when used in a descending $^6_3$ sequence.

35. Page 79, Example 174, m. 1, beat 2. In this example, II should be a diminished chord (an artificial dominant applied to V), spelled E–G♮–B♭–D♭. Still, the G♯ in the grand-staff example could be a passing tone, although this would fail to lend it harmonic status. Example EN 35, above, presents an alternative version with G♮.

36. Page 81, Example 190, m. 4. The + sign refers to the thickening of the accompaniment in m. 4 compared to m. 2. In this case, Schoenberg did not consider the change of harmony per se or the transposition to a new degree to accommodate this new harmony as an "alteration." If he had, then m. 3 would likely also feature a +, since its harmony and scale degrees are altered to accommodate the motive on V.

37. Page 83, Example 208, m. 6. In Example 208, the C in parentheses refers to the reduction of the motive, illustrating what its rhythmic value would be had this motive been continued as a half note as in mm. 1–5. Instead, the two quarter notes (♭2) that punctuate the two-measure phrase from m. 3 are immediately followed by *c2* (a variation of *a*), thus producing an acceleration of the pattern. Whereas a duration of four quarter notes (from mm. 4–5) separates the original motive *b* from the next *a2* in m. 5, these two motives are directly juxtaposed in m. 6.

38. Page 83, Example 210, m. 8. The bracket of motive *b1* (m. 8) has been lengthened from the 1943 and 1972 editions of *MBC* to extend across to C (D–D–C). Both earlier editions truncate the bracket after the second D. Its lengthening highlights the correspondence of this motive to the previous *b1* in measure 4 (I thank Áine Heneghan for bringing this inconsistency to my attention). Schoenberg's manuscripts show the same bracketing as the previous published editions. Perhaps the inconsistency was due to haste.

39. Page 85, Example 220, m. 5. A strikethrough has been added to VI, based on Schoenberg's handwritten corrections to manuscript S143.C3 (ASC). Schoenberg's corrections also show a

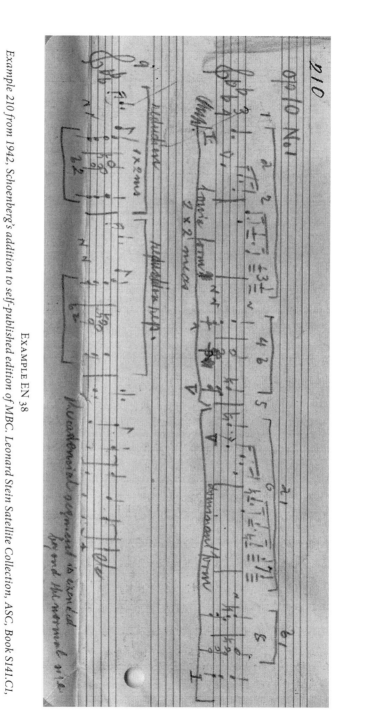

EXAMPLE EN 38

Example 210 from 1942, Schoenberg's addition to self-published edition of MBC. Leonard Stein Satellite Collection, ASC, Book S141.C1, Example 210.

tonic region: V̶

subdominant region: H̶ V   I

mediant region: H̶   I   V   I

(neap.)

EXAMPLE EN 41
Alternative roman-numeral analysis of Example 222 from MBC.

strikethrough in II (m. 5, beats 3–4); however, since this chord is diatonic, it appears without a strikethrough in this edition. Third ending, m. 8, beat 1: a strikethrough has been added to roman numeral III to reflect its chromatic alteration.

40. Page 85, Example 221, m. 8. In Example 221, Schoenberg analyzes the cadential $\frac{6}{4}$ chord as a tonic rather than a dominant harmony. Unlike previously discussed examples, however, here Schoenberg omits the figured bass altogether, so that the cadence is labeled I–V–I.

41. Page 86, Example 222, mm. 6–8. While consistent with Schoenberg's method of roman-numeral analysis, the chord in m. 6, beat 2, considered as an altered dominant, may be more clearly understood as part of an explicit tonicization of the subdominant region, as in Example EN 41.

Specifically, the A° $\frac{4}{6}$ chord on beat 2 of m. 6 is heard as a supertonic in the subdominant region transformed though modal mixture, or what Schoenberg described as the "interchangeability of major and minor" (*SFH*, 51–56). This emphasis of the subdominant region is then followed by a cadence in the mediant region. Also in Example 222, manuscript S143.C3 shows a strikethrough in IV. Because it is diatonic, it appears as IV here, unchanged from the 1943 and 1972 editions.

42. Page 87, Example 225, m. 2, beat 3; and m. 4, beat 3. Based on S142.C3, m. 2, beat 3, E♭ has been changed to E♮. Also based on this source, the D♭s in the final chord of m. 4 have been corrected to D♯s.

43. Page 88, Example 228, m. 1, beats 3–4. Motivic symbols have been added to reflect the immediate parallelism between the motive in the anacrusis and the one on beats 3–4.

44. Page 91, Example 231a, m. 5, third eighth note, inner voice. The 1972 and 1943 editions of *MBC* show B3 here, but this has been changed to A3 based on Schoenberg's corrections in S142.C3.

45. Page 93, Example 237, m. 11. The parenthetical descriptor "plagal" confirms that the dominant region has been tonicized in mm. 10–11. This motion causes the (D–A major) succession in mm. 11–12 to temporarily sound plagal. The fixed tonic orientation with regard to the roman numerals in this passage, however, demonstrates that the passage as a whole is in D major.

46. Page 94, "Harmonic Schemes for Contrasting Middle Section." In S141.C1, underneath this heading Schoenberg has written: "Many of these models can be developed according to advice on page xx."

47. Page 95, Progressions 17–20. When the root of a chord was altered through mode mixture, Schoenberg often used flat signs before the roman numerals, as in Examples 17–20, although he is not entirely consistent in this practice.

48. Page 95, Progression 21. A strikethrough has been added to II in m. 3 of Progression 21 to indicate that this chord has been chromatically altered (as a French sixth transformation). See Appendix 6: Primer in Transformations, 167–87.

49. Page 97, Progression 40. An early draft of the Harmonic Schemes for Contrasting Middle Sections (TBK 1, ASC) shows C4 on beat 2 of the alto in m. 3 (an "Italian augmented-sixth" chord). In the published version of *MBC*, this is changed to a "French sixth" sonority. An additional discrepancy between the early draft and the published version of these harmonic schemes occurs in

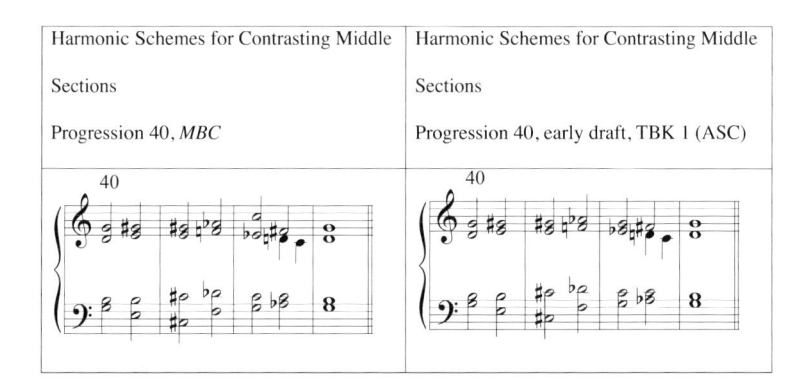

EXAMPLE EN 49

Early draft of Harmonic Schemes for Contrasting Middle Sections compared with published version in MBC *(TBK 1, ASC).*

progression no. 40. In this instance, the smooth soprano line of the draft may indeed be preferable to the Schirmer edition. See below.

50. Page 99, Example 242, "Minuet." Above the "Minuet," in S143.C3, Schoenberg wrote, "Add here more minuet and Scherzo models, themes only." Schoenberg never completed his new edition of *MBC*. See Preface, endnote 19.

51. Page 99, Minuet, m. 18, beat 3. The half-note duration for the major second, B♭–C (inner voices), shown here and in previous editions (1943 and 1972), results in a measure with too many beats. Although no sketches for the Minuet exist, the fair copy in TBK 5, Unnumbered Folder *b*, features the same half-note duration at this point. Because more than one plausible solution exists, I have opted to place both possible corrections below. Solution *a* simply changes the half notes B♭–C to quarter notes, while Solution *b* retains the half-note duration, simply shifting it over so that it is correctly placed within the measure. Although Solution *a* is less intrusive with regard to the placement of the pitches as they now appear in both the fair and the published copies, solution *b* seems more convincing from a tactile and aural perspective.

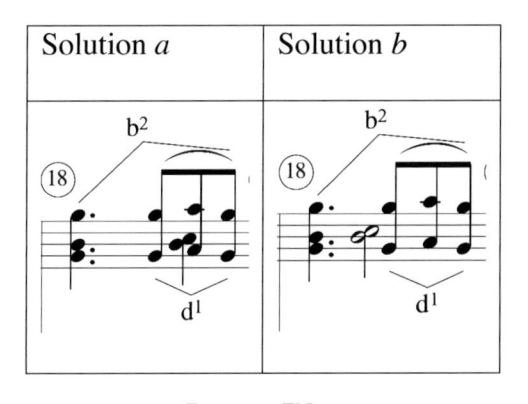

EXAMPLE EN 51

Alternate solutions to m. 18 of Schoenberg's Minuet in MBC.

52. Page 102, Example 245, Alternative ending 1. The key signature of G major has been added to this passage in order to clarify the tonality.

53. Page 106, the quarter notes in Examples 12 and 13 have been changed to dotted quarter notes, based on S142.C2, and S143.C3 (compare Editorial Notes, xxv–xxviii).

Notes to Schoenberg's Glossary

54. Because VII has a dominant function in Schoenberg's harmonic system, it is usually labeled as V. Thus, as Schoenberg suggests here, it typically lacks an independent label. See Appendix 6: Primer in Transformations, 167–87.

55. That is, cadences sometimes occur on unexpected degrees.

56. See Appendix 6: A Primer in Transformations, 167–87, "The German Sixth Transformation."

57. In this case, the transformation of II, marked "?" in Schoenberg's example, is a Neapolitan chord. See Appendix 6: Primer in Transformations, "The Neapolitan Transformation."

58. Schoenberg described the process through which a motive gradually gives rise to new motive forms as developing variation. See Commentary, endnote 41.

59. For a discussion of sentences, see Commentary, "The Two-Measure Phrase as a New Model" and "Models for Harmonizing the Two-Measure Phrase."

60. Schoenberg discusses liquidation in *MI, FMC,* and even as early as *TH.* See Commentary, endnote 54.

Appendix 1 Notes

1. In correspondence with the author, Therese Muxeneder at the ASC has confirmed that Schoenberg's typing projects were generally completed by assistants or secretaries. Since Stein was Schoenberg's assistant for *MBC,* it is highly probable that he typed at least some of the manuscripts for this text.

2. Because he had self-published an earlier edition of the book in 1942, Schoenberg referred to this 1943 version of *MBC* as the "second edition."

3. For a discussion of the 1943 errata sheet, see Preface, "On the History of *MBC*," xvi–xvii.

4. The handwritten musical additions in S141.C1 contain the following examples: 47a, 48a, 49a, and 67a ("Two Measure Phrases on Two- and Three-Harmonies"); 86a, 90a, 91a, and 93a ("Building Two-Measure Phrases on more than Three Harmonies"); 130a and 144a ("Various other Ways of Utilizing Motival Features"); 162a–b, 167–77 ("Models of Harmonies for Two-Measure Phrases enriched by insertion of one or more Harmonies"); 207–11, "Sentences from the Literature"; 212–15, "Completion of Sentence"; 228a–b ("Periods"); footnote on p. 33, under "Periods"; 229a–b, 230a–b, and 231a–b ("Periods"); 233–234 ("Harmonic Schemes for Contrasting Middle Section"); and 421, "The Recapitulation." To create this new section from the 1942 edition, Schoenberg simply pasted in several examples, including period #3, Example 230, the contrasting middle section from Example 239, and a newly composed recapitulation: Examples 243–44 ("Alternatives to Phrases from the Minuet"); Example 246 ("Alternative to mm. 5–16 of the Scherzo"); "Ending to Alternative *a* [and *b*]" from Example 247; and "Recomposition of melodies 27 and 36 from Phrases, Half-Sentences, Antecedents, and 'a' Sections of Ternary Forms."

5. See TBK 8, 001r.

6. In a letter to Schoenberg dated October 6, 1942, Felix Greissle mentions these editors as having gone over Schoenberg's text "very carefully." He explains that in completing their work, they "met with great difficulties." (Greissle to Arnold Schoenberg, October 6, 1942, Library of Congress.) It is surprising that these were not the only editors involved with Schoenberg's text; Schoenberg's annotations for the Glossary (copies 1 and 2) contain a note to a "Mr. O'Brien," and a "Mr. Boelke" (Walter Boelke). The latter is now best known as a founding member of Boelke-Bomart, the publishers of the 1949 edition of Schoenberg's *A Survivor from Warsaw*. As editors for Schirmer, Boelke and O'Brien were primarily responsible for musical examples and matters of "type combination" and formatting.

Appendix 2 Notes

1. It is possible that there are omissions in these documented courses. There may be one or two courses that Schoenberg taught which are not listed—perhaps added late. Or perhaps there were one or two cancellations that are not accounted for in this list.

Appendix 3 Notes

1. These two sheets of notes contained in Folder 103 of the Leonard Stein Satellite Collection (UCLA notes) seem to be preparatory lecture notes for Beginning Composition 105a, rather than class notes taken *during* lectures. The neatness of the notes, the careful numbering of examples, the absence of student names from the notes, and the lack of dates make them unique among the notes from Composition 105 in this folder. In the sense that they lay out the plans, methods, and assignments of Composition 105, these manuscripts may be viewed as prototypes for *MBC*.

2. This assignment is also featured in Eike Fess's booklet *Examinations: Der Lehrer Arnold Schönberg*. Eike Fess, "Examinations: Der Lehrer Arnold Schönberg," in *Das magische Quadrat: Eine Annäherung an den Visionär Arnold Schönberg; Materialien zu einem Leben mit vielen Talenten*, ed. Musikhochschule Luzern and the Arnold Schönberg Center (Lucerne: Edizioni Periferia, 2006), Appendix, unpaginated.

3. *FMC*, 121. At several points in *FMC*, Schoenberg describes dwelling, or standing, on the dominant as a method for organizing the contrasting middle section of a small ternary form. See also *FMC*, 142–43, 153, 179, and 186. In *TH*, Schoenberg describes two kinds of dominant emphases: the

first, pedal point, "reinforces" the dominant by sustaining its root in the bass (206–9); the second, described as "lingering on the dominant," emphasizes this degree "by means of a *sustained voice* in the upper parts" (212).

Appendix 5 Notes

1. Lewin, "Inversional Balance as an Organizing Force."

2. Ibid., 3.

3. Dieter Rexroth, "Arnold Schönberg als Theoretiker der tonalen Harmonik" (Ph.D. diss., University of Bonn, 1971).

4. Wason, *Viennese Harmonic Theory*.

5. For a general overview of Patricia Carpenter's contribution to Schoenberg scholarship and to the field of music theory in general, see the introduction to Janna K. Saslaw and James P. Walsh, "Patricia Carpenter: A Commemoration," *Theory and Practice* 30 (2005): 1–4.

6. Patricia Carpenter, "*Grundgestalt* as Tonal Function," *Music Theory Spectrum* 5, no. 1 (April 1983): 15–38.

7. Severine Neff, "Aspects of *Grundgestalt* in Schoenberg's First String Quartet, Op. 7," *Theory and Practice* 9, nos. 1–2 (July–December 1984): 7–56.

8. Severine Neff, "Schoenberg and Goethe: Organicism and Analysis," in *Music Theory and the Exploration of the Past*, ed. Christopher Hatch and David Bernstein (Chicago: University of Chicago Press, 1993), 409–433.

9. Severine Neff, "Schoenberg as Theorist: Three Forms of Presentation," in *Schoenberg and His World*, ed. Walter Frisch (Princeton, NJ: Princeton University Press, 1999), 55–84.

10. Ibid., 60.

11. Severine Neff, "Editing Schoenberg's Music-Theoretical Manuscripts: Problems of Incompleteness and Authorship," in *Arnold Schoenberg in seinen Schriften: Katalog—Fragen—Editorisches*, ed. Hartmut Krones (Vienna: Böhlau Verlag, 2011), 193–216.

12. Dineen's 2005 article "Schoenberg's Modulatory Calculations" relates to Lewin's 1968 premise. Dineen argues for the advantages of the system of modulatory measurement in *TH* (one based on the circle of fifths). This method allowed the possibility of calculating modulatory patterns through simple mod-12 arithmetic. For example, a move to the second circle upward might be achieved through a compound modulation involving a move to the first circle downward, followed by a modulation to third circle upward. (This pattern could be expressed succinctly as: -1 + 3 = 2). Schoenberg himself notes this possibility in *TH*, and Dineen demonstrates that Schoenberg used such calculations in his lessons with Berg. Further, Dineen discusses how these "modulatory contours" and their properties of inversional symmetry and equivalence prefigure the kinds of manipulations normally associated with Schoenberg's twelve-tone music. In many ways, Schoenberg's Chart of the Regions clarifies the kinds of crucial parallel relationships that remain only implicit in his system of circles. However, such a clarification need not devalue the advantages that Dineen finds in Schoenberg's system of circles. Perhaps what the Chart of the Regions gains in the clarification of parallel relationships, it loses through an obscuration the earlier modulatory calculations. Ultimately, as Dineen demonstrates in his discussion of Schoenberg's analysis of the song "Lockung" in *Structural Functions of Harmony*, these two systems need not be incompatible. See Phillip Murray Dineen, "Schoenberg's Modulatory Calculations: Wn Fonds 21 Berg 6/III/66 and Tonality," *Music Theory Spectrum* 27, no. 1 (2005): 97–112.

13. Phillip Murray Dineen, "Problems of Tonality: Schoenberg and the Concept of Tonal Expression" (Ph.D. diss., Columbia University, 1989).

14. See also Dineen article, "Schoenberg on the Modes: Characteristics, Substitutes, and Tonal Orientation," *College Music Symposium* 33–34 (1993), 140–54; in many ways, it is a distillation of his 1989 dissertation. In this article, Dineen again clearly lays out the process through which substitution led to extended tonality, transformation, the theory of regions, and even, in some sense, to the ultimate consequence of the chromatic scale as a basis for all tonal material—the twelve-tone system (150).

15. David Bernstein, "Schoenberg contra Riemann: *Stufen*, Regions, *Verwandtschaft*, and the Theory of Tonal Function," *Theoria* 6 (1992): 23–53.

16. Dudeque, *Music Theory and Analysis in the Writings of Arnold Schoenberg*, 33–131.

17. John Spratt, "The Speculative Content of Schoenberg's *Harmonielehre*," *Current Musicology* 11 (Spring 1971): 83–88.

18. In "Schoenberg contra Riemann," David Bernstein points to similarities between the intervallic structure of Schoenberg's chart and Hermann Erpf's 1920s-era *Tonnetz*—a similarity later also noted in Dudeque, *Music Theory and Analysis in the Writings of Arnold Schoenberg*, 54–69. Schoenberg owned and heavily annotated a copy of Erpf's 1927 *Studien zur Harmonie*, now held at the Arnold Schönberg Center, Vienna (call number E10). Most of Schoenberg's annotations are highly critical; however, toward the end of the book, on page 185, his opinion seems to be somewhat tempered. He writes: "Angered by his criticism, I have apparently done this author somewhat wrong. I have read the points marked, only superficially, and now that I look at them again I see, that he shows a perfectly decent, respectable attitude with much understanding. Why should he not occasionally miss the mark? September 1936 Sch." [Es scheint, ich habe diesem Autor, erzürnt durch seine Kritik, einigermassen Unrecht getan. Ich habe die angezeichneten Stellen nur oberflächlich gelesen und sehe jetzt, wo ich dieselben nochmals anschaue, dass er eine durchaus anständige respectvolle Haltung mit viele Verständnis bezeigt. Warum sollte er nicht gelegentlich daneben hauen? September 1936 Sch] Later, in a letter to Hugo Leichtentritt, Schoenberg included Erpf's book in a list of German books that strongly interested him. (Arnold Schoenberg to Hugo Leichtentritt, December 3, 1938, Library of Congress).

19. The Chart of the Regions in the minor mode features this same symmetrical balancing about the tonic by fifth-related regions along the vertical plane and third-related regions along the horizontal plane. However, the labels of the regions are adjusted to fit the minor-mode orientation. See Example 8.5.

20. The symmetrical structure of Schoenberg's Chart of the Regions has been discussed in David Lewin, "Inversional Balance as an Organizing Force in Schoenberg's Music and Thought," *Perspectives of New Music* 6, no. 2 (Spring–Summer 1968): 1–21; Patricia Carpenter, "*Grundgestalt* as Tonal Function," *Music Theory Spectrum* 5, no. 1 (April 1983): 15–38; Severine Neff, "Aspects of *Grundgestalt* in Schoenberg's First String Quartet, Op. 7," *Theory and Practice* 9, nos. 1–2 (July–December 1984): 7–56; Dineen, "Problems of Tonality"; David Bernstein, "Schoenberg Contra Riemann: *Stufen*, Regions, *Verwandtschaft*, and the Theory of Tonal Function," *Theoria* 6 (1992): 23–53; Dudeque, *Music Theory and Analysis in the Writings of Arnold Schoenberg*; and many others.

21. *SFH*, 21, 68. Schoenberg's Classification of Relationship is summarized below.

22. This is in fact implied by Schoenberg's concept of the "interchangeability of major and minor." See *SFH*, 51–56.

23. *SFH*, 68.

24. The major scale at T6 retains one common tone, while at T1 it retains two; enharmonic equivalent spelling may obscure this difference. Unfortunately, Schoenberg's rationale for the Classification of Relationship—based on common tones—does not work equally well for all regions. For example, the Dorian region, which shares six tones in common with the tonic, would seem to be a direct and close relation—as is its relative major (the subdominant). However, in Schoenberg's system of classification, it is described as "Indirect and Remote" (*SFH*, 69). Although Schoenberg fails to explain the reason for this label, it may stem from the potential cross-related degrees in establishing this region: in C major, the C♯ leading tone of the Dorian region cancels the original tonic degree, while the B♭ cancels its leading tone. Thus, establishing the Dorian region involves first neutralizing, then altering, two crucial, key-defining degrees in the tonic region. This may explain why the Dorian region is classified as indirect and remote, despite the large number of common tones its unaltered scale shares with the tonic. This idea of cross-related degrees as a means of explaining the "Indirect and Remote" classification of the Dorian region was suggested to me by Severine Neff, who has in turn credited her mentor, Patricia Carpenter, for bringing this to her attention.

25. *MBC*, 55.

26. For another instance of an abbreviated Chart of the Regions, see also *PEC*, 81–83.

Appendix 6 Notes

1. As Wason explains in his landmark study *Viennese Harmonic Theory*, certain essential characteristics of Schoenberg's analytic nomenclature derive from the theories of Simon Sechter (1788–1867), a highly influential Viennese theorist and composer whose students included such luminaries as Henri Vieuxtemps, Anton Bruckner, and even—for one lesson—Franz Schubert. Owing to the way in which his theory categorizes each harmony according to the scale degree of its root, Sechter's method is often described as *Stufentheorie*, or "scale-degree theory." Schoenberg refers to Sechter at several points in *TH*, even citing *Die Grundsätze der musikalischen Komposition* (*TH*, 270), and he seems to have attended at least one of Bruckner's harmony lectures at the University of Vienna sometime before the latter's death in 1896 (*TH*, 39) (see also Wason, *Viennese Harmonic Theory*, 31). Indeed, like Sechter's notation, Schoenberg's highlights the diatonic root of each chord within the main key. And also like Sechter's notation, Schoenberg's symbols disregard inversions and chromatic alterations. Considering this shared nomenclature, we might assume the fixed roman numerals to refer to some essential diatonic framework. This is undoubtedly the message behind Sechter's diatonic roman numerals. For Sechter, tonality was *naturally* diatonic. However, this is not the case with Schoenberg, who viewed his examples within the context of his own fully chromatic species of monotonality, one whose most extreme possibilities may not always be realized in practice, but which nevertheless leaves such options open.

2. Like Schoenberg's roman-numeral approach, the idea of the implied fundamental seems once more to bear the influence of Sechter, who most likely encountered this principle secondhand, through summaries of Rameau's writings by earlier Viennese theorists.

3. Schoenberg insisted that these altered scale degrees do not change "the functional quality of the degree" (*MBC*, 54). I use the description "scale-degree class" here only loosely, to refer to the multiple variants that each scale degree contains in Schoenberg's system. Schoenberg never used this term in his theoretical writings.

4. *TH*, 29.

5. See Thomas Christensen, "Fétis and Emerging Tonal Consciousness," in *Music Theory in the Age of Romanticism*, ed. Ian Bent (New York: Cambridge University Press, 1996), 50. Schoenberg's

progressive portrayal of history is reminiscent of Fétis's Hegelian account of the development of common-practice tonality. Christensen's summary of Fétis's view could easily describe Schoenberg's explanation for the demise of modality. See also Michael Cherlin, "Dialectical Opposition in Schoenberg's Music and Thought," *Music Theory Spectrum* 22, no. 2 (Autumn 2000): 157–76. As Cherlin explains, Schoenberg's view of human history and its key figures has much in common with Hegel's notion of the "world-historical individual." Cherlin notes that there are many similarities between Schoenberg's portrayal of his own role in music history and that of Hegel's "world-historical individual."

6. *TH*, 389.

7. In *TH*, Schoenberg did in fact predict a further evolutionary state of chromaticism, one that would ultimately extend beyond the confines of the chromatic scale. Perhaps one day, he conjectured, a "new division of the octave will even be untempered and will not have much left over in common with our scale" (25). Ultimately, Schoenberg devoted only a few pages to this vast expansion of pitch space, known as microtonality, except for a brief discussion of a few possible divisions of the octave into twenty-four, thirty-six, forty-eight, or fifty-three parts, possibilities he attributed to a young scholar named Robert Neumann (*TH*, 423). A brief letter of praise from Neumann regarding Schoenberg's expert pedagogical skill is found in *SW*, 254.

8. Although no derivation for D♯ is shown in 9.2, Schoenberg's earlier chart of substitute tones from *TH* (175–76) includes D♯ as a derivation from the Phrygian mode. Schoenberg's ambivalence regarding this substitute tone is understandable; all of the other substitute tones are derivable from traditional contrapuntal cadences. The E Phrygian mode, however, did not traditionally close melodically from D♯ to E, but rather either from F to E, or D to E. As a dissonance, the interval D♯–F is not allowed in first-species counterpoint. Although problematic in this context, D♯ can be derived as the chord factor of an artificial dominant of E. In *SFH*, however, no "modal" derivation of D♯ is given. Instead, D♯ is listed as one of five substitute tones, but now it is omitted from the scale. Note: in *SFH*, G♯ is given both an Aeolian and a Phrygian derivation. In the former instance, it is an artificial leading tone, while in the latter, it was for Schoenberg no doubt linked to the typical major treatment of E in Phrygian chorales, such as Bach's "Aus tiefer Not schrei' ich zu dir" (BWV 38/6). See Example 9.2, Appendix 6: Primer in Transformations.

9. *TH*, 384–89.

10. According to Norton Dudeque, the strikethrough notation was Schoenberg's own. However, there is a long tradition of the use of slash notation in figured bass to indicate alterations. Dudeque, *Music Theory and Analysis in the Writings of Arnold Schoenberg*, 74.

11. The first specific mention of the term "transformation" that I have found appears in Stein's notes from Schoenberg's 1941 harmony course, Music 106B (Structural Functions of Harmony), although it is possible that earlier instances exist. An excerpt from these notes, illustrating transformation applied to tonic harmony, is reproduced in Facsimile 9.1.

12. For a discussion of transference, see Dineen, "Problems of Tonality," 146–56.

13. Schoenberg's initial discussion of transformations in *SFH* (35) contains triads without extensions; however, the chart of transformations features only seventh chords. Schoenberg provides no rationale for this limitation, but perhaps it is motivated by the simple desire to include the most basic chordal dissonance common to each harmony.

14. For an instance of the V7(♯5) in *SFH*, see Example 77, *k* (61).

15. Several other chords in Schoenberg's chart are no more distant than the mm7 transformation on the tonic (Cm7). For example, applied to the tonic, both the Neapolitan and mm7 transformations belong to same region: B♭ (♭MD). Since it is no more remote than many other transformations in

Schoenberg's chart, the mm7 transformation in Example 9.7 is included on I–III and VI–VII for the sake of comprehensiveness and consistency, but with parentheses to highlight its supplemental status.

16. *SFH*, 42.

17. *SFH*, 51–56. Described alternatively in *TH* as "the relationship of keys with the same name" (207).

18. As explained in endnotes 1 and 2, Schoenberg most likely learned Rameau's theories indirectly, through Sechter and Bruckner. Schoenberg's use of implied roots is here compared directly with Rameau's in order to clarify its relation to the source of these procedures.

19. Lester, *Compositional Theory in the Eighteenth Century*, 115.

20. *TH*, 193.

21. *SFH*, 36.

22. Even without the A on the second eighth note of beat 3 (m. 6, Example 9.10), the C♯°7 chord on the final eighth note of the measure would retain its roman numeral of V in Schoenberg's notational system.

23. See the earlier discussion of harmonic variation (28–29).

24. This final step in Schoenberg's illustration, i.e., respelling ♭3 as ♯2, is not always taken. In fact, *MBC* almost exclusively features the ♭3 spelling.

25. Although Schoenberg occasionally refers to other inversions of the augmented sixth, namely $\frac{6}{5}$ and $\frac{4}{2}$, he nearly always uses the $\frac{6}{5}$ inversion in his pedagogical texts.

26. *SFH*, 44–50.

27. *SFH*, 44.

28. *SFH*, 44. $\frac{6}{5}$ and $\frac{4}{3}$ are Schoenberg's figures for the German and French augmented-sixth chords respectively.

29. Like the Ger 6 transformation (including Schoenberg's implied root), Mm7(♭5)/Fr.6 transformation has four possible interpretations—not counting the interchangeability of major and minor.

30. Although Schoenberg never applied the descriptive term "artificial" to Neapolitan chords, it would seem logical to do so in instances where new regions are established via this transformation.

31. *SFH*, 41–42.

32. In her 2006 analysis of Schoenberg's Second String Quartet, Op. 10, in F♯ minor, Severine Neff discusses the use of the flatted tonic (F major) at the beginning of the recapitulation of this landmark work—an interpretation corroborated by Schoenberg's own analysis of the work (included in Neff's edition). As Neff aptly puts it, the flatted tonic is "a radical 'tonic' that is not the tonic, a key ignored or considered an impossibility in virtually all theoretical literature." She goes on to cite a strikingly similar instance of the same harmonic relationship (at pitch) in Brahms's Violin Sonata in D Minor, Op. 108. See Arnold Schoenberg, *The Second String Quartet in F♯ Minor, Op. 10*, ed. Severine Neff (New York: W. W. Norton, 2006), 129.

Select Bibliography

Alderman, Pauline. "Schoenberg at USC." *Journal of the Arnold Schoenberg Institute* 5, no. 2 (November 1981): 203–11.

Antokoletz, Elliott. "Theories of Pitch Organization in Bartók's Music: A Critical Evaluation." *International Journal of Musicology* 7 (1998): 259–300.

Auner, Joseph. "Schoenberg's Handel Concerto and the Ruins of Tradition." *Journal of the American Musicological Society* 49, no. 2 (Summer 1996): 222–36.

Auner, Joseph, ed. *A Schoenberg Reader: Documents of a Life.* New Haven, CT: Yale University Press, 2003.

Babbitt, Milton. *Words about Music.* Edited by Stephen Dembski and Joseph Straus. Madison: University of Wisconsin Press, 1987.

Bailey, Walter, ed. *The Arnold Schoenberg Companion.* Westport, CT: Greenwood, 1998.

Bernstein, David. "Schoenberg contra Riemann: *Stufen*, Regions, *Verwandtschaft*, and the Theory of Tonal Function." *Theoria* 6 (1992): 23–53.

Bestor, Dorothea N. "Schoenberg Teaches: An Interview with Arnold Schoenberg." *Musical Review* 3 (October 1934): 3 and 6.

Boss, Jack. "Mahler's Musical Idea: A Schenkerian-Schoenbergian Analysis of the Adagio from Symphony No. 10." In *Analyzing the Music of Living Composers (and Others)*, edited by Jack Boss, Brad Osborn, Tim S. Pack, and Stephen Rodgers, 115–31. Cambridge: Cambridge Scholars, 2012.

———. "Schoenberg's Op. 22 Radio Talk and Developing Variation in Atonal Music." *Music Theory Spectrum* 14, no. 2 (Autumn 1992): 125–49.

———. *Schoenberg's Twelve-Tone Music: Symmetry and the Musical Idea.* New York: Cambridge University Press, 2014.

Cahn, Stephen J. "Schoenberg, the Viennese-Jewish Experience and Its Aftermath." In *The Cambridge Companion to Schoenberg*, edited by Jennifer Shaw and Joseph Auner, 191–206. Cambridge: Cambridge University Press, 2010.

Calico, Joy. "Schoenberg as Teacher." In *The Cambridge Companion to Schoenberg*, edited by Jennifer Shaw and Joseph Auner, 137–46. Cambridge: Cambridge University Press, 2010.

Caplin, William E. *Analyzing Classical Form: An Approach for the Classroom.* New York: Oxford University Press, 2013.

———. *Classical Form: A Theory of Formal Functions for the Instrumental Music of Haydn, Mozart, and Beethoven.* New York: Oxford University Press, 1998.

———. "Harmony and Meter in the Theories of Simon Sechter." *Music Theory Spectrum* 2, no. 1 (Spring 1980): 74–89.

Carpenter, Patricia. "*Grundgestalt* as Tonal Function." *Music Theory Spectrum* 5, no. 1 (April 1983): 15–38.

———. "Schoenberg's Theory of Composition." In *The Arnold Schoenberg Companion*, edited by Walter Bailey, 209–22. Westport, CT: Greenwood Press, 1998.

———. "Tonality: A Conflict of Forces." In *Music Theory in Concept and Practice*, edited by David Beach, James Baker, and Jonathan Bernard, 97–129. Rochester, NY: University of Rochester Press, 1997.

Cherlin, Michael. "Dialectical Opposition in Schoenberg's Music and Thought." *Music Theory Spectrum* 22, no. 2 (Autumn 2000): 157–76.

———. "Schoenberg and Chamber Music for Strings." In *The Cambridge Companion to Arnold Schoenberg*, edited by Jennifer Shaw and Joseph Auner, 30–52. Cambridge: Cambridge University Press, 2010.

———. *Schoenberg's Musical Imagination.* Cambridge: Cambridge University Press, 2007.

Christensen, Thomas. "Fétis and Emerging Tonal Consciousness." In *Music Theory in the Age of Romanticism*, edited by Ian Bent, 37–56. New York: Cambridge University Press, 1996.

Conlon, Colleen. "The Lessons of Arnold Schoenberg in Teaching the Musikalische Gedanke." Ph.D. diss., University of North Texas, 2009.

Crawford, Dorothy. "Arnold Schoenberg in Los Angeles." *Musical Quarterly* 86, no. 1 (Spring 2002): 6–48.

Cross, Charlotte. "Three Levels of 'Idea' in Schoenberg's Thought and Writings." *Current Musicology* 30 (Fall 1980): 24–36.

Dineen, Phillip Murray. "Gerald Strang's Manuscript Notes to Arnold Schönberg's Classes (1935–37): Construction and the Two Learnings." In *Arnold Schoenberg in America: Report of the Symposium, May 2–4, 2001*, edited by Christian Meyer, *Journal of the Arnold Schönberg Center* 4 (2002), 104–18.

———. "Problems of Tonality: Schoenberg and the Concept of Tonal Expression." Ph.D. diss., Columbia University, 1989.

———. "Schoenberg's Modulatory Calculations: Wn Fonds 21 Berg 6/III/66 and Tonality." *Music Theory Spectrum* 27, no. 1 (Spring 2005): 97–112.

———. "Schoenberg on the Modes: Characteristics, Substitutes, and Tonal Orientation." *College Music Symposium* 33–34 (1993–94): 140–54.

———.

———. "The Tonal Problem as a Method of Analysis." *Theory and Practice* 30 (2005): 69–96.

Dudeque, Norton. *Music Theory and Analysis in the Writings of Arnold Schoenberg.* Burlington: Ashgate, 2005.

Dunsby, Jonathan. "Schoenberg and Present-Day Theory and Practice." In *Constructive Dissonance: Arnold Schoenberg and the Transformation of Twentieth-Century Culture*, edited by Juliane Brand and Christopher Hailey, 188–95. Berkeley and Los Angeles: University of California Press, 1997.

———. "Schoenberg on Cadence." *Journal of the Arnold Schoenberg Institute* 4, no. 1 (June 1980): 41–49.

Fess, Eike. "Examinations: Der Lehrer Arnold Schönberg." In *Das magische Quadrat: Eine Annäherung an den Visionär Arnold Schönberg; Materialien zu einem Leben mit vielen Talenten*, edited by Musikhochschule Luzern and the Arnold Schönberg Center, Appendix, unpaginated. Lucerne: Edizioni Periferia, 2006.

Feisst, Sabine. "Arnold Schoenberg and America." In *Schoenberg and His World*, edited by Walter Frisch, 285–336. Princeton, NJ: Princeton University Press, 1999.

———. "Dane Rudhyar on Arnold Schoenberg: About European Seeds in America." *Twentieth-Century Music* 6, no. 2 (February 1999): 13–17.

———. *Schoenberg's New World: The American Years*. New York: Oxford University Press, 2011.

Forte, Allen. *The Structure of Atonal Music*. New Haven, CT: Yale University Press, 1973.

Frisch, Walter. *Brahms and the Principle of Developing Variation*. Berkeley and Los Angeles: University of California Press, 1984.

———. *The Early Works of Arnold Schoenberg, 1893–1908*. Berkeley and Los Angeles: University of California Press, 1993.

Frisch, Walter, ed. *Schoenberg and His World*. Princeton, NJ: Princeton University Press, 1999.

Goehr, Alexander. "The Theoretical Writings of Arnold Schoenberg." *Perspectives of New Music* 13, no. 2 (Spring–Summer 1975): 3–16.

Gradenwitz, Peter. *Arnold Schönberg und seine Meisterschüler: Berlin 1925–1933*. Vienna: Paul Zsolnay Verlag, 1998.

Green, Douglass M. *Form in Tonal Music*. 2nd ed. New York: Holt, Rinehart and Winston, 1979.

Gruber, Gerold, ed. *Arnold Schönberg: Interpretation seiner Werke*. 2 vols. Laaber: Laaber Verlag, 2002.

Haimo, Ethan. *Schoenberg's Serial Odyssey: The Evolution of His Twelve-Tone Method, 1914–1928*. Oxford: Clarendon, 1990.

———. *Schoenberg's Transformation of Musical Language*. Cambridge: Cambridge University Press, 2006.

Heneghan, Áine. "The 'Popular Effect' in Schoenberg's Serenade." In *Schoenberg's Chamber Music, Schoenberg's World*, edited by James K. Wright and Alan M. Gillmor, 37–51. Hillsdale, NY: Pendragon Press, 2009.

———. *Schoenberg on Form*. New York: Oxford University Press, forthcoming.

———. "Tradition as Muse: Schoenberg's Musical Morphology and Nascent Dodecaphony." Ph.D. diss., University of Dublin, Trinity College, 2006.

Hilmar, Rosemary. *Alban Berg: Leben und Wirken in Wien bis zu seinen ersten Erfolgen als Komponist*. Vienna: Böhlau, 1978.

———. "Alban Berg's Studies with Schoenberg." *Journal of the Arnold Schoenberg Institute* 8, no. 1 (June 1984): 7–29.

Hoffmann, Richard. "A Schoenberg Centennial Symposium at Oberlin College (March 2, 1974)." *Journal of the Arnold Schoenberg Institute* 8, no. 1 (June 1984): 59–77.

Jacob, Andreas. *Grundbegriffe der Musiktheorie Arnold Schönbergs*. 2 vols. Hildesheim: Olms, 2005.

Jenkins, J. Daniel, ed. *Arnold Schoenberg: Program Notes and Analyses (1902–1951)*. New York: Oxford University Press, 2016.

———. "Schoenberg's Concept of *ruhende Bewegung.*" *Theory and Practice* 34 (2009): 87–109.

Kelly, Dorothea. "Arnold Schoenberg's Sixtieth Birthday in Chautauqua." *Journal of the Arnold Schoenberg Institute* 11, no. 2 (November 1988): 154–57.

Knight, Lovina M. "Classes with Schoenberg January through June 1934." *Journal of the Arnold Schoenberg Institute* 13, no. 2 (November 1990): 137–63.

Kopp, David. *Chromatic Transformations in Nineteenth-Century Music*. New York: Cambridge University Press, 2006.

Krämer, Ulrich. *Alban Berg als Schüler Arnold Schönbergs: Quellenstudien und Analysen zum Frühwerk*. Vienna: Universal Edition, 1996.

———. "Schoenberg's Concepts of *Kompositionslehre* (1904–1911) and The Nineteenth-Century German Tradition." *Revista de Musicología* 16, no. 6 (1993): 13–31.

Krehl, Stephan. *Musikalische Formenlehre (Kompositionslehre)*. Berlin: G. J. Göschen, 1914.

Krones, Hartmut, ed. *Arnold Schönberg in seinen Schriften: Verzeichnis, Fragen, Editorisches*. Vienna: Böhlau, 2011.

Langlie, Warren. "Arnold Schoenberg as an Educator." In *Arnold Schönberg: Gedenkaussтellung1974*, edited by Ernst Hilmar, 92–99. Vienna: Universal Edition, 1974.

———. "Arnold Schoenberg as a Teacher." Ph.D. diss., University of California, Los Angeles, 1960.

Lerdahl, Fred, and Ray Jackendoff. *A Generative Theory of Tonal Music*. Cambridge, MA: MIT Press, 1983.

Lester, Joel. *Compositional Theory in the Eighteenth Century*. Cambridge, MA: Harvard University Press, 1992.

Leibowitz, René. *Schoenberg and His School: The Contemporary Stage of the Language of Music*. Translated by Dika Newlin. New York: Philosophical Library, 1949.

Lewin, David. "Inversional Balance as an Organizing Force in Schoenberg's Music and Thought." *Perspectives of New Music* 6, no. 2 (Spring–Summer 1968): 1–21.

Lobe, Johann Christian. *Katechismus der Musik*. Leipzig: J. J. Weber, 1881.

Mann, Alfred. "Schubert's Lesson with Sechter." *19th-Century Music* 6, no. 1 (Autumn 1982): 159–62.

Marx, Adolf Bernhard. *Die Lehre von der musikalischen Komposition, Praktisch-theoretisch*, vol. 1. Leipzig: Breitkopf und Härtel, 1863.

———. *Musical Form in the Age of Beethoven: Selected Writings on Theory and Method*. Edited and translated by Scott G. Burnham. New York: Cambridge University Press, 1997.

McDonald, Malcolm. *Schoenberg*. London: Dent, 1976. Reprint, New York: Oxford University Press, 2008.

Meyer, Christian, and Therese Muxeneder, eds. *Arnold Schönberg: Catalogue raisonné*. Vienna: Christian Brandstätter, 2005.

Monod, Jacques–Louis. "Interview: Patricia Carpenter and Her Studies with Arnold Schoenberg." *Gamut: Journal of the Georgia Association of Music Theorists* 7 (1997): 61–74.

Morris, Robert. *Composition with Pitch Classes*. New Haven, CT: Yale University Press, 1987.

Neff, Severine. "Aspects of *Grundgestalt* in Schoenberg's First String Quartet, Op. 7." *Theory and Practice* 9, nos. 1–2 (July–December 1984): 7–56.

———. "Editing Schoenberg's Music-Theoretical Manuscripts: Problems of Incompleteness and Authorship." In *Arnold Schoenberg in seinen Schriften: Katalog—Fragen—Editorisches*, edited by Hartmut Krones, 193–216. Vienna: Böhlau, 2011.

———. "Schoenberg and Goethe: Organicism and Analysis." In *Music Theory and the Exploration of the Past*, edited by Christopher Hatch and David Bernstein, 409–33. Chicago: University of Chicago Press, 1993.

———. "Schoenberg as Theorist: Three Forms of Presentation." In *Schoenberg and His World*, edited by Walter Frisch, 55–84. Princeton, NJ: Princeton University Press, 1999.

Severine Neff, ed. *Preliminary Exercises in Counterpoint*. New York: Oxford University Press, forthcoming.

Newlin, Dika. *Schoenberg Remembered: Diaries and Recollections, 1938–1976*. New York: Pendragon Press, 1980.

Nono, Nuria Schoenberg. *Arnold Schönberg, 1874–1951: Lebensgeschichte in Begegnungen*. Klagenfurt, Austria: Ritter, 1992.

Pisk, Paul. "Arnold Schoenberg as Teacher." *American Society of University Composers: Proceedings of the Annual Conference* 2 (1967): 51–53.

Rahn, John. *Basic Atonal Theory*. New York: Longman, 1980.

Ratz, Erwin. *Einführung in die musikalische Formenlehre*. Vienna: Universal Edition, 1968.

Reich, Willi. *Schoenberg: A Critical Biography*. Transated by Leo Black. New York: Praeger, 1971.

Rexroth, Dieter. "Arnold Schönberg als Theoretiker der tonalen Harmonik." Ph.D. diss., University of Bonn, 1971.

Rosen, Charles. *Arnold Schoenberg*. Chicago: University of Chicago Press, 1996.

Rubsamen, Walter. "Schoenberg in America." *Musical Quarterly* 37, no. 4 (October 1951): 469–89.

Rufer, Josef. *Composition with Twelve Tones Related Only to One Another*. Translated by Humphrey Searle. Westport, CT: Greenwood Press, 1979.

———. *The Works of Arnold Schoenberg: A Catalogue of His Compositions, Writings and Paintings*. Translated by Dika Newlin. London: Faber and Faber, 1962.

Saslaw, Janna K. and James P. Walsh. "Patricia Carpenter: A Commemoration." *Theory and Practice* 30 (2005): 1–4.

Schoenberg, Arnold. "Analysis of the Four Orchestral Songs, Op. 22." Translated by Claudio Spies. In *Perspectives on Schoenberg and Stravinsky*, edited by Benjamin Boretz and Edward T. Cone, 25–45. New York: W. W. Norton, 1972.

———. *Coherence, Counterpoint, Instrumentation, Instruction in Form (Zusammenhang, Kontrapunkt, Instrumentation, Formenlehre)*. Edited by Severine Neff. Translated by Charlotte M. Cross and Severine Neff. Lincoln: University of Nebraska Press, 1994.

———. *Fundamentals of Musical Composition*. Edited by Gerald Strang and Leonard Stein. London: Faber and Faber, 1967.

———. *Harmonielehre*. Vienna: Universal Edition, 1911.

———. *Harmonielehre*. 3rd ed. Vienna: Universal Edition, 1922.

———. *Letters*. Edited by Erwin Stein. Translated by Eithne Wilkins and Ernst Kaiser. London: Faber and Faber, 1967.

———. *Modelle für Anfänger im Kompositionsunterricht*. Edited and translated by Rudolf Stephan. Vienna: Universal, 1972.

———. *Models for Beginners in Composition*. Los Angeles: Self-published, 1942.

———. *Models for Beginners in Composition*. New York: G. Schirmer, 1943.

———. *Models for Beginners in Composition*. New York: G. Schirmer, 1947.

———. *Models for Beginners in Composition*. Edited by Leonard Stein. Los Angeles: Belmont Music Publishers, 1972.

———. *The Musical Idea and the Logic, Technique, and Art of Its Presentation*. Edited and translated by Patricia Carpenter and Severine Neff. Bloomington: University of Indiana Press, 2006.

———. "New and Outmoded Music, Style, and Idea." In *Style and Idea: Selected Writings of Arnold Schoenberg*, edited by Leonard Stein, 113–24. Berkeley and Los Angeles: University of California Press, 1984.

———. *Preliminary Exercises in Counterpoint*. Edited by Leonard Stein. London: Faber and Faber, 1963.

———. *Sämtliche Werke*. Edited by Joseph Rufer et al. Mainz: B. Schott's Söhne and Vienna: Universal Edition AG,1966–.

———. *The Second String Quartet in F♯ Minor, Op. 10*. Edited by Severine Neff. New York: W. W. Norton, 2006.

———. *Structural Functions of Harmony*. Edited by Leonard Stein. New York: W. W. Norton, 1969.

———. *Style and Idea: The Selected Writings of Arnold Schoenberg*. Edited by Leonard Stein. Translated by Leo Black. Berkeley and Los Angeles: University of California Press, 1975.

———. *Style and Idea: The Selected Writings of Arnold Schoenberg*. Edited by Leonard Stein. Translated by Leo Black. With a foreword by Joseph Auner. 60th anniversary ed. Berkeley and Los Angeles: University of California Press, 2010.

———. *Theory of Harmony*. Translated by Roy E. Carter. Berkeley and Los Angeles: University of California Press, 1978.

———. *Theory of Harmony*. Translated by Roy E. Carter. With a foreword by Walter Frisch. 100th anniversary ed. Berkeley and Los Angeles: University of California Press, 2010.

Sechter, Simon. *Die Grundsätze der musikalischen Komposition, Erste Abtheilung*. Leipzig: Breitkopf und Härtel, 1853.

Shaw, Jennifer, and Joseph Auner, eds. *The Cambridge Companion to Schoenberg*. Cambridge: Cambridge University Press, 2010.

Simms, Bryan. "Arnold Schoenberg, *Theory of Harmony*—Commentary" [review of *Theory of Harmony*]. *Music Theory Spectrum* 4 (Spring 1982): 155–62.

———, ed. *Schoenberg, Berg, and Webern: A Companion to the Second Viennese School*. Westport, CT: Greenwood Press, 1999.

Smith, Peter. "Brahms and Schenker: A Mutual Response to Sonata Form." *Music Theory Spectrum* 16, no. 4 (Autumn 1994): 94.

Scharenberg, Sointu. *Überwinden der Prinzipien: Betrachtungen zu Anrold Schönbergs unkonventioneller Lehrtätigkeit zwischen 1898 und 1951*. Saarbrücken: Pfau, 2002.

Sobaskie, James. "Associative Harmony: The Reciprocity of Ideas in Musical Space." *In Theory Only* 10, nos. 1–2 (August 1987): 31–64.

Spratt, John. "The Speculative Content of Schoenberg's *Harmonielehre.*" *Current Musicology* 11 (Spring 1971): 83–88.

Stein, Erwin. *Praktischer Leitfaden zu Schönbergs Harmonielehre: Ein Hilfsbuch für Lehrer und Schüler.* Vienna: Universal Edition, 1923.

Stein, Leonard. "Five Statements." *Perspectives of New Music* 14, no. 1 (Autumn–Winter 1975): 169–72.

Straus, Joseph, N. *Introduction to Post-Tonal Theory.* Upper Saddle River, NJ: Pearson Prentice-Hall, 2005.

Stuckenschmidt, Hans Heinz. *Arnold Schoenberg: His Life, World and Work.* Translated by Humphrey Searle. New York: Schirmer, 1977.

Swift, Richard. "Tonal Relations in Schoenberg's *Verklärte Nacht.*" *19th-Century Music* 1, no. 1 (July 1977): 3–14.

van den Toorn, Pieter. "What's in a Motive? Schoenberg and Schenker Reconsidered." *Journal of Musicology* 14, no. 3 (Summer 1996): 370–99.

Wason, Robert W. *Viennese Harmonic Theory: From Albrechtsberger to Schenker and Schoenberg.* Ann Arbor, MI: UMI Research Press, 1984.

Watkins, Holly. "Schoenberg's Interior Designs." *Journal of the American Musicological Society* 61, no. 1 (Spring 2008): 123–206.

Weiss, Adolph. "The Lyceum of Schönberg." *Modern Music* 9, no. 3 (March–April 1932): 99–107.

Index

Printed and bound by CPI Group (UK) Ltd, Croydon, CR0 4YY